Actes du XIVème Congrès UISPP, Université de Liège, Belgique, 2-8 septembre 2001

Acts of the XIVth UISPP Congress, University of Liège, Belgium, 2-8 September 2001

SECTION 9

NÉOLITHIQUE AU PROCHE ORIENT ET EN EUROPE

NEOLITHIC IN THE NEAR EAST AND EUROPE

Colloque / Symposium 9.3

Production and Management of Lithic Materials in the European Linearbandkeramik

Gestion des matériaux lithiques dans le Rubané européen

Édité par / Edited by

Laurence Burnez-Lanotte

BAR International Series 1200
2003

Published in 2016 by
BAR Publishing, Oxford

BAR International Series 1200

Acts of the XIVth UISPP Congress, University of Liège, Belgium, 2-8 September 2001
Colloque / Symposium 9.3

Production and Management of Lithic Materials in the European Linearbandkeramik /
Gestion des matériaux lithiques dans le Rubané européen

ISBN 978 1 84171 565 0

BAR Publishing is the trading name of British Archaeological Reports (Oxford) Ltd.
British Archaeological Reports was first incorporated in 1974 to publish the BAR
Series, International and British. In 1992 Hadrian Books Ltd became part of the BAR
group. This volume was originally published by Archaeopress in conjunction with
British Archaeological Reports (Oxford) Ltd / Hadrian Books Ltd, the Series principal
publisher, in 2003. This present volume is published by BAR Publishing, 2016.

Printed in England

BAR
PUBLISHING

BAR titles are available from:

BAR Publishing
122 Banbury Rd, Oxford, OX2 7BP, UK
EMAIL info@barpublishing.com
PHONE +44 (0)1865 310431
FAX +44 (0)1865 316916
www.barpublishing.com

Table of contents

FOREWORD

This conference discusses lithic production in the Linearbandkeramik (LBK) communities of Europe : exploitation and processing of siliceous rocks, characterization of different strategies for knapping blanks for tools at site level and of their mode of production (domestic, specialized, surplus production), differentiation of settlements (producers, users), networks of regional and extra-regional exchange (of raw materials, cores, blanks or tools), modes of distribution, geographical and chronological evidence, and problems involved in reconstructing the socio-economic context of lithic production.

I warmly thank the participants for replying to my invitation to share the results of their current research, through discussions during which practice and theory, applied to different sets of data, were confronted to highlight the relevance of lithic assemblages for study of the LBK. The question addressed was to what extent technical treatment of siliceous materials signifies phenomena of coherence and/or uniformity, involving a certain variability of choice as regards the management, transformation and use of these materials. The reader will find regional models of site differentiation in accordance with control of raw material sources and/or of circulation of nodules or artefacts at different stages of the *"chaînes opératoires"* of manufacture. Research shows how the circulation of siliceous products presents comparable modalities within the LBK, in more or less distant regions, along networks which reflect economic and/or social aspects of the human groups involved.

At the western end of this culture, inter-regional links revealed by flint exchange contradict the definition of relations between groups proposed solely on the basis of stylistic analyses of pottery. Clearly, the spatial and chronological patterning which emerges from lithic studies alters the picture established through examination of other categories of material culture. The articulation of these different levels of understanding of LBK culture in specific environmental contexts is an issue of major interest for current research.

On the scale of a single site, particular cultural phenomena have been revealed. An example here is proof of micro-regionally organized surplus production of blades in fine-grained Hesbaye flint, in proportions previously unknown in the LBK. A possible correlation is also suggested between lithic technology, a mechanical device and raw materials economy, involving recuperation and selective reuse of flint artefacts from one Danubian culture (LBK) by another (Blicquy-Villeneuve-Saint-Germain).

The outcome of this meeting was to confirm once again that lithic artefacts and technical systems are essential for our understanding of the LBK.

Acknowledgements

This conference would not have been possible without the support of the institutions that funded the congress. Their help is gratefully acknowledged. The practical organization of our meeting owed a great deal to the efficiency of Emmanuel Delye, who also helped to harmonize and improve presentation of the published papers. I extend my warmest thanks to him, on behalf of all the participants. Last but not least, I should like to thank Mike Ilett (University of Paris I and UMR 7041 CNRS) for helpful comments and for translating this foreword in english.

Laurence Burnez-Lanotte

DISTRIBUTION OF RAW MATERIALS USED IN THE CHIPPED STONE INDUSTRY OF THE WESTERN LINEAR BAND POTTERY CULTURE AND THE EASTERN LINEAR POTTERY CULTURE IN THE CIRCUM-CARPATHIAN AREA

Malgorzata KACZANOWSKA*

Résumé

La comparaison, dans une perspective diachromique, de systèmes d'approvisionnement en matières premières lithiques dans les deux complexes linéaires, oriental et occidental, relève aussi bien des similitudes que de différences. Le caractère commun de ces systèmes est le fait que les nodules non-décortiqués ont été fourni dans les sites et les chaînes opératoires complètes sont enregistrées dans les sites. Néanmoins dans certains sites de deux complexes les supports laminaires ont été importés surtout dans les sites éloignés des gisements de matières premières. Les plus importantes différences entre les deux complexes apparaissent dans les aires de distribution : dans le Complexe Linéaire Oriental (Slovaquie de l'Est) la distribution est limitée à 30–40 km, surtout dans les bassins intra-montagneux, par contre dans le Rubané (Linéaire Occidental) les matériaux provenant des sources éloignées sont fréquents. Cette différence dans le système d'approvisionnement résulte du caractère plus conservatif et plus isolé des sociétés du Linéaire Oriental, par rapport au caractère plus ouvert aux influences extérieures et plus novateur des groupes du Rubané (Linéaire Occidental).

Abstract

Comparison of the diachronic perspective of raw material distribution patterns in the Eastern and Western Linear Complexes is showing some similarities and some differences. Common feature is the supply of unworked nodules to the sites and complete operational chain performed on the sites. But in both complexes exist some sites where ready blanks has been imported, mostly sites situated outside the raw material sources. Most important differences between both complexes appear in the distances from raw material sources: in the Eastern Linear Complex (Eastern Slovakia) the distance from raw material sources was from 30 to 40 km, generally in the limits of intramountain basins. In the western (Bandkeramik) complex raw materials originating from distant sources are frequent. These fundamental difference is the result of more conservative, regionally limited societies of the Eastern Linear Complex, opposed to the more open to external influences and more innovative, but internally connected societies of the Bandkeramik (Western Linear) complex.

The emergence of the Linear Pottery Complex was one of the most important events in the growth of food–producing economy in Central Europe, in particular, in the northern part of the central Danube basin and in the circum-Carpathian area. This complex can be divided into two branches. The eastern cultures inhabited the upper and central section of the Tisza basin and basically developed on its native territory, while the western cultures expanded across Europe, reaching Moldavia, to the east, and the Parisian Basin and Belgium to the west. The boundary between the two branches of the Linear Band Pottery Complex runs along the upper section of the River Ipel, the River Zagyva and further to the south along the River Tisza. This boundary was respected by almost all prehistoric cultures. It seems that examples of overlapping of both Linear Pottery Complexes can be found in the area of Spiš and Lesser Poland (Sub-Carpathian foot-hills). The purpose of this paper is to discuss differences and similarities as well as mutual relations between the two branches of the Linear Pottery Complex by examining the pattern of distribution of raw materials used in the chipped stone industry.

Before the proper Eastern Linear Band Pottery Complex came into being Szatmár group appeared, which can roughly be regarded as a transition between the Balkan cultures – the Starcevo-Körös complex and the Eastern Linear Pottery Culture. The inventories of the Szatmár group differ from those of the Körös culture, both in respect to the type of

(*) Muzeum Archeologiczne w Krakowie, Oddzial w Nowej Hucie, Os. Zielone 7, 31-968 Kraków.

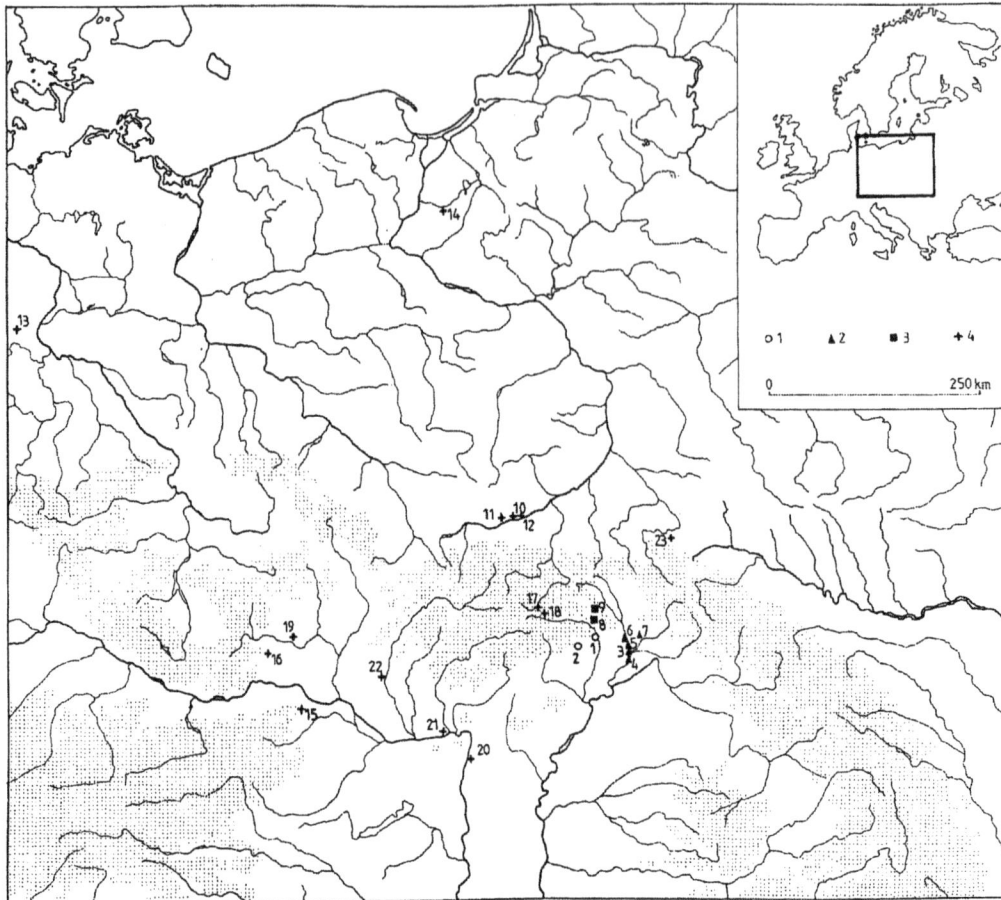

Figure 1. Index map of discussed sites : 1. Eastern Linear Culture, Košice basin Protolinear and Barca III group, 2. Eastern Linear Culture, Slovakian Lowland Proto-Kopčany and Kopčany group, 3. Eastern Linear Culture, Šariš valley, Tiszadob group, 4. Bandkeramik (Western Linear Pottery). 1. Košice-Cervený Rak, 2. Čečejovce, 3. Kopčany, 4. Raškovce, 5. Slavkovce, 6. Zbudza, 7. Zalužice, 8. Prešov-Šarišské Lúky, 9. Šarišské Michal'any (Tiszadob group and Bükk culture), 10. Mogilya, 11. Olszanica, 12. Pleszów, 13. Eilsleben, 14. Boguszewo, 15. Brunn, 16. Rosenburg, 17. Matejovce, 18. Strana pod Tatrami, 19. Vedrovice, 20. Budapest Aranyhegyi, 21. Šturovo, 22. Borovce, 23. Fredropol.

raw materials used and the manner in which such materials were supplied. For the sites of the Starčevo-Körös complex, of great importance was the characteristic wax coloured, spotted flint, which probably comes from the Pre-Balkan platform. However, it is not the raw material itself which is the most distinct feature, but rather the manner in which it was provided. Raw material was initially worked in specialised workshops, probably near deposits, while in settlements finished blades and tools have been recovered. Single cores were exploited in several chipping episodes. When necessary, they were also often repaired. Such raw material management is the reason why only a small number of artefacts have been found on the site, with the predominance of tools and blades. The distribution of raw materials in the inventories of the Szatmár group is different. Representatives of this group started to exploit on a massive scale Slovakian and Hungarian obsidian deposits. What differentiates assemblages of the typical Starčevo-Körös complex and the Szatmár group is not the fact that new deposits were discovered and exploited, as obsidian was known even before that period, but first of all a quite different manner of obtaining raw materials. Instead of the multi-stage high intensity raw material exploitation of

carefully prepared cores, unworked nodules of raw materials have been supplyed on sites. Such nodules were reduced in settlements, which is why there are so many flakes. This change was taking place gradually on the sites of the Szatmár group, however, such a supply system of raw materials was becoming increasingly popular on some late sites of the Körös culture, in particular, where obsidian predominated (Méhtelek - Starnini 1994). This method of supplying raw material can be associated with a model proposed several years ago by C. Renfrew, (Renfrew *et al.* 1966), who defined the concept known as a "zone of supply", i.e., an area from where expeditions were sent to the deposits of raw materials, and the zone of contact, i.e., an area where raw materials were bartered. With respect to the Szatmár group, area of a direct supply measured less than 100 km to the south-east off the deposits. Apart from obsidians, the Szatmár community also exploited in the same area, to a smaller extent, limnoquarzite. Single artefacts from other extralocal materials indicate that the Szatmár group indirectly maintained links with other cultural groups.

The Eastern Linear Pottery Culture relied on the same

6

method of supply, i.e. raw materials in the form of nodules were brought to settlements and then worked. Even in the oldest phase of this culture local groups used different raw materials. This particularity of these groups has been confirmed by the slightly different style of pottery decoration (fig.2 and 3). The mentioned groups inhabited naturally separated geographical units – mountain valleys (fig. 1). In its oldest phase, the group inhabiting the Košice basin used mainly local silica rocks, such as limnoquarzite (Košice-Cerveny Rak – 93.3% - Šiška 1989). In younger inventories the proportion of local siliceous rocks falls as compared to obsidian (Čečejovce 62.9% - Kozlowski 1989). Limnoquarzite was brought to settlements from locations as far as 30-40 km away, thus, as compared to the older inventories, the zone of supply was shorter.

Representatives the other branch of the Eastern Linear Pottery Culture inhabiting the East Slovakian Lowland, open to the south and east, exploited manly obsidian deposits. Even in the oldest phase of development of settlements raw material was brought in the form of nodules. A collection of such nodules of obsidian, i.e. 34 specimens, of the total weight of 13 kg has been discovered on the site at Slavkovce, within about 30 km from the deposits (Kaczanowska, Kozlowski 1997). On the site at Zbudza, chronologically later than to Slavkovce we observe the first signs of a functional diversification of the settlement. In some areas of the settlement a complete reduction sequence have been recovered while in others at least a certain amount of finished blades were brought to the site (Kaczanowska, Kozlowski 1997).

Settlements further to the east, on the territory of Trans-Carpathian Ukraina also used chiefly obsidian, however, at the present stage of research it is not possible to determine whether this material was bartered or whether it was brought from expeditions to obsidian deposits. At the beginning of the middle phase of its development, the Eastern Linear Pottery Culture expanded as far as Gemer, i.e., the Rimava valley and Slovensky Kras. The Šariš valley, in the northern part of Eastern Slovakia was inhabited by groups which earlier occupied the Košice valley. The small inventory from the site at Šarišské Michal'any indicates that the new inhabitants adapted to the local conditions and used the local radiolarite (about 20 km from the site). Obsidian found on the site is evidence that the group maintained contact with the south (Kaczanowska, Kozlowski, Šiška 1993).

The system of supply developed by the Eastern Linear Pottery Culture is characterised by the exploitation of local deposits of raw materials, a relatively short zone of supply and the fact that raw material was worked in settlements, near dwelling places. This situation may illustrate the thesis of J. Pavúk (1996) concerning the development of small isolated early Neolithic communities in closed valleys which continued pre-Neolithic traditions. This hypothesis is not that simple as it seems at first sight, as:
1. we are not able to define these pre-Neolithic traditions. This statement has not been changed by new discoveries of Mesolithic sites by R. Kertész in the Jaszag region (Kertész 1996a, Kertész 1996b, Kertész et al. 1994); which represent exclusively Early and Middle Phase of the Mesolithic.

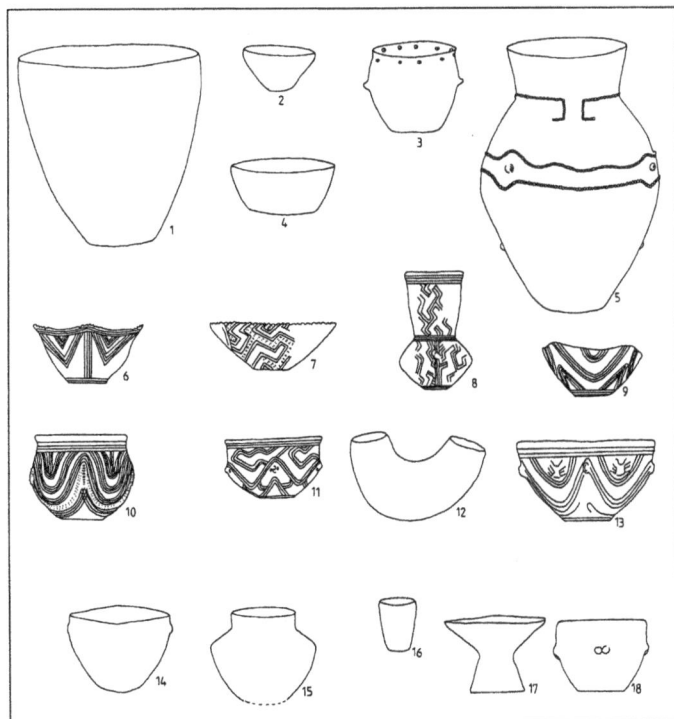

Figure 2. Pottery of the Eastern Linear Cultur. 1-5. Early phase, Barca III group, Košice basin; 6-13. Younger phase, Tiszadob group; 14-18. Early phase, Kopčany group, Slovakian Lowland.

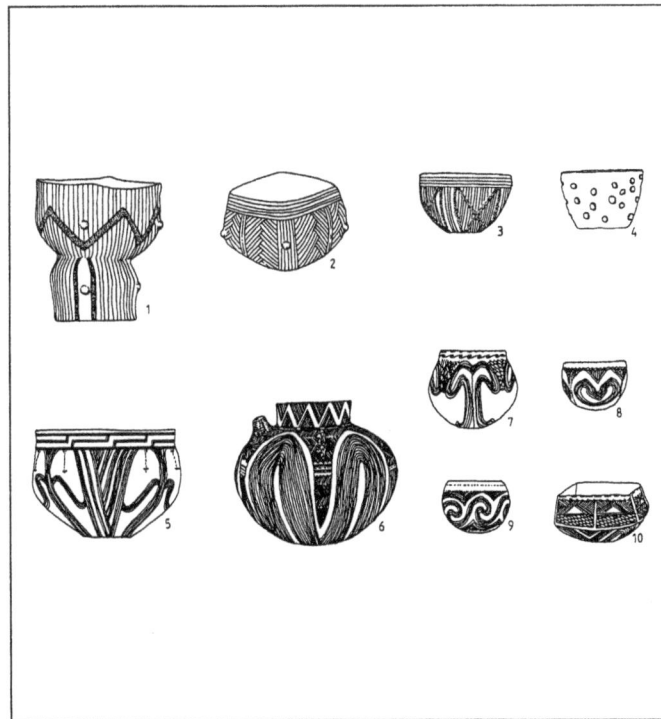

Figure 3. Pottery of the Eastern Linear and Bükk Cultures. 1-4. Younger phase, Raškovce group, Slovakian Lowland; 5-10. Bükk Culture.

2. an analysis of the raw material composition of the inventories found at the specific sites indicates that a certain amount of raw material was moved between the particular groups and that the Linear Pottery Culture maintained links, albeit to a limited extent, with other cultures.

The Bükk culture, regarded by some scientists (Kalicz, Makkay 1977) as the youngest group of the Eastern Linear Pottery Culture continued the existing traditions with respect to the distribution of raw materials and lithic technology and typology. In this case, the zone of supply does not exceed 20–30 km, which is a day's march from a settlement. Within the same distance there are also sites where the predominance of blades and a high proportion of tools indicate that items were less often worked on the spot and half-products were rather purchased. Thus in terms of the distribution of raw materials, sites can be divided into these where material was worked locally and those where this practice was less common. It seems, however, that relations between local groups were increasingly stronger, as suggests a more dynamic movement of certain raw materials, including obsidian. In the relevant literature one can often come across an opinion about the vital role of the Bükk culture in the production, processing and distribution of obsidian. In Central Europe this raw material was the most widely used in the early phase of the Lengyel Culture (Kaczanowska 1980a; Šiška 1998). In the Prešov basin, in the northern part of Eastern Slovakia, like in the earlier period, Jurrasic flint from southern Poland can be found (3.7% - Šarišské Michal'any). As compared to the earlier phases of development, the proportion of obsidian on sites in Western Slovakia and the Lesser Poland area, so beyond the scope of the Bükk culture, suggests that this culture was also increasingly active outside of its own territory.

Even in its oldest phase (here I mean the per-Notenkopf phase) the system of distribution of raw materials in the LBPC, i.e., in the western Linear Pottery Complex, was much more complex. Several models of material supply can be differentiated.
1. the use of local deposits from the beginning of the development of these culture. A number of sites representing this culture has been discovered in the vicinity, or even directly on flint deposits, and the local raw material constitutes 98-100%. The structure of inventories, with a large proportion of flakes, indicates that flint was locally processed (Mogila, Pleszów, Olszanica, Eilsleben). In the relevant literature one can find an opinion about the role of these settlements in the process of production and distribution of flint (Lech 1989). This thesis has not be satisfactorily proved. It should be noted that at least in Lesser Poland these settlements are also located in the most favourable areas in terms of ecological and soil conditions.
2. the major raw material comes from extra-local deposits even in the earliest phase of these culture. The first thought that immediately comes to mind is that a group came to a given location with their own stock of raw material, mainly in the form of nodules or cores. Only when the inhabitants got used to the local conditions, local raw materials found on the

site started to be used. One should mention here the site as Boguszewo in the Chelm region (Malecka-Kukawka 1992), where the flint from Kraków-Czestochowa Jurassic Plateau (360 km away) makes up 85,3%. Brunn II and Rosenburg (Mateicucová 1997) probably belong to such sites – their inventories include artefacts chiefly made from the Szentgál radiolarite, whose deposits are located 150 km away from these sites. With respect to the younger phases of development of the LBPC, one should mention the Upper Spiš area, approx. 130 km from Jurassic flint deposits, where the proportion of this flint is not lower than 70% (Strana pod Tatrami, Matejovce).
3. a number of the LBPC sites have been discovered where the proportion of extra-local raw materials is high, even though raw material was widely available in their vicinity. First and foremost, one should mention inventories from the graves at Vedrovice (Mateicucová 1997), where in burial inventories from the oldest phase of the LBPC, Jurrasic flint, obtained in locations 270-280 km away, constitutes 36.4%. Certainly, I am well aware of the fact that the comparison of burial and settlement materials may result in errors: – in one case we are dealing with production waste or tools accidentally discarded, while in the other – we have artefacts deliberately selected according to rules which still remain unknown to us. However, the fact that in the Vedrovice settlement assemblages have been found which include a large number of items made from Jurrasic flint shows that this raw material was very important (Kaczanowska 1980b). In the younger development phases of the LBPC, we have a similar situation at Borovce or Šturovo (28.3%), where the distance from the deposits is comparable. In the area between the San River and the River Vistula, a raw material of the Cretaceous flint from the Volhynia-Podolie plateau has been discovered. This material predominates in the upper River San on a site at Fredropol, 200 km away from its deposits (Kaczanowska 1980a). The direction from which extra-local raw materials were brought, opposite to the movement of the first farmers, who were advancing along the Carpathian Mountains to the south-east, as far as Moldavia, clearly indicates that the new settlements maintained strong links with their native areas.

Throughout the whole development of the LBPC in the mentioned area, one can observe a free flow of raw materials. Artefacts made of extra-local flints have been discovered at all the sites representing this culture, and even at those located near the deposits. On areas beyond the zone of supply, i.e. in the case of the region discussed here, 100 – 150 km away, items made of other raw materials were brought as finished blade blanks, possibly also as single tools. This hypothesis is confirmed by the fact that at many sites a specific type of retouched tools is mostly made of the particular extra-local raw material, for example trapezes at Vedrovice, perforators in the settlement at Vedrovice, end-scrapers at Šturovo. The reason for such an intense exchange activity was definitely not economic. Extra-local raw materials were obtained during expeditions to very remote locations, sometimes in areas inhabited by groups characterised by a differ-

Figure 4. Pottery of the Bandkeramik (Western Linear) Culture. 1-6, 8. oldest phase; 1. Slovakia, 2, 8. Hungary, 3-7. Poland; 7, 9, 10, 12, 13. Middle phase; 7. western Poland, 9. Moravia, 10. Slovakia, 12. Lesser Poland, 13. Hungary, 11, 14-20. Youngest phase; 11, 18. Lesser Poland; 16, 17. Slovakia, (Željiezovce group); 19. Moravia, 14, 15, 20. western Poland, Lower Silesia (Šarka group).

ent style of pottery decoration (fig. 4) (e.g. flint from the Kraków-Czestochowa Jurassic Plateau was supplied to sites located in Lower Silesia). This only suggests that relations within the whole LBPC community were constantly renewed and that information was freely exchanged. An issue that provokes animated discussions and heated debates is the question whether the aforementioned phenomena are a reflection of old pre-Neolithic structures, manifesting themselves with a fresh impetus in the adapted system of food-producing economy, or they are evidence of the allochtonic origin of the Neolithic in the circum-Carpathian area.

Certain similarities and quite distinct differences can be identified in the pattern of distribution of raw materials in the western and eastern branch of the Linear Pottery complex. A common feature of this complex is the fact that unworked nodules of raw materials were brought to settlements and worked there. In the units of both branches of the Linear Pottery there are sites where a certain amount of blanks which were supplayed ready-made. These are settlements located in areas with no deposits of raw materials or located within some distance from them.

The most striking difference is the extension of the zone of supply, i.e. area from where expeditions were sent to obtain raw material. In the archaeological material available it is reflected by a high, according to C. Renfrew, (Renfrew *et al.* 1966) proportion (80 %) of raw material and, in my view,

the fact that items were fully worked on a site. The extension of the zone of supply varied in different directions depending on whether "competitive" resources of raw material and natural geographical obstacles existed. Generally in the area of the Eastern Linear Pottery Complex, the zone did not exceed 30-40 km, closing in naturally separated mountain valleys, while with respect to the western Linear Band Pottery Complex its radius was generally over 100 km, sometimes not respecting the boundaries marked by a distinct style of pottery decoration. In the assemblages of both branches we can observe that extra-local materials were found even in the oldest phases. In the eastern complex these are mainly single items and their proportion does not exceed 3-4 %, whereas in the western complex, within a distance of about 200 km, they make up 1/3 of an inventory, and even more, for example at Bylany (300 km from the deposits), where in the II b and II c phases the proportion of Jurassic flint was respectively 58 and 59% (Lech 1989). Interestingly enough, the western LBPC groups often came to new locations with their own stock of raw material, and then they adopted to local flints, however, still maintaining strong links with their native regions. A widespread free flow of raw materials is indicative of the existence of close, social relations. This difference between the eastern and western branch of the Linear Pottery Complex, reflected for example in a different manner of distribution of raw materials, which suggests, on the one hand, that the eastern community was rather conservative, closed and applied only one model, and on the other hand, the LBPC community, which was open and adapted certain new traditions in chipped stone industry, and at the same time maintained, as research in Western Europe shows, strong internal links reflected in the free flow of raw materials, can provide an answer as to why the Eastern Linear Pottery Culture stopped its expansion on the Carpathian Mountains while the western LBPC spread across vast areas of Europe.

Bibliography

KACZANOWSKA, M., 1980a, *Rohstoffe, Technik und Typologie der neolithischen Feuersteinindustrien im Nordteil des Flussgebietes der Mitteldonau*. Warszawa : PWN.

KACZANOWSKA, M., 1980b, Steinindustrie der Kultur der Linienbandkeramik. In *Problèmes de la néolithisation dans certaines régions de l'Europe*: Ossolineum. Wroclaw Warszawa Kraków Gdansk, p. 79-96.

KACZANOWSKA, M., KOZLOWSKI, J. K., 1997, Lithic industries. In *The early Linear Pottery Culture in Eastern Slovakia*, edited by J. K. Kozlowski, Kraków, p. 177-253.

KACZANOWSKA, M., KOZLOWSKI, J. K., ŠIŠKA, S., 1993, *Neolithic and eneolithic chipped stone industries from Šarišské Michal'any, Eastern Slovakia*, Kraków: Instytute of Archaeology Jagellonian University.

KALICZ, N., MAKKAY, J., 1977, *Die Linienbandkeramik in der Großen Ungarischen Tiefebene*. Budapest : Akadémiai Kiadó.

KERTÉSZ, R., 1996a, The Mesolithic in the Great Hungarian Plain.

In *At the Fringes of three Worlds Hunter-Gatheres and Farmers in the middle Tisza Valley*, edited by L. Tálas. Szolnok, p. 5-34.

KERTÉSZ, R., 1996b, A new site of the Northern Hungarian Plain Mesolithic Industry in the Jászság Area (Jászberény IV). *Tiscum* IX, p. 27-49.

KERTÉSZ, R., SÜMEGI, P., KOZÁK, M., BRAUN, M., FÉLEGYHÁZI, E., HERTELENDI, 1994, Mesolithikum im nördlichen Teil der Großen Ungarischen Tiefebene. *Jósa András Múzeum Évkönyve* XXXVI, p. 15-63.

KOZLOWSKI, J. K., 1989, The lithic industry of the Eastern Linear Pottery Culture in Slovakia. *Slovenská Archeológia* XXXVII-2, p. 377-410.

LECH, J., 1989, A Danubian raw material exchange network: a case study from Bylany. In *Bylany seminar. 1987*, edited by J. Rulf. Praha. p. 111-120.

MALECKA-KUKAWKA, J., 1992, *Krzemieniarstwo spolecznosci wczesnorolniczych ziemi chelminskiej (2 polowa VI – IV tysiaclecie p.n. e.).* Torun.

MATEICUCOVÁ, I., 1997, Štipaná industrie na pohrebišti kultury s LNK ve Vedrovicich. *Pravek* 7, p. 77-103.

RENFREW, C., DIXON, J. E., CANN, I. R., 1966, Obsidian and Early cultural contacts in the Near East. *Proceedings of the Prehistoric Society*, NS 32, p. 319-331.

PAVÚK, J., 1996, Zur Frage der Verbreitung des Neolithikums auf dem Zentralbalkan und in Mitteleuropa. In *The Vinca Culture, its Role and Cultural conection*, Timisoara, p. 23-40.

STARNINI, E., 1994, Typological and technological analyses of the Körös Culture chipped, polished and ground stone assemblages of Méhtelek-Nádas (North Eastern Hungary). *Atti della Societa per la Preistoria e Protoistoria della regione Friuli-Venezia Giulia,* p. 29-96.

ŠIŠKA, S., 1989, *Kultura s vychodnou linearnou keramikou na Slovensku.* Bratislava.

ŠIŠKA, S., 1998, Obsidián v prostredi spoločenstiev doby kamennej na strednom a západnom Slovensku. *Východoslovenský Pravek* V, p. 63-88.

TEVEL FLINT : A SPECIAL CONSTITUENT OF THE CENTRAL EUROPEAN LBC LITHIC INVENTORIES

Katalin T. BIRÓ*

Résumé

Le silex, "flint", au sens propre, signifie une roche siliceuse qui s'est formée dans des eaux marines superficielles issue de l'âge Crétacé et Terciaire, composé en majorité de l'éponge siliceuse. Ces conditions ci-dessus, on ne peut pas les rencontrer souvent en Hongrie parmi les matières premières. En fait, il n'y a qu'une seule source géologique dont on a des informations sur la présence du silex. Cette source est située dans la région occidentale de la Hongrie, plus exactement sur le côté ouest des montagnes Bakony (composé en majorité du calcaire), près de la ville Pápa, tout près de la colline Tevel (Nagytevel). Plusieurs mottes de silex – de dimension jusqu'à 40 cm – surgissent à la surface du solide calcaire blanc de l'âge Senonian. Cette notice vise à fournir des renseignements archéologiques sur la distribution de cette matière première assez spéciale. Le surgissement était identifié comme une source d'une matière première préhistorique par un géologue, D. Bihari. Des éclats façonnés ont été trouvés dans les couches sablées d'âge Würm supérieur près de cette source, ce qui sont parmi les traces les plus âgées de l'activité humaine dans la région. Comme la source est relativement petite, apparemment ce n'était pas connue et en usage tout au long des différentes périodes de la Préhistoire. Cette matière est connue principalement issue de la Culture Danubienne Supérieure et du contexte de Lengyel antérieur, généralement dans la région Nord-Ouest de la Transdanubie bien que quelques pièces aient été trouvées à Aszód et à Zengővárkony à 300 km de distance de la source. À nos connaissances actuelles il y a un site d'atelier de cette matière première à Kup-Egyes où il était trouvé une certaine partie des plus larges nucléus coniques de la Préhistoire hongroise. La première trouvaille était découverte à Kup par S. Mithay dans les années 1970, la documentation était publiée en 1990. Tout récemment plusieurs trouvailles de silex ont été découvertes au cours des enquêtes superficielles et pour cette raison des nouvelles fouilles étaient commencées à l'initiative du Musée National Hongrois.

Abstract

"Flint" in the strict sense means shallow-water marine siliceous rocks of Late Cretaceous/Early Tertiary age, composed mainly of siliceous sponges. These conditions are very seldom met in the Hungarian raw material spectrum. In fact there is only one geological source where s.s. flint is known to occur. This source is located in W Hungary, western flanks of the Bakony Mts. close to the town Pápa, Tevel-hill at Nagytevel. Large flint nodules up to the size of 40 cm crop out in hard white limestone of Senonian age. This paper aims at presenting the archaeological data on the distribution of this very special raw material. The outcrop was identified as a source of prehistoric raw material by D. Bihari, geologist. In the Late Würm sandy deposits close to the source, some worked flakes were found which are among the earliest traces of human activity in the region. As the source is very small, it was seemingly not known and in use during all periods of prehistory. The material is known mainly from Late LBC and Early Lengyel context, prevailingly from North-Western parts of Transdanubia though some pieces got as far as Aszód or Zengővárkony, about 300 km from the source. So far we know about one workshop site of this material at Kup-Egyes, where some of the most beautiful large conical cores in Hungarian prehistory were found. Old material from Kup was excavated by S. Mithay in the 1970-ies and published in 1990. Recently, more flint material came forth from surface collections and new excavations started by the Hungarian National Museum.

(*) Hungarian National Museum, Dept. of Archaeology, H-1088 Budapest,
Múzeum krt. 14-16, Hungary, tbk@ace.hu

Introduction

The systematical investigation of chipped stone inventories of Holocene (Prehistoric) in Hungary started in the last quarter of the 20th century. Following the pioneering study of E. Bácskay (1976), a survey of Early and Middle Neolithic chipped stone tools was performed by 1985 (Bácskay-Simán 1987; Biró 1987) on the occasion of the conference "Chipped stone industry of early farming communities in Europe". The latter work was specially consecrated to the study of LBC chipped stone industries (Biró 1987). In the following years, several studies – both large regional surveys (Biró 1998) and individual case studies (Mencshely, Kup, Kustánszeg etc: Biró 1989, Biró 1991, 1991a) added much to the knowledge on LBC lithic inventories and large lithic assemblages are under investigation currently. By now, we know about the most important local and regional sources used in Hungary and specific studies concerning the use and distribution of certain elements of the raw material spectrum can be analysed. The present study is dedicated - in accordance with the general theme of this Colloque - to the study of the only s.s. "flint" variety, the source of which is in North-Central Transdanubia, at the NW part of the Bakony Mts., i.e., Tevel flint.

Raw materials sources for LBC chipped stone artefacts in Hungary

The growing interest in the "pottery period" lithic assemblages was in close relation with the emerging provenance studies, getting new impetus in the mid-eighties (see especially Proceedings and Papers of the Sümeg Conference (International conference on prehistoric flint mining and lithic raw material identification in the Carpathian Basin, Biró ed. 1986, 1987) and the foundation of the comparative raw material collection of the Hungarian National Museum, the Lithotheca (Biró-Dobosi 1991, Biró-Dobosi-Schléder 2000). The basic features of LBC raw material economy were summarised in (Biró 1998 : 49)

According to present data, LBC lithic assemblages rely on local resources for most of their supply. The most important raw material types were obsidian and limnic silicites on the areas East of the Danube (Alföld and North-Hungarian Mid-Mountain Range) while on the areas West of the Danube, i.e., Transdanubia, the most important material was Transdanubian radiolarite with absolute dominance of Szentgál radiolarite. The system of evaluation applied in the cited monograph (Biró 1998) concentrated more on the Alföld than other parts of the country, thus some important details like e.g. the use of Tevel flint, the subject of the present paper could be easily lost.

Tevel flint : its outcrop, physical qualities and potentials of exploitation

Hungarian raw materials used for the production of chipped stone tools include a wide variety of rocks: obsidian, radiolarite, hydrothermal and limnic silicites, hornstone, quartzite etc. Flint in the strict sense (marine, shallow water siliceous rock composed mainly of silica from sponge spicules; relatively young (typically, of Cretaceous/Tertiary age)) is a rare constituent, imported from outside the Carpathian Arch in most cases (e.g., Prut flint, Volhynian flint).

The only occurrence of s.s. flint in Hungary is connected with the Upper Cretaceous (Senonian) Ugod Limestone Formation. It is a light, thick bedded limestone of platform and platform slope facies. Contains large flint nodules to my best information only at Tevel Mt., in the vicinity of Nagytevel close to the city Pápa in Western Hungary (fig 1). The flint looks very much like Upper Cretaceous/Tertiary flint known from wide regions of Europe mainly North from our region (Poland, Germany, etc.). It is grey with chalk white cortex, with concentrically darkening pattern (fig. 2). Flint occurs in the form of large nodules within the light coloured limestone, sometimes up tho the length of 40 cms. Some parts may be translucent but on the

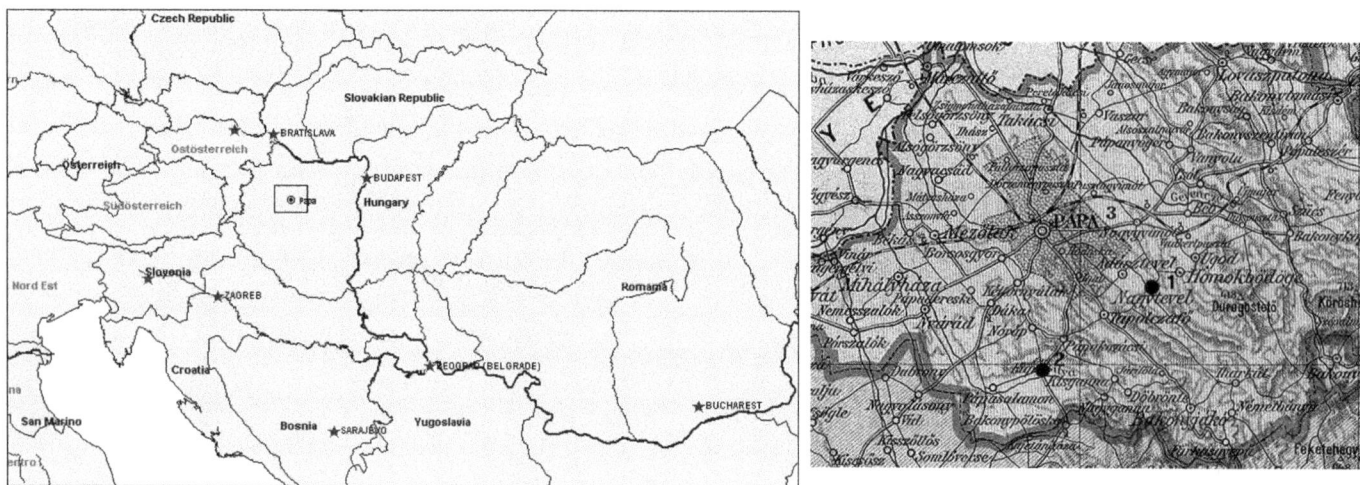

Figure 1. Location of Nagytevel (1) and Kup (2) near Pápa, West-Central Hungary.

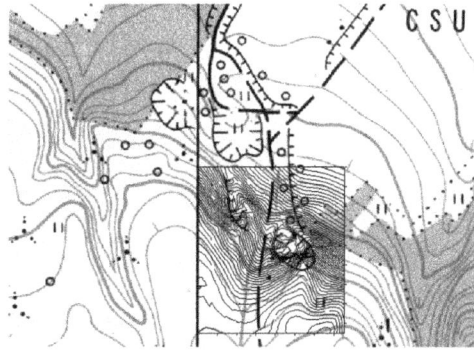

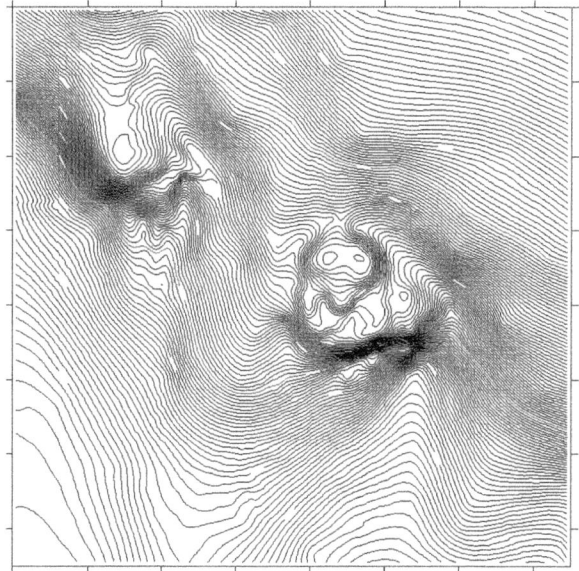

Figure 3. Tevel flint – outcrop opened by a small village quarry.

Figure 4. Geodetic survey of the Tevel flint outcrop.

whole it is non-transparent and has a dull lustre. Today it is opened on the surface by a small (limestone) village quarry (fig. 3). For long time, the outcrop was not accessible for archaeological research as a Russian military excercise ground for tanks was operating just over the flint-bearing layers. Due to re-organisation of the landscape following the sand mining and military use, we have lost the site from view for some time. István Wenczel, local collector helped us to locate the source again as well as added some workshop fields and regular archaeological sites to the list of distribution. In April 2001, the environs of the source were visited several times and a geodetic survey of the region was made (fig. 4).

Analytical studies on the material include petrographical thin section on geological reference sample and archaeological specimens from Aszód and Zengővárkony (fig. 5), optical emission spectroscopy data (Bácskay-Bihari 1989), neutron activation analysis (Varga 1991) (tabl. 1). Recently, prompt gamma activation analysis was performed by Zsolt Kasztovszky in the Institute of Isotope and Surface Chemistry of the HAS which will be published on the 33rd International Symposium of Archaeometry, Amsterdam.

Tevel flint on archaeological sites

Tevel flint is an important regional constituent among the Transdanubian lithic raw materials. On the "list of popularity" presented in 1992 (Biró 1993), it was ranked 22nd among 80 categories (Biró 1993 : 409, fig. 44.5). Its absolute contribution to the raw material supply of the country can be estimated around 2 %, centred mainly in Western Transdanubia. The distribution range is in the order of some 200 km radius at least (fig. 6); we can count on the appearance of Tevel flint in the neighbouring countries especially Slovakia where it was already recognised by M Kaczanowska at Svodín (Kaczanowska 1985).

The temporal distribution of Tevel flint seems to be centred in the Middle and Late Neolithic period, with a

13

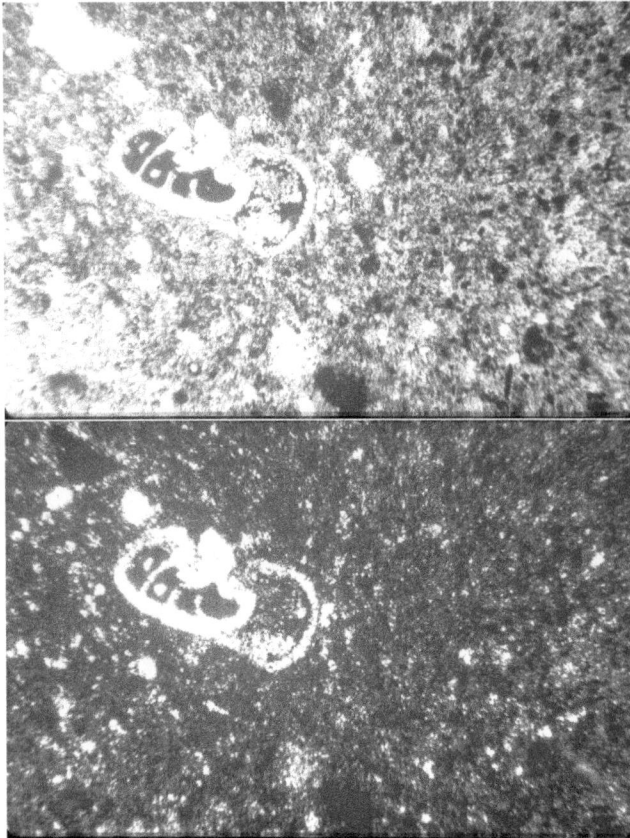

Figure 5. Petrographical thin section of Tevel flint. Foraminifera in cryptorystalline quartz matrix, rich in opal. Above: parallel Nicols, below: crossed Nicols.

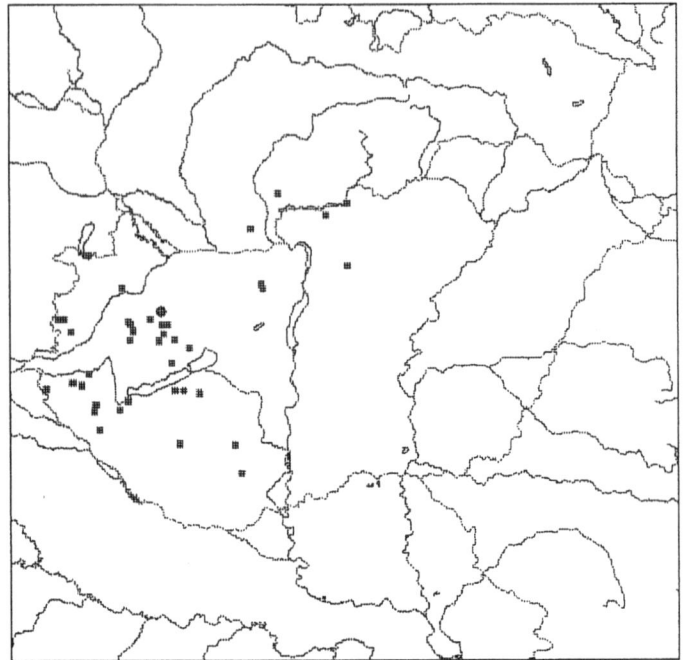

Figure 6. Distribution of Tevel flint on archaeological sites. Source is marked with full circle, archaeological sites with square. See also Table 2.

special preference of Transdanubian LBC Keszthely group (tabl. 2). The earliest appearance of the material, to our best knowledge, can be associated with the Würm 3 period, layers of the exploited sand quarry at the source region (mentioned by Bácskay and Bihari, 1989). As the source is small and unique, we can postulate that for large periods in prehistory it was not known to the inhabitants.

Kup-Egyes: workshop and distribution centre

The renewed interest in the exploitation area is mainly connected to the new excavations started at Kup, workshop site of LBC and Lengyel cultures closely connected to the source. The site was discovered in the seventies, discovered during planting an orchard, reported by Kálmán Szalay to the local museum, excavated by its director, Sándor Mithay (Mithay 1975). Kálmán Szalay still has in his private collection one of the choicest blade cores (fig. 7). Some comparable pieces were found by Mithay and subsequent field surveys in the early 1990-ies by G. Ilon. The archaeological material of the early excavations was published by Regenye et al. 1990, including the above mentioned exceptional cores and some refitting.

The current excavations, which are still in progress, completed our image on the Lengyel culture material mainly, though this year we had significant LBC finds including a

small depot (?) of Tevel flint as well. It is beyond question that the site was in direct connection with the Tevel source region and served as a workshop site and, probably, distribution centre for this material.

Data on the utilisation of Tevel flint

The physical qualities of Tevel flint render it specially suitable for the production of (relatively large) blades and blade derivatives. By simply comparing the main type groups of Hungarian average with the same data on Tevel flint we can see that blade forms were preferentially made of this material (fig. 8.). In the same way, we can investigate the tool forms typically made of Tevel flint. Most of them are made on blade (84 % of all tools). The most typical tool forms made on Tevel flint are truncated blades and blade scrapes, often with sickle polish. Tool form categories made of this material are summarised on figure 9.

A note on large conical cores

The most attractive finds from Tevel flint, known to us from Kup are the large conical cores. Though only part of them were found in excavation context (associated with LBC material), it seems that such type of cores were produced basically in the Middle Neolithic (LBC and derivatives) period in Hungary.

The investigation of about 40 000 pieces of lithic implements proved that full cores, especially large cores (over 10 cms) are extremely rare in Hungary. Lithic material was

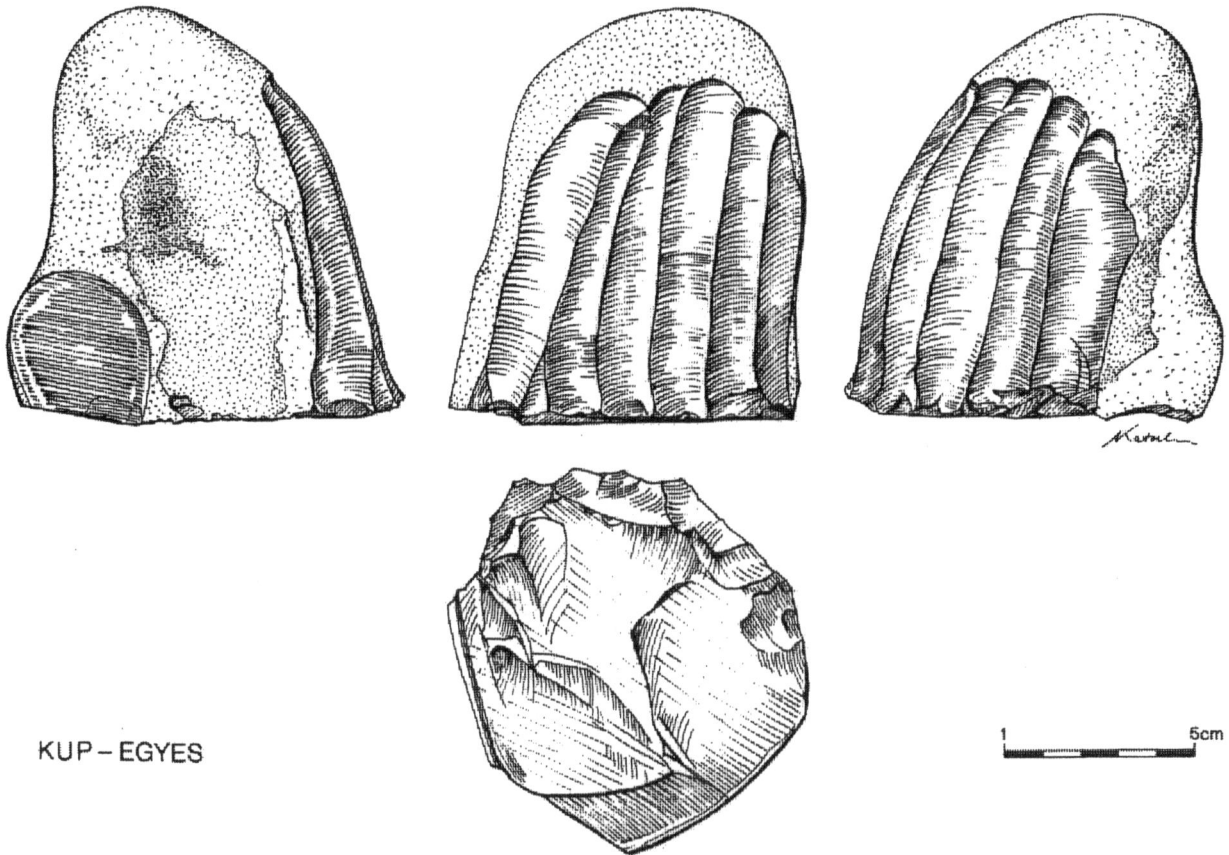

KUP – EGYES

Figure 7. Kup-Egyes: large conical core made of Tevel flint from the collection of K. Szalay.

available at restricted, special places only and typically much smaller size implements could be made of them. Obsidian is typically occurring in much smaller nodules; radiolarite will generally produce micro-cores rather than large conical cores due to the physical qualities of the material. Recent exceptional find (Budakeszi, Balatonszemes-Bagódomb) of large radiolarite cores and pre-cores only underline the connection of LBC assemblages and larger blades. Finds from Kašov published by Bánesz (1993) also connect LBC derivatives – notably, Bükk culture – with the production of large conical cores. As it was expressed elsewhere (Biró 1998), the large obsidian cores from the Nyirlugos depot can also be dated to Middle Neolithic rather than Copper Age.

Anyways, we must bear in mind that such large conical blade-cores are exceptional in our archaeological evidence and were probably representing a very large value for the prehistoric people. Tevel flint, of all, is primarily suited for the production of such cores and, consequently, blades and should be regarded as one of the best quality raw materials in the reach of prehistoric population in Hungary.

Summary

The investigation of Tevel flint, the exploitation area and its role in the prehistoric raw material economy of present-day Hungary is a current, topical task. Our plans include a detailed study of the exploitation are in hope of finding pre-historic mining traces and the elaboration of the Kup-Egyes workshop material which is constantly growing as a result of current excavations.

Aknowledgement

With financial support of Hungarian National Scientific Fund, OTKA T-25086.

Bibliography

BÁCSKAY, E., 1976, Early Neolithic Chipped Stone Implements in Hungary. *DissArch* 4 1-.

BÁCSKAY, E., SIMÁN, K., 1987, Some remarks on chipped stone industries of the earliest Neolithic populations in present Hungary. *Archaeologia Interregionalis* 240, Warsaw - Cracow University press, p. 107-130.

BÁCSKAY, E., BIHARI, D., 1989, Paleolitgyanús leletek a Bakonyból. *A Tapolcai Városi Múzeum Közleményei* p. 21-27.

BÁNESZ, L., 1993, Neolitische Werkstatt zur Herstellung von Obsidianindustrie in Kašov. *Actes du XIIe Congres International des Sciences Préhistoriques.* p. 432-437.

BIRÓ, K., 1987, Chipped stone industry of the Linearband Pottery

15

Katalin T. BIRÓ

Type group distribution of Tevel flint

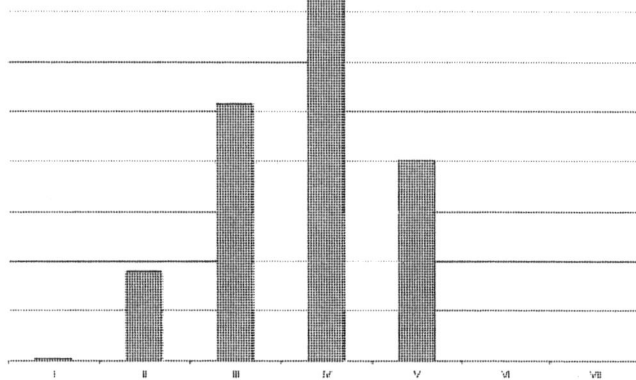

Type group distribution total

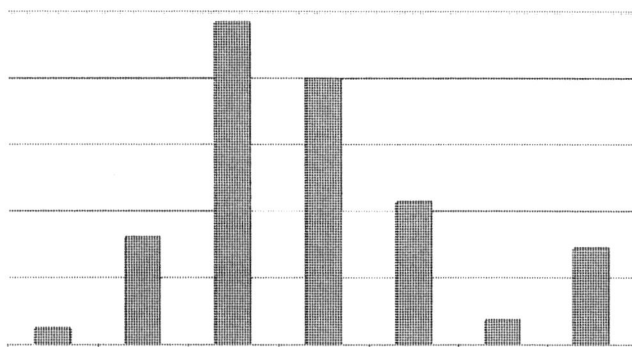

I: raw material   VI: polished stone tools
II: cores   VII: other stone utensils
III: flakes
IV: blades
V: retouched tools

Figure 8. Distribution of main tool type groups in Tevel flint and the Hungarian average.

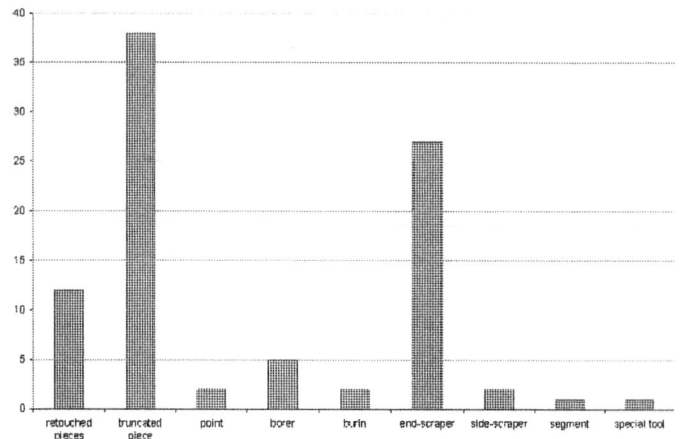

Figure 9. Tool type categories typically made of Tevel flint.

Culture in Hungary. *Archaeologia Interregionalis*, Warsaw - Cracow 240, p. 131-167.

BIRÓ, K., 1988, Distribution of lithic raw materials on prehistoric sites, *Acta Archaeologica Academiae Scientiarum Hungaricae* (Budapest) 40, p. 251-274.

BIRÓ, K., 1989, A kúp-egyesi neolit lelőhely köeszközei / From stone artifacts of neolithic place of accurence of Kúp-egyes. *Veszprémi Történelmi Tár.* Veszprém, 2 p. 34-41.

BIRÓ, K., 1991, Mencshely-Murvagödrök köanyaga (Stein-artefacten aus neue Grabungen von Mencshely) *A Tapolcai Városi Múzeum Közleményei* 2, p. 51-72.

BIRÓ, K., 1991a, Steingerate des Fundortes Kustánszeg-Lisztessarok. *CommArchHung* p. 32-37.

BIRÓ, K., 1993, Good or bad? Raw material procurement criteria in the Carparthian Basin. In: ANDERSON–MADSEN-SCOLLAR, *CAA 1992 Proceedings*, Aarhus, p. 405-413.

BIRÓ, K., 1998, *Lithic implements and the circulation of raw materials in the Great Hungarian Plain during the Late Neolithic Period,* Budapest, Magyar Nemzeti Múzeum 1-350.

BIRÓ, ed. 1986, T. Biró K. (ed), *Ösköri kovabányászat és kőeszköznyersanyag azonosítás a Kárpát medencében (International conference on prehistoric flint mining and lithic raw material identification in the Carpathian Basin)* Sümeg Papers Vol. 1. (1986) Budapest KMI Rota 1-342.

BIRÓ, ed. 1987, T. Biró K. (ed), *Őskori kovabányászat és kőeszköznyersanyag azonosítás a Kárpát medencében (International conference on prehistoric flint mining and lithic raw material identification in the Carpathian Basin)* Sümeg Proceedings Vol. 2. (1987) Budapest KMI Rota 1-.

BIRÓ, K., DOBOSI, V., 1991, *LITOTHECA - Comparative Raw Material Collection of the Hungarian National Museum.* Budapest, Magyar Nemzeti Múzeum, p. 1-268.

BIRÓ, K., DOBOSI, T., & SCHLÉDER, Zs., 2000, *LITOTHECA II. - Comparative Raw Material Collection of the Hungarian National Museum* Budapest Magyar Nemzeti Múzeum /1991/ 1-320.

KACZANOWSKA, M., 1985, *Rohstoffe, Technik und Typologie der neolithischen Feuersteinindustrien im Nordteil des Flussgebietes der Mitteldonau.* Warszawa 1-.

MITHAY, S., 1975, Kup-Egyes. *Régészeti Füzetek* I/1 28, p. 13.

REGENYE, J., GLÄSER, R,. & BIRÓ, K., 1990, Kup-Egyes. *Veszprémi Történeti Tár* 1, p. 18-42.

VARGA, I., 1991, Mineralogical analysis of the lithic material from the Palaeolithic Site of Esztergom-Gyurgyalag. *Acta Archaeologica ASH* 43, p. 267-269.

Analnr	Source or site	Li	V	Cr	Mn	Co	Ni	Cu	Sr	Y	Zr	Mo	Ag	Sn	Ba	La	Pb
1666	Nagytevel	0.16		100	1600		60	60	16			6	0.25		100		
1667	Nagytevel	4		100	600		60	100	16			10	0.16		100		

Optical emission spectroscopy analyses data, ppm (Biró *et al.* 2000, after Bácskay-Bihari 1989).

Analnr	Source or site	La	Na	Sb	Sc	Sm	U
169	Nagytevel	0.2	189	0.29	0.11	0.08	0.51
170	Nagytevel	0.24	191	1.14	0.09	0.07	0.36

Neutron activation analyses data, ppm (Biró *et al.* 2000, after Varga 1991).

Table 1. Analytical data on Tevel flint.

Site	Period	Culture	stone tools total	Tevel flint (pieces)	Tevel flint (%)
Aszód - Papi földek	LN	Lengyel culture	4260	118	2,77
Kup-Egyes	EMP		196	100	51,02
Ajka-Csók u. 3.	LN	Lengyel culture	105	32	30,48
Zalaszentbalázs-Szőlőhegyi m.	LN		414	29	7,00
Csabdi-Télizöldes	LN	Lengyel culture	417	16	3,84
Kustánszeg-Lisztessarok	MN	LBC culture	25	16	64,00
Gellénháza-Városrét	EN, MN	Starcevo, LBC	1227	15	1,22
Németbánya-Felsőerdei dűlő III/5	LB-EIA	Tumulus grave/Urn field culture	555	14	2,52
Balatonmagyaród-Kápolnapuszta	N	LBC, Lengyel	191	13	6,81
Mencshely-Berki kút	MN	LBC	594	12	2,02
Sé-Malomi dűlő	LN	Sopot, Lengyel	70	10	14,29
Nemesvámos-Balácapuszta	MN-LN		613	9	1,47
Nagykanizsa-Sánc	CA	Balaton culture	136	8	5,88
Zalaegerszeg-Gébárti tó	EN-MN	Starcevo, LBC	385	6	1,56
Nagycsepely-Pácsmánd	LN	Lengyel culture	48	5	10,42
Csögle	MN-MBA	LBC, Lengyel	10	4	40,00
Gór-Kápolnadomb	MN-LBA	LBC	123	4	3,25
Zala	LN	Lengyel culture	12	4	33,33
Iszkáz-Rétdombdűlő	MN		9	3	33,33
Szentgál-Füzikút	LN	Lengyel culture	441	3	0,68
Kaposvár-Gyertyános	LN	Lengyel culture	179	3	1,68
Bakonyjákó-Malomoldal	LB		44	3	6,82
Licskóvadamos-Mucsfalu-Dél	MN	LBC	7	3	42,86
Balatonmagyaród - Hidvégpuszta	LN	Lengyel culture	64	2	3,13
Zengővárkony	LN	Lengyel culture	2843	2	0,07
Adorjánháza			3	2	66,67
Veszprémpinkóc	MN-LN	LBC, lengyel	6	2	33,33
Ajka-Pál major	LN	Lengyel culture	236	2	0,85
Svodin (Szőgyén), Slovakia	LN	Lengyel culture	10	2	20,00
Kisunyom-Nádasi tábla	MN-LN	LBC, Lengyel	28	2	7,14
Szécsény - Ültetés	MN	Zseliz culture	438	1	0,23
Csesztve - Stalák	LN		406	1	0,25
Santovka	LN		225	1	0,44
Páli-Homokbánya	MN	LBC	53	1	1,89
Kislőd	LN	Lengyel culture	47	1	2,13
Balatonszölös	MN	LBC	2	1	50,00
Lengyel	LN	Lengyel culture	600	1	0,17
Kisberzseny			2	1	50,00
Bicske-Galagonyás	EN-LN	LBC, Sopot	287	1	0,35
Mencshely-Murvagödrök	MN	LBC	135	1	0,74
Hahót-Szartori I.	LN, CA	Lengyel, Baden	45	1	2,22
Dozmat-Hosszú dűlő	MN-LN	LBC, Lengyel	46	1	2,17
Dozmat-Csompatka	MN-BA	LBC	45	1	2,22
Szentgyörgyvölgy-Pityer	EN	Starcevo	379	1	0,26
Látrány-homokbánya	MN	Zseliz culture	14	1	7,14
Ajka-Szent István u. 6.	LN	Lengyel culture	6	1	16,67
Vörs-Máriaasszonysziget	N-CA	Lengyel culture	45	1	2,22

Table 2. Occurrences of Tevel flint.

17

MINING AND SILICEOUS ROCK SUPPLY TO THE DANUBIAN EARLY FARMING COMMUNITIES (LBK) IN EASTERN CENTRAL EUROPE : A SECOND APPROACH

Jacek LECH*

Résumé

Cet article résume les recherches dans l'extraction du silex et l'approvisionnement en matières siliceuses au sein des communautés LBK. Les roches siliceuses clairement différenciées dans la partie orientale de l'Europe centrale offrent une bonne opportunité aux recherches dans ce domaine. Il semble que les méthodes d'extraction peu élaborées étaient fréquentes parmi les communautés LBK. En comparant les matières premières et les compositions des assemblages lithiques LBK des différents sites implantés à des distances variées des gîtes de matière siliceuse, on peut reconstituer l'organisation de l'approvisionnement en silex. Les sites responsables de l'exploitation et de la transformation des roches siliceuses et les sites des consommateurs étaient liés dans un réseau multi-directionnel d'échanges directs et indirects. Il semble qu'un système de circulation équivalent n'existe pas sur une telle échelle dans les périodes plus récentes du Néolithique.

Abstract

This paper summarizes research into flint mining and siliceous rock supplies among LBK communities. The clearly differentiated siliceous rocks in the eastern part of central Europe provide good opportunities for research in this field. It seems that simple mining methods were common among LBK communities. By comparing the raw material and morphological structures of LBK chipped inventories from different sites located at various distances from the deposits of siliceous rocks, one can reconstruct the organisation of flint supply. The settlements dealing with the exploitation and processing of siliceous rocks and the settlements of users were connected by a network of multi-directional direct and indirect exchanges. It seems that such networks did not exist on such a scale in the later periods of the Neolithic.

From the history of research

Without depreciating the importance of theoretical revolutions in science, we must not forget that the advance of knowledge also takes place through accumulation. This is certainly true in the area which was the subject of our conference.

In the second half of the 20th century chipped materials became one of the subjects to be included in studies of LBK communities. It seems that the first noteworthy work in this field was done in the Netherlands, Poland and Great Britain (Bohmers & Bruijn 1958-1959; Tringham 1968; Newell

1970). In Poland such studies of LBK chipped material were initiated by A. Dzieduszycka-Machnikowa (1961) and J.K. Kozłowski (1970; 1971 ed.; 1974 : 8-22; Kozłowski & Kulczycka 1961) in second half of the fifties.

Nevertheless, at the beginning of the seventies our knowledge concerning the long-distance distribution of many kinds of siliceous rock was still limited, as becomes evident when we read R. Tringham's (1972) article on the famous site at Bylany in eastern Bohemia (see Lech 1989); and when it come to flint mining we knew nothing at all. We owe our knowledge concerning such areas as mining, the morphological structure of chipped inventories at LBK sites and the great variety of siliceous rocks utilized by LBK communities to the contemporary generation of researchers working in Europe in the last thirty years, whose notable representation participated

(*) Institute of Archaeology and Ethnology, Polish Academy of Sciences, Al. Solidarności 105, PL 00-140 Warszawa.

Jacek LECH

Figure 1. Sümeg-Mogyorósdomb, Veszprém dist. The Neolithic radiolarite mine in the SW end of the Transdanubian Mid-Mountains (Bakony Mountains) in western Hungary. A. Part of the open air museum with outlines of exploitation pits (white places). December 1981. B. Part of the shallow exploitation pit. Scale 20 cm (see Bác-skay 1995).

in the XIV International Congress of Prehistoric and Protohistoric Sciences held at Liège, and specially in the symposium 9.3. : *Gestion des matières premières dans le Rubané européen*.

In this paper I am returning to a subject which I devoted much time to in the eighties (Lech 1987; 1988; 1989; 1990; 1991). Today, I wish to present to what extent research done in the last decade of the twentieth century has added to our knowledge of mining and long-distance distribution of siliceous rocks among LBK communities. I will limit myself to the area of eastern Central Europe and to those varieties of siliceous rock which were important on an interregional level. By eastern Central Europe I mean present-day Poland, the Czech Republic, Slovakia, Eastern Austria and Hungary.

Raw materials

The easily differentiated siliceous rocks that occur in eastern Central Europe provide good opportunities for research of flint supply to prehistoric communities. The straighforward division of siliceous rocks used by LBK communities enables us to differentiate raw material of interregional, regional and local importance (Lech 1988 : 370). In eastern Central Euro-

pe the most important siliceous rocks were Middle Jurassic Szentgál radiolarite (Bath-Kallovian period) of pelagic origin from the Transdanubian Central Mountains - the Bakony Mountains, obsidian from the Zemplin-Tokay Mountains and Jurassic-Cracow flint from the southern part of the Polish Jura (Lech 1981a : 7-17; Kaczanowska 1985 : 16-24; Biró 1986; 1987; 1995; Biró & Regenye 1991).

Several other raw materials were also distributed interregionally but were lesser importance. Among them were other varieties of radiolarite from the Bakony Mountains (fig. 1), Skršín type quartzites, Tušimice and Bečov from northwestern Bohemia (fig. 6 - g), and "chocolate" (fig. 2 and fig. 6 - c), and grey white spotted flints from the Świętokrzyskie Mountains (Holy Cross Mountains - fig. 6 - k-a) region in central Poland (Schild 1980; 1987; 1995; Lech 1981a:7-13; Vencl 1989; Biró 1987 : 150-151; Lech & Mateiciucová 1995a; 1995b). Further research may show that hornstone from the Krumlovský Les area in southern Moravia was also important on an interregional scale (Mateiciucová 1995; 1997; Oliva 1997; Oliva *et al* 1999 : 257-269).

Moreover, very good quality cretaceous flint, known as Volhynian and Dnestr (Dniester, Dniestr) flint, was important from the east, from western Ukraine, while Bavarian tabular banded hornstone - *plattensilex* (fig. 3) was brought in from the west (Sulimirski 1960 : 299-304; Kozłowski 1974:9-15; Lech 1981a:8-9 and 17; 1989; 1990; Kaczanowska 1985 : 23 and Karte 2; Engelhardt & Binsteiner 1988; Groot 1994; 1995). In the period when LBK communities inhabited Central Europe the area over which various raw materials distributed underwent certain changes. This can be best observed in the multi-phase settlement of Bylany in East Bohemia (Lech 1989; 1990).

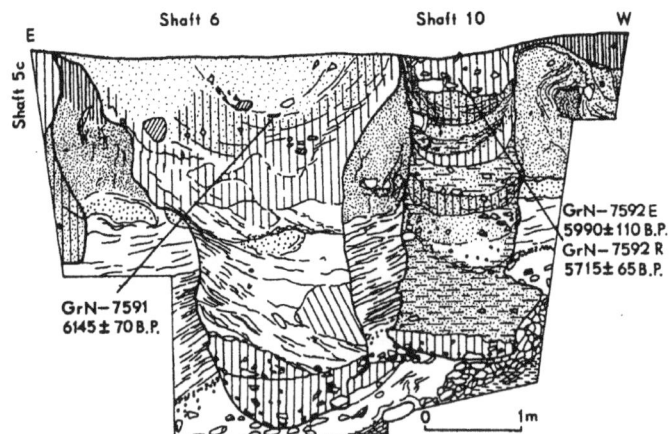

Figure 2. Tomaszów, Radom dist. The Neolithic mine of the "chocolate" flint in central Poland. Cross-section of shafts no 6, 10, and part of shaft 5c with radiocarbon dating. According to R. Schild *et al* 1985.

20

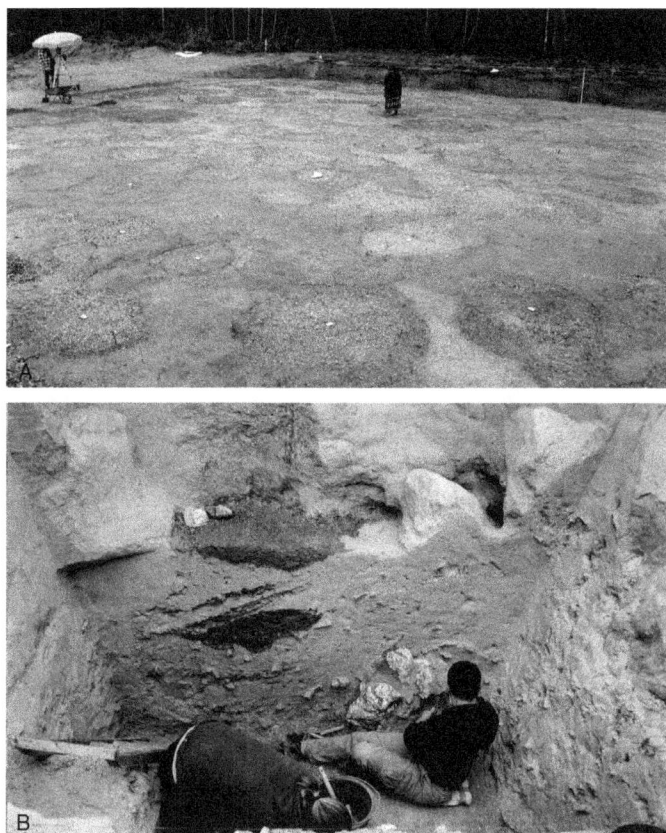

Figure 3. Abensberg-Arnhofen, Kelheim dist. The Neolithic mine of the Bavarian tabular banded hornstone. Excavation conducted by Dr. Michael M. Rind, *Kreisarchäolog.* A. The cutting from 2001 with the narrow shafts visible in the cutting floor. B. Cross-section of a shaft during excavation.

Mining

It seems that simple mining exploitation of siliceous rocks was a characteristic feature of the culture of LBK communities in those regions where deposits of raw material occurred (Lech 1981a : 47; 1988 : 370-374; Schild 1987 : 139; 1995; Engelhardt & Binsteiner 1988; Engelhardt 1989; Groot 1995). It would also seem that studies of the oldest LBK settlements, which have been carried out in the last decade, provide convincing proof that mining and long-distance distribution of raw materials began during the earliest LBK phase in eastern Central Europe. I am basing my surmise on the analysis of chipped inventories from Szentgyörgyvölgy-Piterdomb settlement, Zala district, to the west of the southern edge of Lake Balaton (Hungary) - material from the excavations carried out by Dr. Eszter Bánffy in 1996 - and the inventories from the settlement at Brunn am Gebirge, site Wolfholz in Lower Austria, directly south of Vienna - excavations by Dr. Peter Stadler in 1999 (Lenneis *et al* 1996 : 101-104; Lenneis 1999; Stadler 1999). In both cases the dominant material is Szentgál radiolarite from the Bakony Mountains which lie 100 km from the Piterdomb site and 180 km from Brunn.

Other mined raw materials also occur at Brunn, as, for instance, different varieties of radiolarites from the Bakony

Mountains. Hornstone from the Krumlovský Les area in southern Moravia was also found at the Fundstelle III settlement, 100 km away. This particular raw material was massively exploited by a later LBK community from the Vedrovice-Zábrdovice settlement, Znojmo district, in southern Moravia.

We know of only a few mining features connected with LBK communities, but conclusions concerning mining can also be based on a geological analysis of deposits and the characteristics of the raw materials which were used. Siliceous rocks could have been extracted from shallow exploitation units. There were several possibilities :
1.- systematic extraction from eluvial clays, from glacial or aluvial gravel trains, together with casual soil working;
2.- shallow pits where only one man could work, as in the mining field of Sümeg-Mogyorósdomb in the Bakony Mountains (fig. 1-B.), where the beginning of radiolarite extraction is connected with the LBK communities (Bácskay 1995 : 392-393);
3.- open shafts, maybe also with side workings; this type of flint exploitation by LBK communities was first discovered by R. Schild at Tomaszów in central Poland (Schild 1980; 1987; 1995; Schild *et al* 1985) where "chocolate" flint was exploited. Among this category of workings we can observe a clear division into two groups:
- wide shafts at the mouth, as, for instance, at Tomaszów, Radom dist. (fig. 2);
- narrow shafts with best examples at Abensberg-Arnhofen (fig. 3), Kelheim dist. (Engelhardt & Binsteiner 1988; Engelhardt 1989).

North of Sudetic Mountains the oldest LBK settlements appear approximately in the horizon of Fundstelle III at Brunn, as, for instance, at Gniechowice, Wrocław dist. The flint industry of Gniechowice is similar to that of Brunn though at Gniechowice only local erratic "Baltic" flint occurs. Soon after, in the 1b phase of LBK, in the Vistula and Oder catchment area, mined Jurassic-Cracow flint of the Sąspów variety appears in settlements in Chełmno-land, 400 km north of deposits (Lech 1990:54; Małecka-Kukawka 1992:61) and, probably in the same early phase, at Kazimierza Mała, 50 km east of Sąspów (material from recent excavations by Dr. Krzysztof Tunia). The connection between the beginnings of exploitation of the Sąspów mining field and LBK communities was already noted some time ago (Lech 1975 : 71; 1980 : 619; 1988 : 371-374; 1990 : 50-53).

Flint working on the site of mine or in related encampments and settlements near to the mine, comes under the general heading of mining. The social framework of siliceous rock mining in LBK communities was determined by tribal organization, probably similar to the segmentary tribal design with the familial mode of production described by Sahlins (1968; 1974; see Lech 1981b; 1990; Whittle 1996 : 162-167; Milisauskas 2002 : 185-186) which in the case of LBK communities was comprehensively characterized by Dr. Marjorie de Grooth (1994; 1995; 1997).

Functional variations among LBK sites and settlements

The key to understanding the organization of work linked with mining, raw material processing and distribution in the early farming communities lies in comparative analysis of production remains in settlements, encampments, mines and workshops - that is sites where intensive working of raw materials was carried out. The workshops are distinguished by the number of chipped materials together with their distribution and structure. They are known from LBK sites. The excavation of the LBK settlement at Vedrovice-Zábrdovice, Znojmo dist., in South Moravia, has provided the most interesting example (Ondruš 1976; Lech 1983 : 49-52; Mateiciucová 1997). Analysis of chipped remains which bear the attributes of assemblages, or their representative parts, based on comparison of the general structure of the materials and observable changes in their fundamental characteristics, is the best way to reconstruct the organization of work on the site and the model, or models, supplying settlements with siliceous rocks. The starting point for analysis must always be the reconstruction of the end product, or products, of the workshop and the techniques by which they were produced (Lech 1983 : 48-49).

Therefore, by comparing the raw material and morphological structures of LBK chipped inventories from different sites located at various distances from the deposits, one can reconstruct also the organization of siliceous rock supply (Lech 1975; 1983; 1989; 1991; 1997). The validity of the division of chipped materials into four morphological groups has been confirmed by the latest use-ware analyses of LBK inventories from Chełmno-land in northern Poland. They show that specimens from the second and fourth morphological groups - blades and blade fragments and retouched tools (fig. 4) - were primarily utilized as tools (Małecka-Kukawka 2001:32-50). We may conclude that LBK communities distinguished partly similar categories of specimens to those distinguished by contemporary researches. Comparison of samples of chipped materials from the oldest LBK settlements at Szentgyörgyvölgy-Piterdomb and Brunn shows a strikingly similar structure (table 1 - see p. 30).

Both settlements utilized Szentgál radiolarite. In spite of the considerable distance to the Bakony Mountains, the raw material reached them mainly in the form of natural pieces and, probably, pre-cores and cores. It is not known whether the radiolarite was obtained by means of exchange or through independent excursions to the mining field. Piterdomb and Brunn lie at a distance of considerably more than one day from the Szentgál radiolarite deposits. Brunn and Piterdomb were secondary producers centres as both settlements can be considered as secondary centres processing and distributing Szentgál radiolarite.

A comparison, according to the same criteria, of the general morphological structure of chipped materials from twelve later LBK settlements, lying in various regions north of the Danube, leads to further conclusions (fig. 4 and 5). All the settlements given here used Jurassic-Cracow flint. It dominated in Olszanica (fig. 4-A and 5-A), Strachów (fig. 4-B and 5-B), Bylany (fig. 4-G and 5-B), Topolčany (fig. 4-I and 5-I) and Boguszewo (fig.4-L and 5-L). At Vedrovice (fig. 4-H and 5-H) and Żalęcino (fig. 4-K and 5-K) its share was small. In all the settlements siliceous rocks coming from long-distance distribution were found.

Materials from Cracow-Olszanica (A) and Vedrovice-Zábrdovice (H) are only samples of the far richer inventories from settlements exploiting deposits of Jurassic-Cracow flint, in the case of Olszanica (Milisauskas 1986), and Krumlovský Les hornstone, in the case of Vedrovice (Lech 1983 : 49-52; Mateiciucová 1995; 1997). Excavations at Olszanica yielded over 42 thousand flint artifacts from an area of 15579 sq. m, which means an average of 2.7 specimens from one sq. m. As S. Milisauskas (1986:83) writes: "This number would be higher if the modern plow zone had not been removed with a bulldozer". The deposits of raw materials exploited by the two settlements were within the sphere of economic activities of the communities from Olszanica and Vedrovice, no farther than two hours walking distance in the case of Vedrovice and six hours in the case of Olszanica (see Bakels 1978 : 6-9 and 128-142). When compared with secondary production centres such as Brunn and Piterdomb, there are fewer blades and blade fragments, as well as fewer retouched tools. The share of pieces from the first morphological group may differ because of differences in the frequency of natural nodules, of which many were found at Vedrovice. Olszanica and Vedrovice are settlements of primary producers (see Lech 1997 : 623-630).

The third clearly defined group of settlements are settlements of users, lying far from deposits of good quality raw materials. The most important siliceous rocks reached them through long-distance distribution, primarily in the form of pre-core and core forms, blade blanks and ready tools. A characteristic feature of these settlements is the increased share of blades, blade fragments and tools which together make up about 45% or more of the whole inventory and the smaller share of flakes and waste, comprising less than 50%. Among the settlements of users are Strachów (B) - 220 km from the deposits of Jurassic-Cracow flints (Kulczycka-Leciejewiczowa 1997), Samborzec (C), Rzeszów (D), Tarnoszyn (E), Kormanice (F), Bylany (G), Topolčany (I) and Brześć Kujawski (J).

A separate commentary is needed in the case of the morphological structure of chipped materials from three settlements - Żalęcino (K), Boguszewo (L) and Topolčany (I). The Żalęcino (K) settlement (fig. 4, 5, and 6) is located in West Pomerania (Poland). The flint materials here the remains of processing of poor quality local erratic "Baltic" flint which makes up 94.8% specimens. Jurassic-Cracow flint comprise only 0.6% (2 specimens) and chocolate flint 4.6% (15 specimens). The structure of the inventory reflects these circumstances. The high frequency of specimens from the

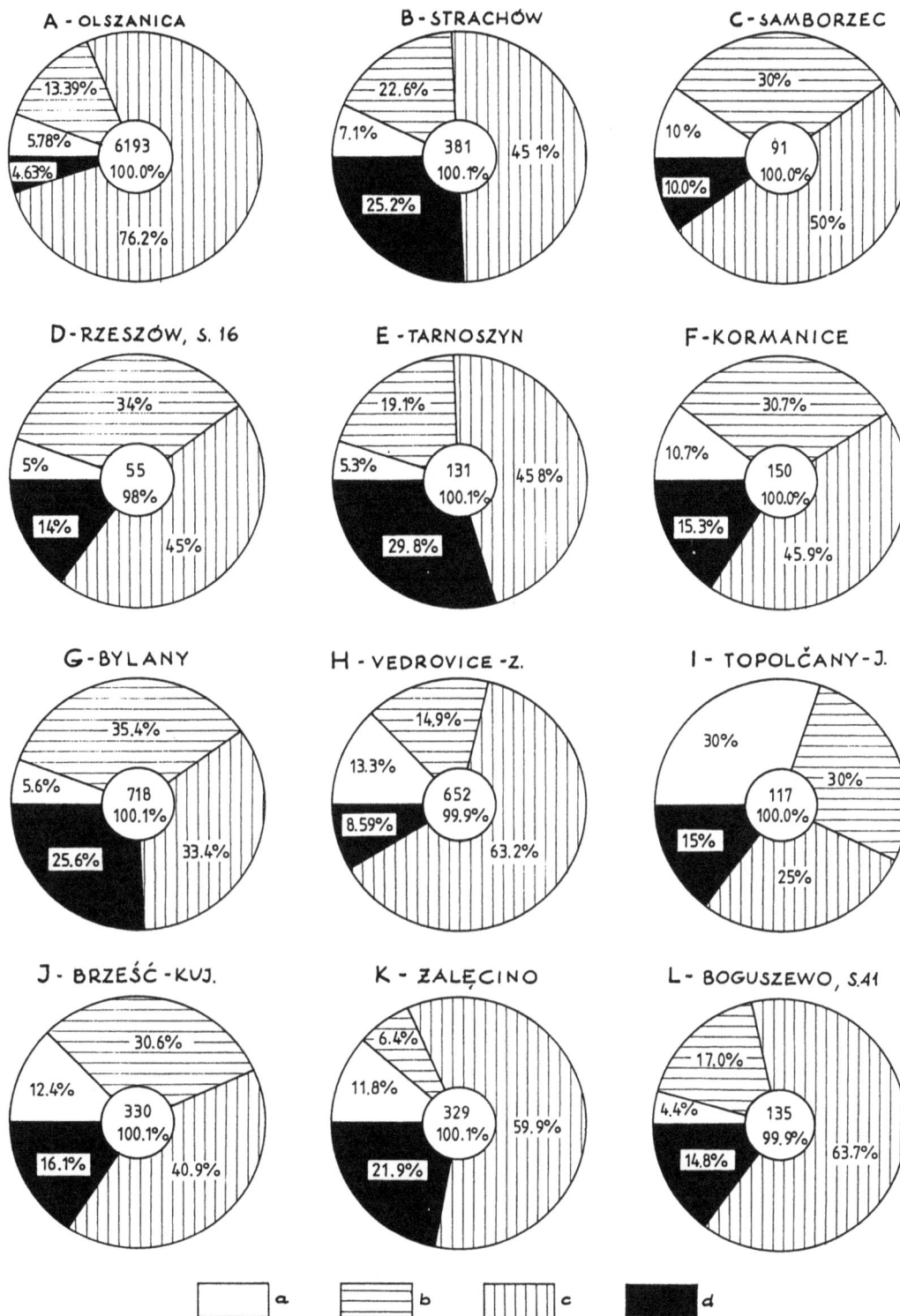

A - OLSZANICA
13.39%
5.78%
4.63%
6193
100.0%
76.2%

B - STRACHÓW
22.6%
7.1%
381
100.1%
45 1%
25.2%

C - SAMBORZEC
30%
10%
91
100.0%
10.0%
50%

D - RZESZÓW, S. 16
34%
5%
55
98%
14%
45%

E - TARNOSZYN
19.1%
5.3%
131
100.1%
45 8%
29.8%

F - KORMANICE
30.7%
10.7%
150
100.0%
15.3%
45.9%

G - BYLANY
35.4%
5.6%
718
100.1%
25.6%
33.4%

H - VEDROVICE - Z.
14.9%
13.3%
652
99.9%
8.59%
63.2%

I - TOPOLČANY - J.
30%
30%
117
100.0%
15%
25%

J - BRZEŚĆ - KUJ.
30.6%
12.4%
330
100.1%
16.1%
40.9%

K - ZALĘCINO
6.4%
11.8%
329
100.1%
59.9%
21.9%

L - BOGUSZEWO, S.41
17.0%
4.4%
135
99.9%
14.8%
63.7%

a   b   c   d

Figure 4. General structures of the chipped materials from twelve later LBK settlements, lying in various regions in eastern Central Europe (see fig. 5), according to the basic morphological groups: a - natural nodules, pre-cores and cores; b - blades and blade fragments; c - flakes and waste; d - retouched tools and hammerstones.

23

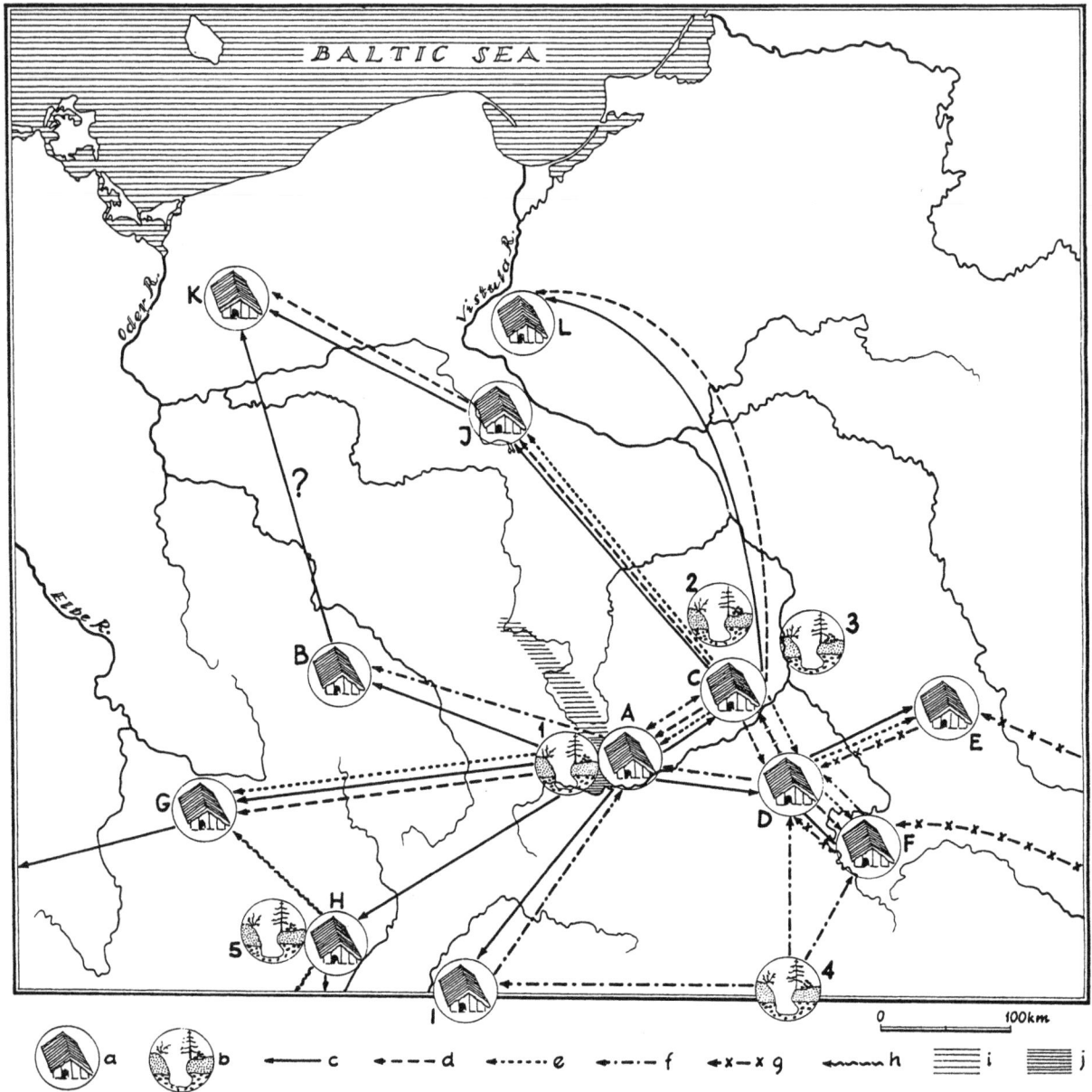

Figure 5. Supply of siliceous rocks to the twelve later LBK settlements (see fig. 4) and some mining sites, lying in various regions in eastern Central Europe, north of the Danube: a - settlements (see fig. 4); b - mines; c - directions of Jurassic-Cracow flint distribution; d - directions of "chocolate" flint distribution; e - directions of grey white spotted flint (Świeciechów flint) distribution; f - directions of obsidian distribution; g - directions of Volhynian and Dnestr flint distribution; h - directions of hornstone from the Krumlovský Les area distribution; i - the Polish Jura; j - southern part of the Polish Jura with deposits of Jurassic-Cracow flint. A - Cracow-Olszanica; B - Strachów; C - Samborzec; D - Rzeszów, site 16; E - Tarnoszyn; F - Kormanice; G - Bylany; H - Vedrovice-Zábrdovice; I - Topolčany-Jacovce, site Medzivody; J - Brześć Kujawski; K - Żalęcino; L - Boguszewo, site 41. 1 - Sąspów; 2 - Tomaszów; 3 - Świeciechów; 4 - exploitation of obsidian deposits in southeastern Slovakia; 5 - exploitation of hornstone from the Krumlovský Les area. See also fig. 6.

first and third morphological group and the low frequency of blades indicate that low quality raw material was processed. Whereas the large share of prepared tools indicates that the inventory comes from a settlement suffering from an inadequate supply of good quality siliceous rock (see Kaczanowska 1985 : 25-73).

The settlement at Boguszewo site 41 (L) in Chełmno-land, located far from good quality raw material, has an inventory structure characteristic of settlements lying on Cra-

cow loess, near deposits of Jurassic-Cracow flint. Two factors were influential here. The Jurassic-Cracow flint which dominates in the inventory (63.7%) reached Boguszewo in the form of prepared pre-cores and cores. Local erratic "Baltic" flint (25.9%), in two variants, was also processed here (Małecka-Kukawka 1992:37 and Pl. 1-3). The working of this poor quality raw material provided more flakes and waste than in the case of Jurassic-Cracow flint which Jacques Pelegrin in 1989 rated in the lower group of average quality European flint.

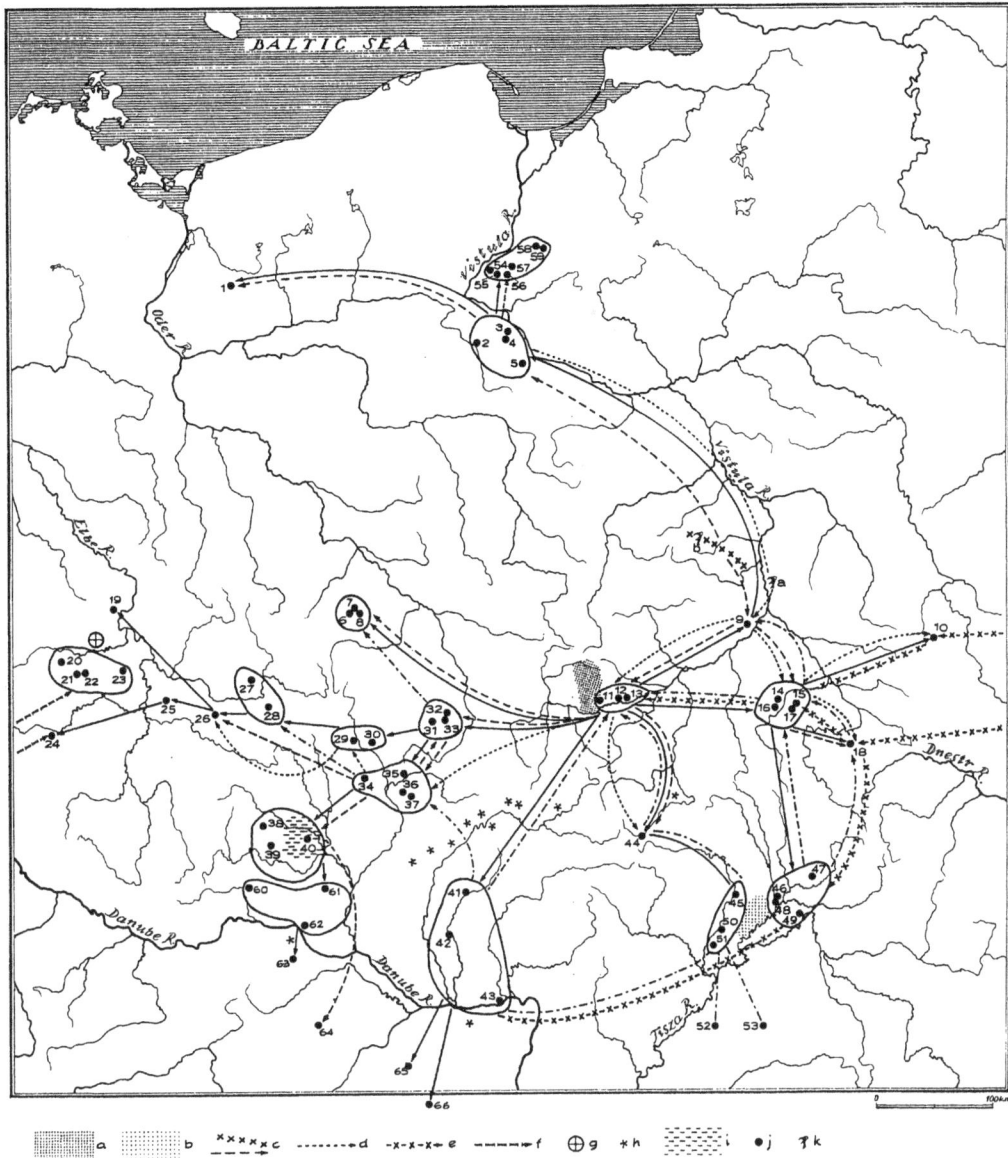

Figure 6. The distribution of siliceous rocks to the first farming communities in eastern central Europe, north of the Danube (without Szentgál radiolarite): a - Jurassic-Cracow flint deposits and directions of raw material distribution (see fig. 5 - c); b - obsidian deposits and directions of raw material distribution (see fig. 5 - f); c - "chocolate" flint deposits and directions of raw material distribution; d - directions of grey-white spotted Świeciechów flint distribution; e - directions of Volhynian and Dnestr flint distribution; f - directions of Bavarian striped hornstone distribution from Abensberg-Arnhofen flint mine; g - Skršín, Tušimice and Bečov quartzites from north-western Bohemia; h - radiolarite deposits; i - exploitation of hornstone from the Krumlovský Les area; j - archaeological sites; k - flint mines. Sites (j) : **Poland** 1 - Żalęcino, dist. Szczecin; 2 - Łojewo, dist. Bydgoszcz; 3 - Przybranowo, dist. Włocławek; 4 - Straszewo, dist. Włocławek; 5 - Brześć Kujawski, dist. Włocławek; 6 - Niemcza, dist. Wałbrzych; 7 - Strachów, dist. Wrocław; 8 - Skoroszowice, dist. Wrocłw; 9 - Samborzec, dist. Sandomierz; 10 - Tarnoszyn, dist. Zamość; 11 - Cracow-Olszanica; 12 - Cracow-Mogiła; 13 - Cracow-Pleszów; 14 - Rzeszów, site 16; 15 - Łańcut, dist. Rzeszów; 16 - Boguchwała, dist. Rzeszów; 17 - Kraczkowa, dist. Rzeszów; 18 - Kormanice, dist. Przemyśl, site 1; 54 - Stolno, dist. Toruń, site 2; 55 - Kornatowo, dist. Toruń, site 2; 56 - Lisewo, dist. Toruń, site 31; 57 - Wielodząc, dist. Toruń, site 31; 58 - Boguszewo, dist. Toruń, site 41; 59 - Boguszewo, dist. Toruń, site 43a; **Czech Republik** 19 - Chabařovice, dist. Ústí nad Labem, site důl Petri; 20 - Chotěbudice, dist. Louny; 21 - Malá Černoc, dist. Louny; 22 - Velká Černoc, dist. Louny; 23 - Slaný, dist. Kladno; 24 - Křimice, dist. Pilsen-North; 25 - Říčany, dist. Praha-East; 26 - Bylany, dist. Kutná Hora; 27 - Libčany, dist. Hradec Králové; 28 - Úhřetice, dist. Chrudim; 29 - Mohelnice, dist. Šumperk; 30 - Brníčko, dist. Olomouc; 31 - Otice, dist. Opava; 32 - Neplachovice, dist. Opava; 33 - Kravaře-Kouty, dist. Opava; 34 - Mostkovice, dist. Prostějov; 35 - Lipnik, dist. Prerov; 36 - Prusy, dist. Přerov; 37 - Žopy, dist. Kroměříž; 38 - Bohušice, dist. Třebíč; 39 - Bojanovice, dist. Znojmo; 40 - Vedrovice-Zábrdovice, dist. Znojmo; **Slovakia** 41 - Topolčany-Jacovce, site Medzivody; 42 - Nitra, site 'Přemyslova ulíca'; 43 - Štúrovo, dist. Nové Zámky; 44 - Poprad-Matejovce; 45 - Ždana, dist. Košice, site Baxaser; 46 - Kopčany, dist. Michalovce; 47 - Krčava, dist. Michalovce, site Stoček; 48 - Malé Raškovce, dist. Trebišov; 49 - Velké Trakany, dist. Trebišov, site Szélmalomdomb; **Hungary** 50 - Boldogkővaralja, dist. Borsod-Abaúj-Zemplin; 51 - Megyaszó Nagy Répás, dist. Borsod-Abaúj-Zemplin; 52 - Hortobágy near Debrecen, site Árkuspart; 53 - Debrecen-Tocopart; 65 - Kúp, dist. Veszprém; 66 - Mencshely-Murvagödrök, dist. Veszprém; **Eastern Austria** 60 - Mold , dist. Horn; 61 - Hadersdorf; dist. Poysdorf; 62 - Würnitz, dist. Kornenburg; 63 - Brunn am Gebirge, dist. Mödling; 64 - Neckenmarkt, dist. Oberpullendorf. Flint mines (k) : a - Świeciechów-Lasek near Annopol, dist. Kraśnik; b - Tomaszów, dist. Radom.

Finally, we must return to the structure of the inventory from Topolčany-Jacovce (I) in western Slovakia. The inventory is extremely interesting because of the large share of Jurassic-Cracow flint (40.2%) which arrived here in the form of pre-cores and cores. The settlement was probably a secondary centre of processing and distribution of this particular flint. Radiolarite (33.3%) and obsidian (16.2%) were also important as raw materials. The inventory comes from systematic surface collection so its structure is evidently disturbed (fig. 4). There are more large specimens (including pre-cores and cores) and much fewer small and medium-sized specimens from the group of flakes and waste. Among the 117 specimens there are 14 cores and 2 splintered pieces (*pieces esquiliées*) from Jurassic-Cracow flint, 6 cores from radiolarite, 8 from obsidian and 4 from other materials.

The LBK flint supply and exchange network

In the Mesolithic the distribution of siliceous rock in eastern Central Europe had a similar range to the one determined for western Central Europe (Cyrek 1981; Zimmermann 1991 : 3). Irrespective of the importance of Mesolithic traditions (Tringham 1968; Kozłowski 1980; Vencl 1986; Kaczanowska 1989; Gronenborn 1990; 1997; 1997; Whittle 1996:150-156; Mateiciucová 2001; Milisauskas 2002 : 153-157), the LBK communities seem to have created, from the beginning, an exceptional, for the Stone Age, system of long-distance flint supply and exchange network of siliceous rock. The system was characterized by multi-directional exchange of many kinds of siliceous rock, connecting in one network nearly all LBK regions and settlements. The Piterdomb and Brunn settlements indicate that the system began to be introduced at the same time when the culture of the LBK communities was forming. Exchange of siliceous rock on such a scale and in such a form has never been observed in this area either earlier or later.

When discussing mining I presented data suggesting the importance of long-distance distribution of Szentgál radiolarite (S). The area where this raw material occurs and the two settlements of Piterdomb (P) and Brunn (B) form a triangle with sides:

B - 180 km - S; S - 110 km - P; P- 150 km - B.

In the case of Szentgál radiolarite from Piterdomb and Brunn, it is possible the communities obtained raw material from the deposits by themselves or that supplies reached them through exchange, with several middlemen involved (see Lech 1989; 1990). Irrespective of the means by which Szentgál radiolarite was obtained (see Grooth 1994:103-135), the existence of exchange is evidence by the presence of small amounts of hornstone from the Krumlovský Les area (southern Moravia) in the Brunn settlement and of grey, mat silex of the Becsehely type (0.93%), probably from Croatia or Slovenia, at Piterdomb.

A comparative study of the morphological structures and differentiation of siliceous rocks in eastern Central Euro-

pe (see also Kaczanowska 1985 : 25-73), shows that in those settlement regions where ample good quality raw material occurred they were extracted in amounts far exceeding the needs of the settlement (fig. 5 : Olszanica - A; Vedrovice-Zábrdovice - B). A similar situation in western Central Europe, the Dutch Limburg and Belgium has been confirmed in studies by A. Zimmermann (1991), M. de Grooth (1994; 1995; 1997), D. Cahen, J.-P. Caspar & M. Otte (1986), and by L. Burnez-Lanotte's & P. Allard (1998) new research at Harduémont (Verlaine), site "Petit-Paradis". Those regions which lacked good quality siliceous rocks obtained flint through exchange, including the exchange of gifts (Mauss 1990 [1923-1924]; Lech 1989; 1990). This explains the systematic use of Jurassic-Cracow flint in the settlements of Lower Silesia (e.g. Strachów - fig. 5-B), eastern Bohemia (Bylany - fig. 5-G) or the Chełmno-land in northern Poland (e.g. Boguszewo - fig. 5-L). The fundamental role of the social and symbolic context of multi-stage, long-distance exchange among LBK communities is certified by the occurrence of small amounts of various siliceous rocks of interregional significance at such settlements as Samborzec (fig. 5-C), Rzeszów (fig. 5-D), Tarnoszyn (fig. 5-E) and Kormanice (fig. 5-F), and the presence of thirteen kinds of siliceous rocks at Bylany (fig. 5-G; see Lech 1989; 1990). The context of this exchange is difficult to define on the basis of archaeological data, but social anthropology is extremely helpful (Malinowski 1922; Mauss 1990 [1923-1924]; Firth 1939; 1956; Strathern 1971; 1984; Sahlins 1974; Godelier 1986; Lederman 1986; Lech 1990; Grooth 1994; Tilley 1994; McBryde 1997). Archaeological sources have their own logic and limitation (Lech 1997 : 634-635). Looking from this point of view it is certain that the settlements dealing with the exploitation and processing of siliceous rock (settlements of producers) and the settlements of users were connected by a network of multi-directional direct and indirect exchanges (fig. 5 and 6).

There is evidence that LBK communities attached greater importance to raw material of interregional significance than to local material. In recent years Dr. Jolanta Małecka-Kukawka (2001) has been conducting micro-ware studies of chipped inventories from Chełmno-land. It turns out that specimens of raw materials from Little Poland - Jurassic-Cracow and chocolate flint were used as tools much more often than specimens from local erratic "Baltic" flint. J. Małecka-Kukawka (2001 : 161-168 and 173-177) explains this fact as stemming from the magical significance attributed to mined flint (see also Taçon 1991; Whittle 1995). It is true that in distant settlements such as Żalęcino (fig. 5-K) small amounts of these raw materials (a total of 5.2%) had relatively great importance. Żalęcino lies 470 km away from deposits of Jurassic-Cracow flint, to the north-west and 460 km away from deposits of chocolate flint. Flint from Little Poland arrived here through indirect exchange from the Kujavia region or maybe even *via* Lower Silesia (fig. 5).

The distribution map (fig. 6) of the main siliceous rocks in eastern Central Europe shows that all settlement regions of the LBK communities were connected by a network of exchange and consequently by social ties. In the later LBK phase Jurassic-Cracow flint reached the same settlements in Bohemia which obtained Bavarian banded plattensilex from the west (flint mine Abensberg-Arnhofen - fig. 3). It seems that such networks did not exist on such a scale in the later periods of the Neolithic. The network of exchange was created gradually beginning in the early stages of LBK development.

As a result of the most recent studies certain corrections must be introduced concerning the exchange network of Bylany during the oldest phase of LBK settlement there (see Lech 1989; 1990). Szentgál radiolarite from the Bakony Mountains in Hungary (the variety was determined by Dr. Katalina T. Biró) appears, as do Jurassic-Cracow flint and Świeciechów flint from Little Poland. The deposits of radiolarite lie 380 km away and the Polish raw material is located at a distance of 300 and 500 km respectively. All three raw materials reached Bylany through settlement regions in Moravia; Szentgál radiolarite possibly together with Krumlovský Les hornstone. At approximately the same time Jurassic-Cracow flint began to reach the Chełmno-land, travelling along the Vistula - 400 km to the north (fig. 5), maybe *via* the Kazimierza Mała settlement.

Final remarks

The methods of obtaining flint differed between settlement regions and probably also between individual communities. The characteristic feature of flint economics of most LBK communities was the use of various mined raw materials and their wide-ranging distribution. There are no analogies either in the Mesolithic or in the later periods of the Neolithic Age.

Among the LBK archaeological sites it is possible to distinguish flint mines, settlements connected directly with the exploitation of deposits - settlements of producers - which played a special role in supplying flint to other communities and settlements of users, connected with former by means of network of long-distance exchange. In regions lying far from deposits we can distinguish secondary centres of distribution of mined raw materials - Brunn in Lower Austria, Topolčany in western Slovakia and Skoroszowice in Lower Silesia (Wojciechowski 1981).

It would seem that in western Central Europe and further west similar phenomena occurred connected with the supplying of siliceous rocks to Danubian communities (Löhr, Zimmermann & Hahn 1977; Cahen *et al* 1986; Grooth 1994; Ilett *et al* 1982:58-59; Lüning 1982:23; Plateaux 1988; 1990 and unpublished studies by the late Michel Plateaux in1989; Zimmermann 1982; 1991).

Bibliography

BÁCSKAY, E., 1995, The Flint-mine of Sümeg-Mogyorósdomb. *Archaeologia Polona* 33, p. 383-395.

BAKELS, C., 1978, *Four Linearbandkeramik Settlements and Their Environment: A Paleoecological Study af Sittard, Stein, Elsloo and Hienheim*. Leiden: Universitaire Pers Leiden.

BIRÓ, K.T., 1986, The raw material stock for chipped stone artifacts in the Northern Mid-Mountains Tertiary in Hungary. In *International Conference on Prehistoric Flint Mining and Lithic Material Identification in the Carpathian Basin, Budapest - Sümeg, 20-22 Mai, 1986*, edited by K.T. Biró. Budapest: Magyar Nemzeti Muzeum, p. 183-195.

BIRÓ, K.T., 1987, Actual problems of lithic raw material distribution studies in Hungary. Comments on the distribution maps. In *International Conference on Prehistoric Flint Mining and Lithic Material Identification in the Carpathian Basin, Budapest - Sümeg, 20-22 Mai, 1986*, edited by K.T. Biró. Budapest: Magyar Nemzeti Muzeum, p. 141-161.

BIRÓ, K.T., 1995, H 8 Szentgál-Tüzköveshegy, Veszprém County. *Archaeologia Polona* 33, p. 402-408.

BIRÓ, K.T., & REGENYE, J., 1991, Prehistoric workshop and exploitation site Szentgál-Tüzköveshegy. *Acta Archaeologica Hungarica* 43, p. 337-375.

BOHMERS, A., & BRUIJN, A., 1958-1959, Statistische und graphische Methoden zur Untersuchung von Flintkomplexen. IV. Das lithische Material aus den bandkeramischen Siedlungen in den Niederlanden. *Palaeohistoria* 6-7, p. 183-211.

BURNEZ-LANOTTE, L., & ALLARD, P., 1998, Production laminaire originale dans le site rubané du "Petit-Paradis" à Harduémont (Verlaine, Hesbaye liégeoise). Résultats de la campagne 1997. *Anthropologie et Préhistoire* 109, p. 15-26.

CAHEN, D., CASPAR, J.-P., & OTTE, M., 1986, *Industries lithiques danubiennes de Belgique*. Liège. Études et Recherches Archéologiques de l'Université de Liège 21.

CYREK, K., 1981, The problem of flint in the Mesolithic of the Vistula and upper Warta basins. In *Third International Symposium on Flint, 24-27 Mei 1979 - Maastricht*, edited by F.H.G. Engelen, "Staringia" 6: Nederlandse Geologische Vereniging, p. 130-135.

DZIEDUSZYCKA-MACHNIKOWA, A., 1961, Z zagadnień krzemieniarstwa neolitycznego [Research into the Neolithic Flint Industry]. In *Sprawozdania PAN w Krakowie, Styczeń-Czerwiec 1961*, Kraków, p. 29-31.

ENGELHARDT, B., 1989, Das neolithische Silexabbaurevier von Arnhofen, Ldkr. Kelheim in Niederbayern. In *Bylany Seminar 1987. Collected Papers*, edited by J. Rulf. Praha: Archeologický ústav ČSAV, p. 135-139.

ENGELHARDT, B., & BINSTEINER, A., 1989, Vorbericht über die Ausgrabungen 1984-1986 im neolithischen Feuersteinabbaurevier von Arnhofen, Ldkr. Kelheim. *Germania* 66:1-29.

FIRTH, R., 1939, *Primitive Polynesian Economy*. London: Routledge & Kegan Paul.

FIRTH, R., 1956, *Elements of Social Organization*. London : Watts & Co.

Jacek LECH

GODELIER, M., 1986, *The Making of Great Men: Male Domination and Power among the New Guinea Baruya*. Cambridge: Cambridge University Press.

GRONENBORN, D., 1990, Mesolithic-Neolithic Interactions - the Lithic Industry of the Earliest Bandkeramik Cultural Site at Friedberg-Bruchenbrücken, Wetteraukreis (West Germany). In *Contribution to the Mesolithic in Europe. Papers Presented at the Fourth International Symposium 'The Mesolithic in Europe', Leuven 1990*, edited by P.M. Vermeersch & Ph. van Peer. Leuven: Leuven University Press, p. 173-182.

GRONENBORN, D., 1997, *Silexartefakte der ältestbandkeramischen Kultur*. Bonn : Dr Rudolf Habelt GmbH. "Universitätsforschungen zur prähistorischen Archäologie" 37.

GRONENBORN, D., 1999, A Variation on a Basic Theme : The Transition to Farming in Southern Central Europe. *Journal of World Prehistory* 13(2), p. 123-210.

GROOTH, M.E.Th. de, 1990, In Search of Bankeramik Specialist Flint Knappers. In *Rubané et Cardial. Actes du Colloque de Liège, novembre 1988*, edited by D. Cahen & M. Otte. Liège, p. 89-93. Etudes et Recherches Archéologiques de l'Université de Liège 39.

GROOTH, M.E.Th. de, 1994, *Studies on Neolithic Flint Exploitation. Socio-economic interpretations of the flint assemblages of Langweiler 8, Beek, Elsloo, Rijckholt, Hienheim and Meindling*. Maastricht: Scorpio.

GROOTH, M.E.Th. de, 1995, The organization of chert exploitation in Southeastern Bavaria during the Neolithic. *Archaeologia Polona* 33, p. 163-172.

GROOTH, M.E.Th. de, 1997, The Social Context of Neolithic Flint Mining in Europe. In *Man and Flint. Proceedings of the VIIth International Flint Symposium, Warszawa-Ostrowiec Świetokrzyski, September 1995*, edtited by R. Schild & Z. Sulgostowska. Warszawa: Institute of Archaeology and Ethnology Polish Academy of Sciences, p. 71-75.

ILETT, M., CONSTANTIN, C., COUDART, A. & DEMOULE, J.P., 1982, The Late Bandkeramik of the Aisne Valley: Environment and Spatial Organisation. *Analecta Praehistorica Leidensia* 15, p. 46-61.

KACZANOWSKA, M., 1985, *Rohstoffe, Technik und Typologie der neolithischen Feuersteinindustrien im Nordteil des Flussgebietes der Mitteldonau*. Warszawa: Państwowe Wydawnictwo Naukowe.

KACZANOWSKA, M., 1989, Feuersteinindustrie der Linearbandkeramik-Kultur. Ursprungsprobleme. In *Bylany Seminar 1987. Collected Papers*, edited by J. Rulf. Praha: Archeologický ústav ČSAV, p. 121-130.

KOZŁOWSKI, J.K., 1970, Z badań nad wytwórczościa krzemieniarską w kulturze ceramiki wstęgowej rytej [Sum.: Research into the Flint Industry of the Linear Band Pottery Culture]. In *Z badań nad kulturą ceramiki wstęgowej rytej*, edited by J.K. Kozłowski. Kraków : The Polish Archaeological Society - Section at Nowa Huta, p. 73-94.

KOZŁOWSKI, J.K., 1974, Über die Untersuchungen der östlichen Peripherien der Linien-Bandkeramik-Kultur. *Acta Archaeologica Carpathica* 14, p. 5-56.

KOZŁOWSKI, J.K., 1980, Die Frage des Ursprungs der Steinindustrie der bandkeramischen Kultur. *Veröffentlichungen des Museums für Ur- und Frühgeschichte Potsdam* 14-15, p. 83-90.

KOZŁOWSKI, J.K., (ed.) 1971, *Z badań nad krzemieniarstwem neolitycznym i eneolitycznym (Referaty i komunikaty przedstawione na sympozjum w Nowej Hucie dn. 10, 11 maja 1971)* [Études sur industries de la pierre taillée du néo-enéolithique (Rapports et communications du symposium tenu à Nowa Huta le 10 et 11 mai 1971)]. Kraków: Societé Archéologique Polonaise - Section de Nowa Huta & Musée Archéologique de Cracovie.

KOZŁOWSKI, J.K., & KULCZYCKA, A., 1961, Materiały kultury starszej ceramiki wstęgowej z Olszanicy, pow. Kraków [Rés. : Les matériaux de la civilisation de la céramique rubanée plus ancienne à Olszanica, district de Kraków]. *Materiały Archeologiczne*, p. 29-50.

KULCZYCKA-LECIEJEWICZOWA, A., 1997, *Strachów. Osiedla neolitycznych rolników na Śląsku* [Sum.: Strachów. Settlements of Neolithic Farmers in Silesia]. Wrocław : Instytut Archeologii i Etnologii Polskiej Akademii Nauk.

LECH, J., 1975. Neolithic flint mine and workshops at Sąspów, near Cracow. In *Second International Symposium on Flint, 8-11 Mei 1975 - Maastricht*, "Staringia" 3 : Nederlandse Geologische Vereniging, p. 70-71.

LECH, J., PL 15 Sąspów I, Jerzmanowice, Wojew. Kraków. In *5000 Jahre Feuersteinbergbau. Die Suche nach dem Stahl der Steinzeit*, edited by G. Weisgereber, R. Slotta & J. Weiner. Bochum : Verlag des Deutschen Bergbau-Museums, p. 616-619. "Veröffentlichungen aus dem Deutschen Bergbau-Museum" 22.

LECH, J., 1981a, Flint Mining among the Early Farming Communities of Central Europe, *Przegląd Archeologiczny* 28, p. 5-55.

LECH, J., 1981b, Górnictwo krzemienia społeczności wczesnorolniczych na Wyżynie Krakowskiej: koniec VI tysiąclecia - 1 połowa IV tysiąclecia p.n.e. [Sum.: Flint Mining among Early Farming Communities in the Cracow Upland (End of VIth Millenium to Mid - IVth Millenium B.C.)]. Wrocław: Zakład Narodowy im. Ossolińskich, Wydawnictwo PAN.

LECH, J., 1983, Flint Mining among the Early Farming Communities of Central Europe. Part II - The Basis of Research into Flint Workshops, *Przegląd Archeologiczny* 30, p. 47-80.

LECH, J., 1987, Danubian raw material distribution patterns in eastern central Europe. In *The human uses of flint and chert. Proceedings of the fourth international flint symposium held at Brighton Polytechnic, 10-15 April 1983*, edited by G. de G. Sieveking & M.H. Newcomer. Cambridge: Cambridge University Press, p. 241-248.

LECH, J., 1988, Mining and distribution of siliceous rocks among the first farming communities in eastern Central Europe. In *Chipped Stone Industries of the Early Farming Cultures in Europe*, edited by J.K. Kozłowski & S.K. Kozłowski. Warsaw: Wydawnictwo Uniwersytetu Warszawskiego, p. 369-380. "Archaeologia Interregionalis" 9.

LECH, J., 1989, A Danubian raw material exchange network: a case study from Bylany. In *Bylany Seminar 1987. Collected Papers*, edited by J. Rulf. Praha: Archeologický ústav ČSAV, p. 111-120.

LECH, J., 1990, The Organization of Siliceous Rock Supplies to the

Early Farming Communities (LBK): Central European Examples. In *Rubané et Cardial. Actes du Colloque de Liège, novembre 1988*, edited by D. Cahen & M. Otte. Liège, p. 51-59. Études et Recherches Archéologiques de l'Université de Liège 39.

LECH, J., 1991, The Neolithic-Eneolithic Transition in Prehistoric Mining and Siliceous Rock Distribution. In *Die Kupferzeit als historische Epoche. Symposium Saarbrücken and Otzenhausen 6.-13. 11. 1988*, edited by J. Lichardus. Bonn: Dr. Rudolf Habelt GMBH, p. 557-574. "Saarbrücker Beiträg zur Altertumskunde" 55.

LECH, J., 1997, Remarks on Prehistoric Flint Mining and Flint Supply in European Archaeology. In *Siliceous Rocks and Culture*, edited by A. Ramos-Millán & A. Bustillo. Granada: Editorial Universidad de Granada, p. 611-637. "Universidad de Granada. Monográfica Arte y Arqueología" 42.

LECH, J., & MATEICIUCOVÁ, I., 1995a, Cz. 1 Tušimice near Kadań, Chomutov District. *Archaeologia Polona* 33, p. 271-276.

LECH, J., & MATEICIUCOVÁ, I., 1995b, Cz. 2 Bečov, Most District. *Archaeologia Polona* 33, p. 276-278.

LEDERMAN, R., 1986, *What gifts engender. Social relations and politics in Mendi, Higland Papua New Guinea*. Cambridge : Cambridge University Press.

LENNEIS, E., 1999, Altneolithikum: Die Bandkeramik. In *Jungsteinzeit im Osten Österreichs*, by E. Lenneis, Ch. Neugebauer-Maresch & E. Ruttkay. St. Pölten: Verlag Niederösterreichisches Pressehaus, p. 11-56.

LENNEIS, E., STADLER, P., WINDL, H., 1996, Neue 14C-Daten zum Frühneolithikum in Österreich. *Préhistoire Européenne* 8, p. 97-116.

LÖHR, H., ZIMMERMANN, A., HAHN, J., 1977, Feuersteinartefakte. In *Der Bandkeramische Siedlungsplatz Langweiler 9, Gemeinde Aldenhoven, kreis Düren*, by R. Kuper, H. Löhr, J. Lüning, P. Stehli & A. Zimmermann. Bonn: Rheinland-Verlag GMBH, p. 131-266. "Rheinische Ausgrabungen" 18.

LÜNING, J., 1982, Research into the Bandkeramik Settlement of the Aldenhover Platte in the Rhineland, *Analecta Praehistorica Leidensia* 15, p. 1-29.

MALINOWSKI, B., 1922, *Argonauts of the Western Pacific. An Account of Native Enterprise and Adventure in the Archipelagos of Melanesian New Guinea*. London: George Routledge & Sons Ltd.

MAŁECKA-KUKAWKA, J., 1992, *Krzemieniarstwo społeczności wczesnorolniczych ziemi chełmińskiej (2 połowa VI - IV tysiąclecie p.n.e.)* [Sum.: Flintwork of Early Farming Communities in Chełmno Land during the Period of the Second Half of the Sixth - Fourth Millenium B.C.]. Toruń: Uniwersytet Mikołaja Kopernika.

MAŁECKA-KUKAWKA, J., 2001, *Między formą a funkcją. Traseologia zabytków krzemiennych z ziemi chełmińskiej* [Sum.: Between Form and Function. Traseological Analysis of the Neolithic Flint Assemblages from Chełmno Land]. Toruń: Uniwersytet Mikołaja Kopernika.

MATEICIUCOVÁ, I., 1995, CZ 4 Krumlovský Les, Znojmo District. *Archaeologia Polona* 33, p. 281-285.

MATEICIUCOVÁ, I., 1997, Local Hornstones among the First Farmers (LBK) of the Krumlovský Les Area. In *Man and Flint. Proceedings of the VIIth International Flint Symposium, Warszawa-Ostrowiec Świętokrzyski, September 1995*, edtited by R. Schild & Z. Sulgostowska. Warszawa: Institute of Archaeology and Ethnology Polish Academy of Sciences, p. 249-253.

MATEICIUCOVÁ, I., 2001, Silexindustrie in der ältesten Linearbandkeramik-Kultur in Mähren und Niederösterreich auf der Basis der Silexindustrie des Lokalmesolithikums. In *From the Mesolithic to the Neolithic. Proceedings of the International Archaeological Conference held in the Damjanich Museum of Szolnok, September 22-27, 1996*, edited by R. Kertész & J. Makkay. Budapest: Archaeolingua, p. 283-299.

MAUSS, M., 1990, *The Gift. The Form and Reason for Exchange in Archaic Societies*. London: Routledge.

McBRYDE, I., 1997, 'The Landscape is a Series of Stories'. Grindstones, Quarries and Exchange in Aboriginal Australia: a Lake Eyre Case Study. In *Siliceous Rocks and Culture*, edited by A. Ramos-Millán & A. Bustillo. Granada: Editorial Universidad de Granada, p. 587-607. "Universidad de Granada. Monográfica Arte y Arqueología" 42.

MILISAUSKAS, S., 1986, *Early Neolithic Settlement and Society at Olszanica*. Ann Arbor: University of Michigan, Museum of Anthropology. "Memoirs of the Museum of Anthropology. University of Michigan" 19.

MILISAUSKAS, S., 2002, Early Neolithic, The First Farmers in Europa, 7000-5500/5000 BC. In *European Prehistory: A Survey*, edited by S. Milisauskas. New York: Kluwer Academic/Plenum Publishers.

NEWELL, R.R., 1970, The Flint Industry of the Dutch Linearbandkeramik. *Analecta Praehistorica Leidensia* 3, p. 144-183.

OLIVA, M., 1997, Prehistoric Chert Extraction and Distribution in the Krumlovský Les Area (Southern Moravia). In *Man and Flint. Proceedings of the VIIth International Flint Symposium, Warszawa-Ostrowiec Świętokrzyski, September 1995*, edtited by R. Schild & Z. Sulgostowska. Warszawa : Institute of Archaeology and Ethnology Polish Academy of Sciences, p. 109-115.

OLIVA, M., NERUDA, M., & PŘICHYSTAL, A., 1999. Paradoxy těžby a distribuce rohovce z Krumlovského Lesa [Sum.: Paradox in the Excavation and Products Distribution of the Kumlov Forest Chert]. *Památky archeologické* 90, p. 229-318.

ONDRUŠ, V., 1976, Neolitické dílny z Vedrovic-Zábrdovic [Zsf.: Die neolithischen Werkstätten aus Vedrovice-Zábrdovice]. *Sborník prací filosofické fakulty brněnské university. Řada archeologicko-klasická* E 20-21, p. 133-139.

PLATEAUX, M., 1988, L'industrie lithique des premièrs agriculturs dans le Nord de la France. In *Chipped Stone Industries of the Early Farming Cultures in Europe*, edited by J.K. Kozłowski & S.K. Kozłowski. Warsaw : Wydawnictwo Uniwersytetu Warszawskiego, p. 225-245. "Archaeologia Interregionalis" 9.

PLATEAUX, M., 1990, Quelques données sur l'évolution des industries du Néolithique danubien de la vallée de l'Aisne. In *Rubané et Cardial. Actes du Colloque de Liège, novembre 1988*, edited by D.

Cahen & M. Otte. Liège, p. 239-255. Études et Recherches Archéologiques de l'Université de Liège 39.

SAHLINS, M.D., 1968, *Tribesmen*. Englewood Cliffs, New Jersey: Prentice-Hall, Inc.

SAHLINS, M., 1974, *Stone Age Economics*. London: Tavistock Publications Ltd.

SCHILD, R., 1980, PL 2 Tomaszów, Gemeinde Oronsko, Wojęw. Radom. In *5000 Jahre Feuersteinbergbau. Die Suche nach dem Stahl der Steinzeit*, edited by G. Weisgereber, R. Slotta & J. Weiner. Bochum: Verlag des Deutschen Bergbau-Museums, p. 579-580. "Veröffentlichungen aus dem Deutschen Bergbau-Museum" 22.

SCHILD, R., 1987, The exploitation of chocolate flint in central Poland. In *The human uses of flint and chert. Proceedings of the fourth international flint symposium held at Brighton Polytechnic, 10-15 April 1983*, edited by G. de G. Sieveking & M.H. Newcomer. Cambridge: Cambridge University Press, p. 137-149.

SCHILD, R., 1995, PL 2 Tomaszów, Radom Province. *Archaeologia Polona* 33, p. 455-465.

SCHILD, R., KRÓLIK, H., & MARCZAK, M., 1985, *Kopalnia krzemienia czekoladowego w Tomaszowie* [Sum.: A Chocolate Flint Mine at Tomaszów]. Wrocław: Zakład Narodowy im. Ossolińskich, Wydawnictwo PAN.

SULIMIRSKI, T., 1960, Remarks Concerning the Distribution of Some Varieties of Flint in Poland. *Światowit* 23, p. 281-307.

STADLER, P., 1999, Ein Beitrag zur Absolutchronologie des Neolithikums aufgrund der 14C-Daten in Österreich. In *Jungsteinzeit im Osten Österreichs*, by E. Lenneis, Ch. Neugebauer-Maresch & E. Ruttkay. St. Pölten: Verlag Niederösterreichisches Pressehaus, p. 210-224.

STRATHERN, A., 1971, *The Rope of Moka. Big-men and Ceremonial Exchange in Mount Hagen, New Guinea*. Cambridge: Cambridge University Press.

STRATHERN, A., 1984, *A Line of Power*. London: Tavistock Publications.

TAÇON, P.S.C., 1991, The power of stone: symbolic aspects of stone use and tool development in western Arnhem Land, Australia. *Antiquity* 65(247), p. 192-207.

TILLEY, Ch., 1994, *A Phenomenology of Landscape: Places, Paths and Monuments*. Oxford: Berg Publishers.

TRINGHAM, R., 1968, A preliminary study of the early neolithic and latest mesolithic blade industries in southeast and central Europe. In *Studies in Ancient Europe. Essays presented to Stuart Piggott*, edited by J. Coles & D. Simpson. Leicester: Leicester University Press, p. 45-70.

TRINGHAM, R., 1972, The Function, Technology, and Typology of Chipped Stone Industry at Bylany, Czechoslovakia. *Alba Regia. Annales Musei Stephani Regis* 12, p. 464-472.

VENCL, S., 1986, The role of hunting-gathering populations in the transition to farming: a Central-European perspective. In *Hunters in Transition*, edited by M. Zvelebil. Cambridge: Cambridge University Press, p. 43-51.

VENCL, S., 1989, Neolithic quartzite processing site at Žichov, distr. of Teplice. In *Bylany Seminar 1987. Collected Papers*, edited by J. Rulf. Praha: Archeologický ústav ČSAV, p. 131-133.

WHITTLE, A., 1995, Gifts from the earth: symbolic dimensions of the use and production of Neolithic flint and stone axes. *Archaeologia Polona* 33, p. 247-259.

WHITTLE, A., 1996, *Europe in the Neolithic. The creation of new worlds*. Cambridge: Cambridge University Press.

WOJCIECHOWSKI, W., 1981, *Wczesnoneolityczna osada w Skoroszowicach* [Early Neolithic Settlement at Skoroszowice]. Wrocław: Wydawnictwo Uniwersytetu Wrocławskiego. "Studia Archeologiczne" 12.

Morphological groups	Szentgyörgyvölgy-Piterdomb (216 specimens)	Brunn am Gebirge (1150 specimens)
I. Natural nodules, pre-cores and cores	6.96%	5.30%
II. Blades and blades fragments	22.68%	24.52%
III. Flakes and waste	58.33%	56.96%
IV. Retouched tools	12.04%	13.22%
Total	99.99%	100.00%

Table 1. Comparison of samples of chipped materials from the oldest LBK settlements at Szentgyörgyvölgy-Piterdomb and Brunn am Gebirge, site Wolfholz (see p. 22).

EXCHANGE SYSTEMS OF STONE ARTEFACTS IN THE EUROPEAN NEOLITHIC

Nicole KEGLER-GRAIEWSKI[*] & Andreas ZIMMERMANN[**]

Résumé

Pour comprendre les systèmes d'échange de l'outillage lithique entre les habitats de Céramique rubanée, plusieurs inventaires en Rhénanie ont été analysés. Pour la distribution des outils en silex, on peut distinguer deux aspects d'une importance particulière. Apparemment, sur un niveau local, il existe des "habitats centraux" (zentrale Orte). Ceux-ci sont plus intégrés dans le processus d'acquisition de la matière première et de la production des pierres taillées que d'autres sites. Pourtant, sur un niveau interrégional, la répartition du travail est moins remarquable. Dans le voisinage des gisements des matières premières, des rognons et des nucleus sont les objets d'échange les plus importants. Un peu plus loin des gisements, les lames dominent l'échange lithique et, à une distance certaine, les outils prédominent les objets d'échange. La distribution des meules était organisée d'une autre manière : en cas de besoin, on se rendait au gisement des matières premières ou on s'adressait aux populations voisines pour acquérir des pièces en matière brute prêtes à l'emploi. En tout cas, l'échange des meules lourdes devait se faire d'une manière plus directe que celui des silex: il s'agissait d'un transport direct jusqu'au lieu d'utilisation.

Abstract

The assemblages of Linearbandkeramik settlements (5300-5000 BC) between Aachen and Frankfurt have been used as a means of studying the exchange systems which were predominant at that time. For the distribution of flint artefacts two aspects are of importance. On a local scale, certain "central places" (zentrale Orte) seem to have existed. These were more involved in the procurement of raw material and the production of artefacts than other sites. However, in larger areas such systems are less recognisable. In the vicinity of the raw material sources, nodules and cores were the main objects of exchange; however, further away from the sources, blades, and at greater distances, tools are the more dominant features. In many cases the consumer seems to have been engaged in final steps of production. The distribution of querns was organised in another way. People visited the source of raw material or contacted exchange partners in their vicinity in order to obtain pieces of raw material ready for use. Owing to their size and weight, there must have been a more direct way of transporting heavy querns from the source of the raw material to the place of use.

In the Rhineland and surrounding landscapes in depth investigations into the Bandkeramik period have led to the accumulation of large amounts of lithic material. Using statistical methods this material can be used to answer questions of historical importance. One of the most important is how the raw material came into the settlements and how the social context in which this took place was structured.

Different aspects of the stone material from different sites may shed light on the mechanism of raw material distribution (Zimmermann 1995) : a good subject for examination is the flint of Rijckholt-type. This material from the Limburg region in the Netherlands is easily recognizable and widespread in the Rhenish Early Neolithic.

1. The portion of artefacts with cortex shows the use of complete nodules in the settlement. Figure 1 shows, using isolines, the percentage of Rijckholt-flint artefacts with cortex from different sites in Rhineland and Hesse. The star marks

---

(*) Melatengürtel 86, D-50823 Köln.
(**) Institut für Ur- und Frühgeschichte der Universität zu Köln, Weyertal 125, D-50931 Köln.

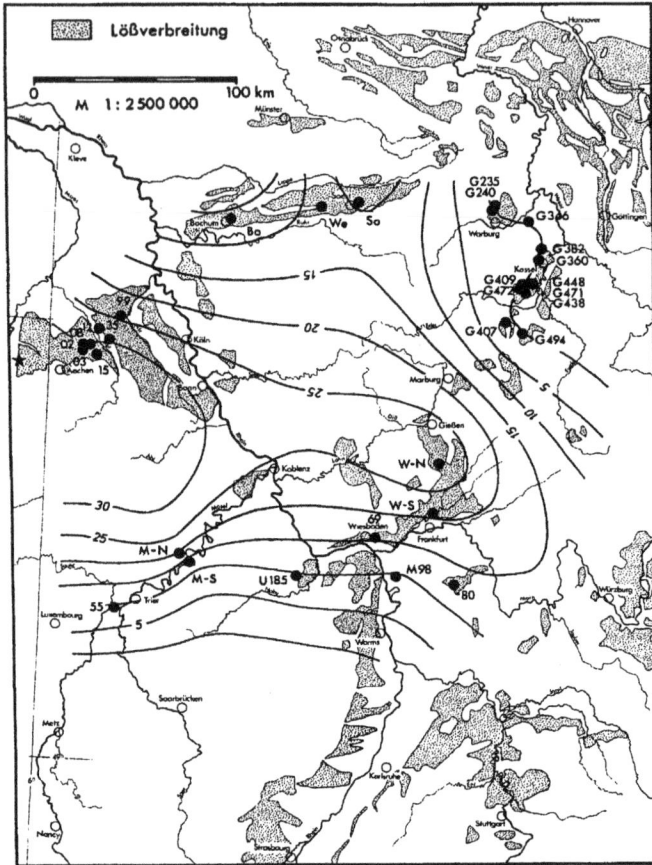

Figure 1. Rijckholt-flint. Percentage of cortex artefacts in Bandkeramik assemblages, isolines made with "minimal curvature" (Zimmermann 1995, fig. 25).

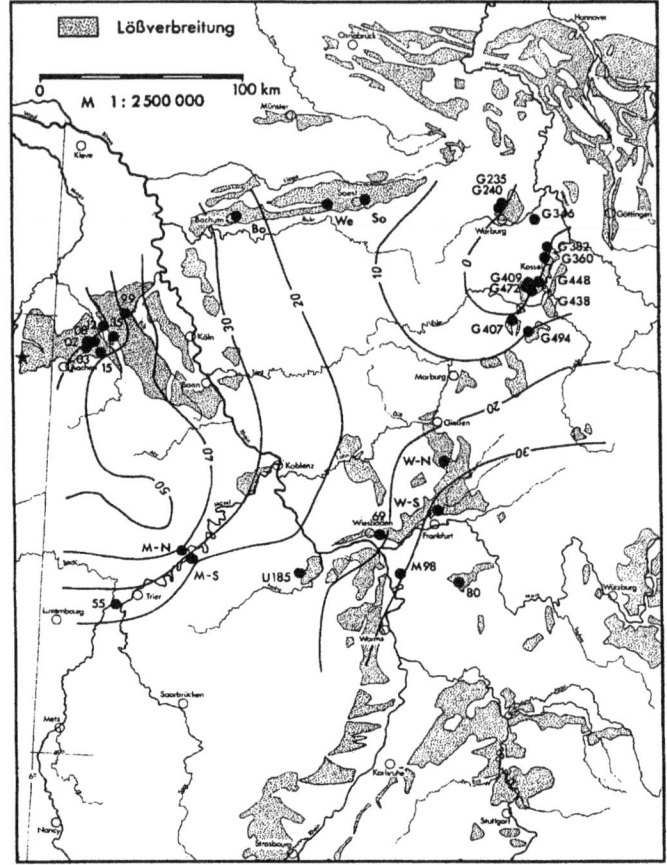

Figure 2. Rijckholt-flint. Percentage of flakes in Bandkeramik assemblages, isolines made with "minimal curvature" (Zimmermann 1995, fig. 26).

the flint deposit. Close to its source the portion of cortex-artefacts is, as expected, high, and at greater distances decreases to zero. Therefore, as the distance from the deposit increases, the use of cortex-nodules decreases. This also applies to the size of the cores and to the size the natural surfaces, which also decrease the further they are away from the source.

2. The portion of flakes which in the Bandkeramik context can mainly be seen as production-waste may indicate the working on cores in the settlement (fig. 2). The second figure visualises the percentage of flakes in the Rijckholt-flint assemblages. When seen as production-waste of blade industry, they serve as an indication of the amount of flint-knapping that took place at the sites. On the northern Lößbörde of the Rhineland flakes can constitute more than 50 percents of the flint inventories. However, further away in the northern Hesse, this figure can drop less than 10 percent. The production on these sites decreases. Thus, on the one hand, there is less waste in form of flakes, but, on the other hand, one finds more tools and blanks ready for use (as can be seen on figure 3 and 4).

3. Blades represent the final product (Zielprodukt) of the production process. If blades dominate, and the corresponding flakes of the production process are missing, a low intensity

of production can be presumed. The percentage of blades is high in an area at an intermediate distance from the source (fig. 3). Therefore, a transmission of these blanks from elsewhere can be deduced.

4. Finally a large portion of tools shows a possible shortage of Rijckholt-flint and, therefore, a more intensive use of other materials that were available (fig. 4). The percentage of tools increases steadily from the region of Aachen to the margins of the distribution area of Rijckholt-flint. On these margins only tools were transmitted.

From these patterns we can conclude that a hand to hand distribution was in operation. The people who lived in the surrounding area of the flint deposits produced a large number of blades, for this reason many more flakes (by-products) are to be found at these production-sites. The inhabitants of these settlements gave away the used, smaller cores and an amount of finished blades to their exchange-partners. Using these cores the recipients could then produce their own blades. They in turn gave on blades and the much smaller cores. The cores were eventually used up in areas far away from the flint source. Consequently only the blades and tools were transmitted. However, in many cases, the end-consumer seems to have been involved in the production process. It

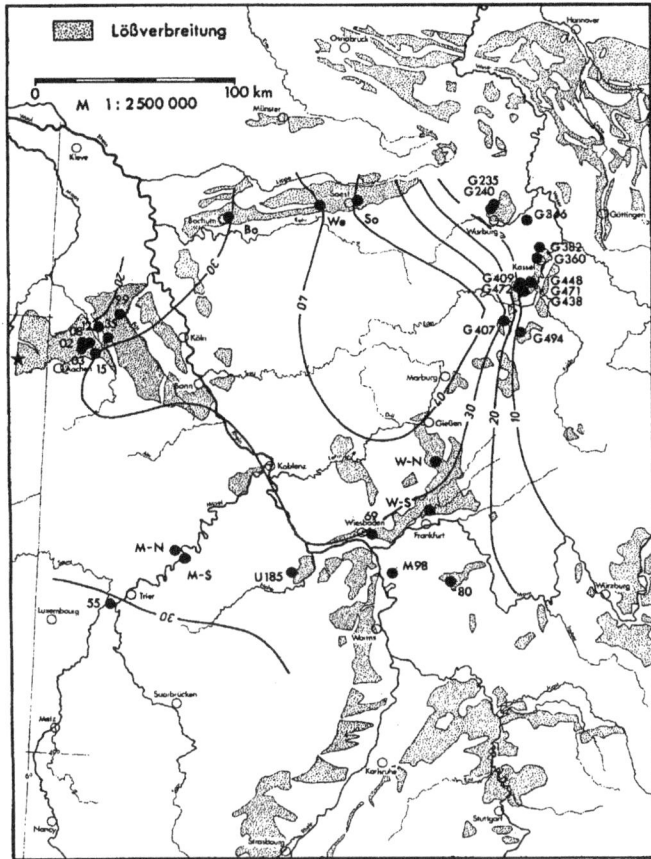

Figure 3. Rijckholt-flint. Percentage of blades in Bandkeramik assemblages, isolines made with "minimal curvature" (Zimmermann 1995, fig. 29).

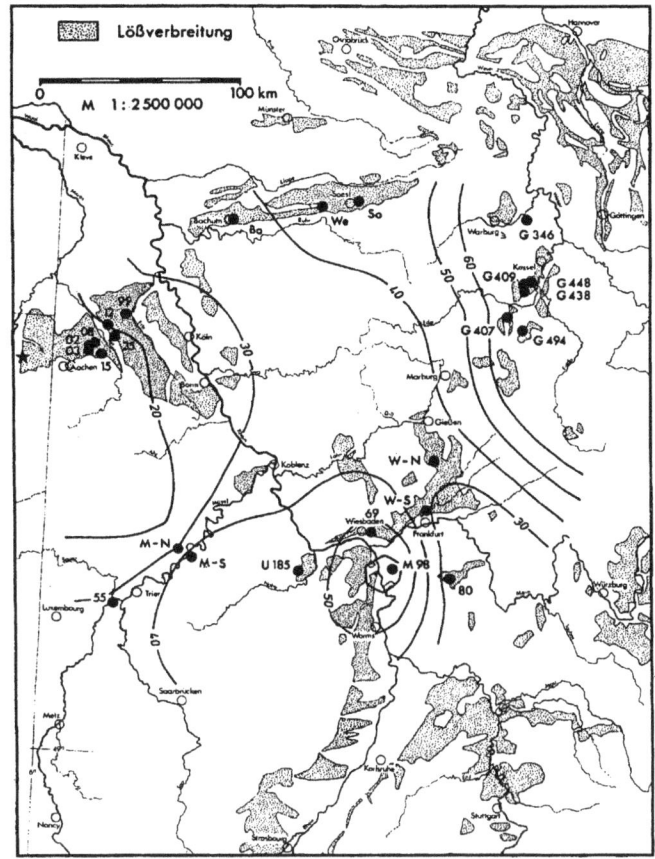

Figure 4. Rijckholt-flint. Percentage of tools in Bandkeramik assemblages, isolines made with "minimal curvature" (Zimmermann 1995, fig. 30).

would appear that this exchange took the form of a balanced reciprocity with a low value of the single flint artefact. Trading with flint artefacts doesn't seem to have been monopolised in any way.

On a smaller scale, for example on the Aldenhovener Platte near Aachen, the exchange system appears somewhat different. Although the settlements of this area are, to a greater extent, the same distance from the Rijckholt deposit, they appear to have had different positions in the exchange system of flint depending on their size. As Chr. Schigiol (1999) and L. Bollig (2000) were able to show, some large settlements seem to have had good access to the deposit, which is roughly 35 km away. These, for example Langweiler 8 and Weisweiler 17, have high portions of cortex-artefacts and flakes. In Lohn 3, a site belonging to a second category of large settlements, cores were used which were partly prepared elsewhere (perhaps at sites of the first category such as Langweiler 8 or Weisweiler 17. However here in Lohn 3 the intensity of production is much more developed than in a third category of large settlements which obtained their artefacts only in a third position of the exchange network (Aldenhoven 3, Lamersdorf 2). Smaller settlements found in the direct vicinity of a large site have a larger percentage of blades and tools. It is possible that they received artefacts

from their larger neighbours in the form of blades and finished products. Of course, flint-knapping took place in these smaller, dependant settlements too. Proof of this is to be found not only in the percentage of flakes, but also in their decreasing size. Whilst the cores, the size of the flakes and self-made blades decreases the more hands they passed, there are still larger blades in the second- and third-category settlements which must have been passed on as blades from the better provided sites. The arrows in figure 5 show a possible distribution network within this local settlement-system.

The distribution of flint did not only take place between direct neighbours but also between neighbours of second and third degree, up to a distance of perhaps 45 km. Otherwise we could expect that the size and number of flakes would decrease much faster with increasing distance in regional and supra-regional scale. The bigger settlements seem to have had good contact to one another.

Querns hint at direct contact between the inhabitants of settlements on a regional scale. The transportation and distribution of these heavy tools, which can weight between 15 and 20 kg each, must have differed from the logistics involved in transporting and distributing small pieces of flint. A quern cannot be divided in order to give a part of it away.

33

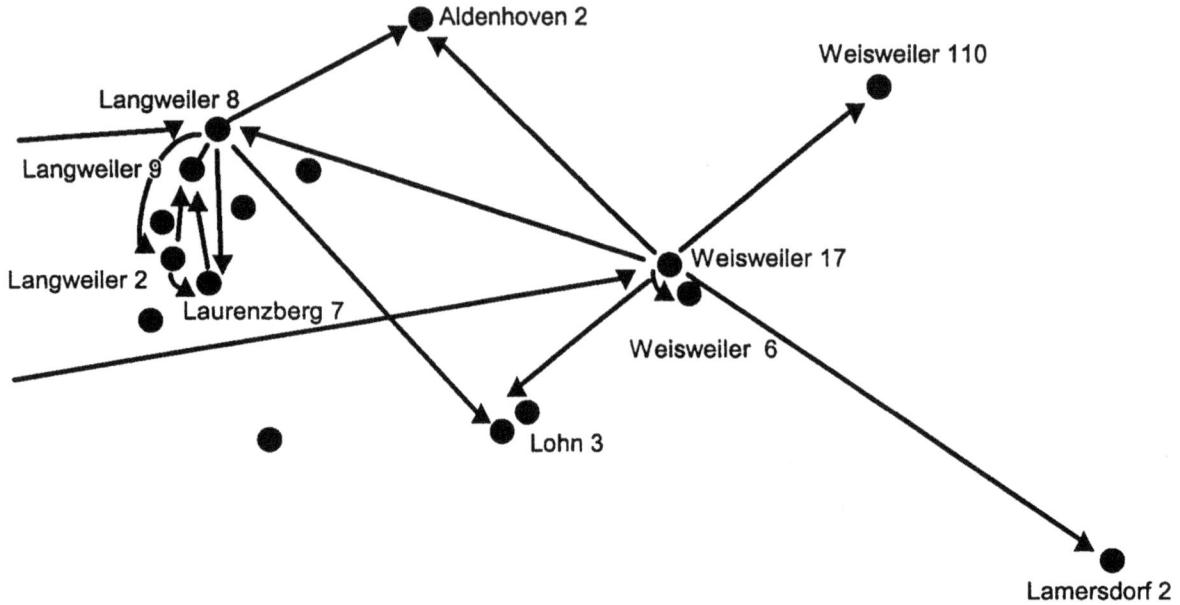

Figure 5. Model of the flint exchange network an the Aldenhovener Platte (after Bollig 2000).

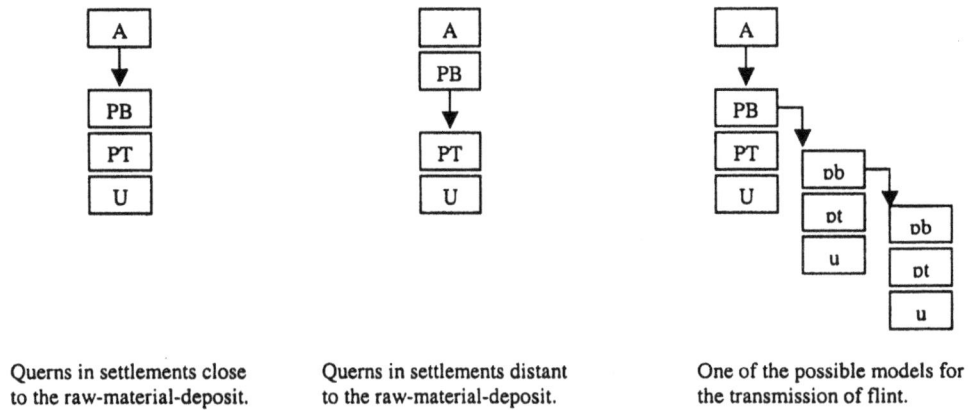

Querns in settlements close to the raw-material-deposit.

Querns in settlements distant to the raw-material-deposit.

One of the possible models for the transmission of flint.

Diagramm 1. Potential models for the transmission of raw materials. A = Acquisition, PB = Production of blanks, PT = Production of tools, U = Use, capital letters = carried out by the group, who did the acquisition, small letters = carried out by other groups, ↓ transport, ⟶ passing on.

For one of the two parts of a quern, one blank is necessary. So it is probable that querns were brought directly from the sandstone deposit to the settlement where they were to be used. The dominant material for querns from settlements at the Jülicher Börde is Eschweiler-Kohlen-Sandstein. The settlements of the Aldenhovener Platte are less then 10 km away from the deposit at the northern border of the Eifel. In this region more than 90 percent of querns are made of Eschweiler-Kohlen-Sandstein. There is some production-waste on the sites. Some of the querns were made in the settlements, where the conditions were more comfortable than at the deposit itself. Diagram 1 shows a model designed after M. E. Th. de Grooths method (1994). It shows the acquisition (A) at the deposit and the production of blanks (PB) and tools (PT) and their use (U) in the settlement. The more distant site of Erkelenz-Kückhoven (fig. 6), about 30 km away from the deposit, has nearly no quern production waste (Graiewski 2000). The pieces must have been well prepared near the deposit of the material, because of the risk of unintentionally breaking the stone during preparation. Thus, the high effort of transportation wouldn't have been in vain. The model for settlements far away from the source shows that the transportation did not take place until the blank had been produced or even the ready tool. According to an estimation proposed by J. Weiner and J. Schalich (2003), 400 tons of Eschweiler-Kohlen-Sandstein where used in the Rhineland during Bandkeramik times. However, no settlements are known which specialised in the production of querns. It would have meant a substantial effort for the people in the vicinity of the deposit to produce the querns for the whole Rhineland and to transport them to the user-settlements. More probable is that the users went to the deposits themselves and the local inha-

34

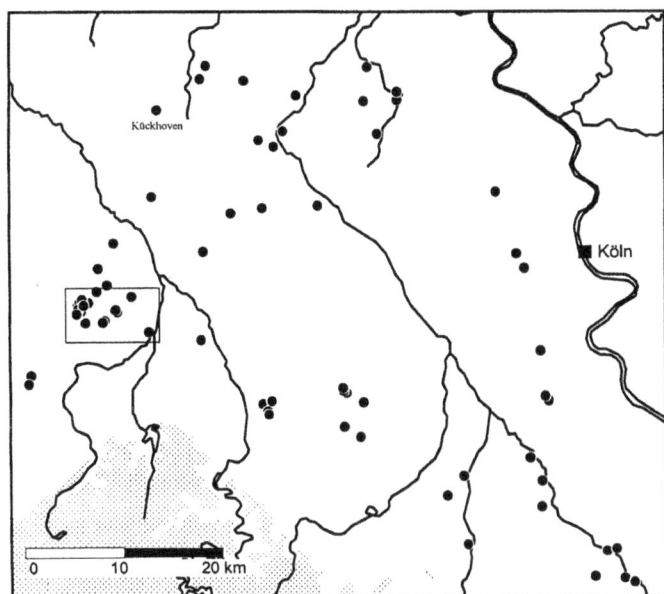

Figure 6. Sites of the Bandkeramik period on the Lössbörde of the northern Rhineland.

bitants showed them the best source and supported them further. The users then transported these heavy tools back to their settlement themselves. This would have meant the direct contact of people in a regional scale of about 30 to 45 km. As a direct result of this contact other material and social goods may also have been transmitted.

To sum up, the distribution mechanism of stone artefacts can be recognised at different levels. The supraregional level shows the transmission of flint-artefacts from hand to hand. On a local scale different properties and duties of neighbouring settlements become visible. However the differentiated network of local and regional contacts between the settlements and settlement-groups prevented that particular settlements were able to monopolize the trading with stone materials and artefacts

Bibliography

BOLLIG, L., 2000, *Die Gesteinsartefakte des bandkeramischen Fundplatzes Weisweiler 110 (Kreis Düren).* Unpublished MA thesis. Köln.

GRAIEWSKI, N., 2000, *Kommunikation an der Peripherie: Rohmaterialien und Grundformen des bandkeramischen Steininventars von Erkelenz-Kückhoven.* Unpublished MA thesis. Köln.

GROOTH, M.E.Th., de, 1994, Die Versorgung mit Silex in der bandkeramischen Siedlung Hienheim "Am Weinberg" (Ldkr. Kehlheim) und die Organisation des Abbaus auf gebänderten Plattenhornstein im Revier Arnhoven (Ldkr. Kehlheim). *Germania* 72, p. 355-407.

SCHALICH, J., & WEINER, J., 2003, On potential Bandkeramik Millstone Quarries in the Rhineland. In *Proceedings of the 8th international flint symposium, September 1999, Bochum. Der Anschnitt,* Beiheft. Edited by G. Weisgerber. Bochum.

SCHIGIOL, Chr., 1999, *Vier bandkeramische Siedlungen im Tal des Schlangengrabens auf der Aldenhovener Platte im Rheinland.* Unpublished PhD thesis. Köln.

ZIMMERMANN, A., 1995, *Austauschsysteme von Silexartefakten in der Bandkeramik Mitteleuropas.* Universitätsforschungen zur Prähistorischen Archäologie 62. Bonn: Habelt.

DEALING WITH BANDKERAMIK CHERTS. PROCUREMENT STRATEGIES IN SOUTH-EASTERN BAVARIA

Marjorie E.Th. de GROOTH*

Abstract

This paper compares the chert procurement strategies employed at two Bandkeramik settlements in South-eastern Bavaria, Hienheim-am-Weinberg (Ldkr. Kelheim) and Meindling (Gde Oberschneiding, Ldkr. Straubing-Bogen). Perceiving material culture as representing the products and consequences of actions and ideas, it documents how two LBK groups showing marked similarities in their material culture and even communicating through the exchange of chert artefacts, nevertheless developed different strategies for dealing with raw material procurement. Thus, it helps to refute the often expressed idea of the 'almost pathological conventionality' of LBK farmers in favour of seeing Bandkeramik lifestyle characterised by 'diversity in uniformity'.

This paper summarises research (de Grooth 1992, 1994) on the chert procurement strategies employed at two Bandkeramik settlements in South-eastern Bavaria (fig. 1). The first, Hienheim-am-Weinberg (Ldkr. Kelheim, Niederbayern) lies in a rather isolated loess-covered region in the southern part of the Franconian Alb. The site has been excavated between 1965 and 1974 by the Institute of Prehistory, University of Leiden (The Netherlands). The main settlement started in the Early Neolithic at c. 5150 cal. BC and ended c. 4600 cal. BC in the Middle Neolithic (Modderman 1977, 1986, van de Velde 1979). In the earlier settlement phases Linearbandkeramik (LBK) pottery was in use. Later on we find decorated pottery belonging to the 'Middle Neolithic of South-eastern Bavaria' (Nadler/Zeeb *et al.* 1994), also known as Stich-Strich-Komplex (van de Velde 1979) and Oberlauterbach Gruppe (Bayerlein 1985).

The second site, Meindling (Gde Oberschneiding, Ldkr. Straubing-Bogen) is situated some 70 km to the east of Hienheim in the *Gäuboden*. The trial excavation performed in 1977 by the Leiden institute yielded the remains of nine houseplans. According to the pottery recovered, Meindling was inhabited from the earliest up to and including the late phases of the Linearbandkeramik (Modderman 1992).

Bandkeramik chert tool manufacture can be summarised in a flow model in the following way (de Grooth 1987 ; cf. Collins 1975). Seven activity sets can be distinguished (outlined with rectangles in fig. 2). Every activity produces its own characteristic product groups (outlined with parallelograms). Blanks intended for further reduction are listed on the left, waste pieces on the right. In practice, however, many stages in the production process can be skipped. Decortication flakes, for example, were shaped into tools, many blades were utilised without further trimming and cores often served as hammerstones. The model shows two important feedback loops: the correction and rejuvenation of cores, and the recycling of worn implements. These can either be maintained in their original function or modified into other tools. The ways these two activities were practised in a settlement may not only reflect knapping skills, but also availability and quality of raw materials.

At the present stage of research, no data on the total number of dated chert artefacts recovered at Hienheim are available. The first series of excavations (up till and including 1970), however, with an excavated surface of 7356 sq. m. (Modderman 1977), yielded 2750 LBK flint artefacts from dated pits alone (de Grooth 1977, 69, Tab. 1), i.e. at least one flint artefact per 2.7 sq. m. In Meindling only 235 LBK flint artefacts were found in 1400 square metres of excavation – surface finds included–, i.e. an average of one flint artefact per 6 sq. m (de Grooth 1992). Thus, the overall density in Hienheim was at least twice as high as that found in Meindling, although the excavation techniques used in Meindling and Hienheim were similar, as were the amount of erosion, and the general character of the settlements in terms of the density of houses and the frequency of refuse pits. The

(*) Bonnefantenmuseum, P.O.Box 1735, NL 6201 BS Maastricht, The Netherlands

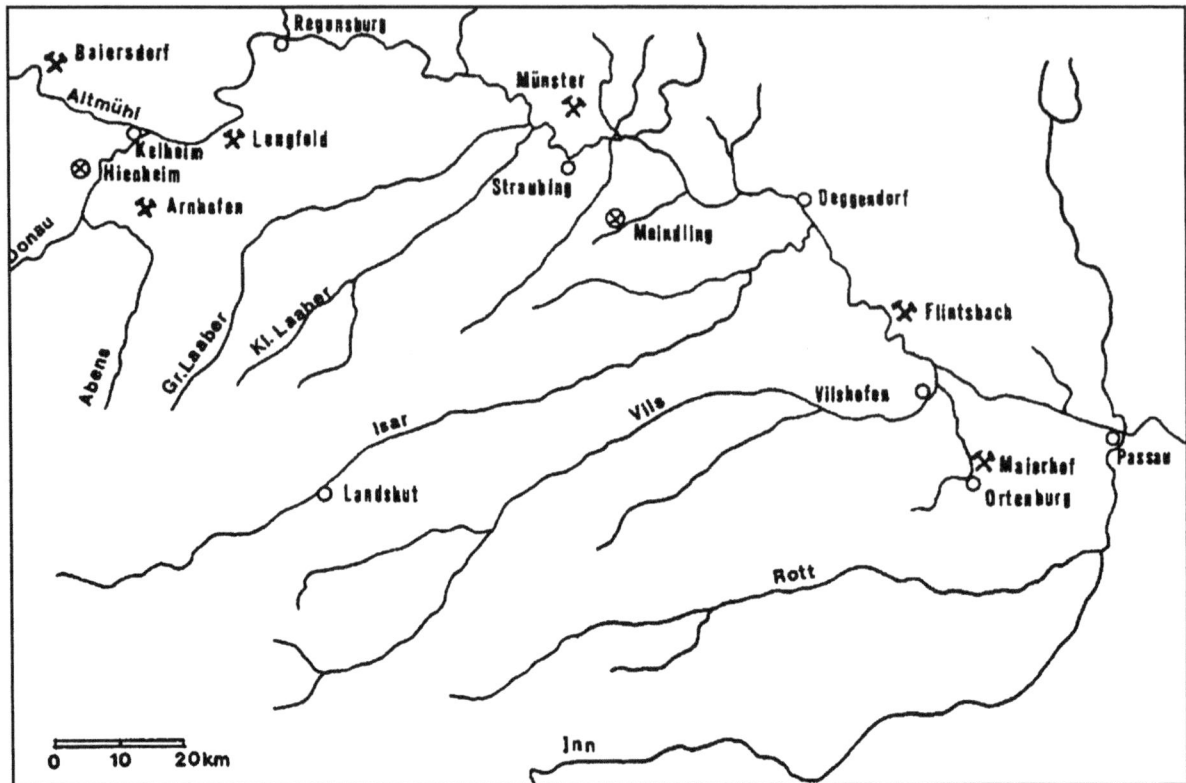

Figure 1. Map showing the location of settlements and chert extraction sites mentioned in the text.

difference in *tool* density, however, is much smaller, Meindling having 1 tool/14.6 sq. m, and Hienheim 1 tool/18.0 sq. m. This indicates that the inhabitants of Meindling displayed behaviour different from those at Hienheim as regards raw material acquisition and tool *production*, but not in tool *consumption*. Differences in the location of available sources of raw material may be regarded as an obvious cause.

The subsoil of the area around Hienheim consists mainly of Jurassic (Malm zeta) Chalk deposits, which contain many varieties of chert. They are present not only in the bedrock, but also in residual loams (*lehmig-kieselige Albüberdeckung*), which cover large parts of the region. At Schwabstetten, 7.5 km to the west of Hienheim, the eluvial clays contain grey nodular cherts (Bakels 1978). This same type of chert was also available at many other localities in the region. Eleven kilometres to the north, i.e. north of the river Altmühl, lies the area of Baiersdorf (in the so-called Paintener Wanne), where brown to greyish brown tabular chert was exploited (Binsteiner 1989). Finally, 9 km to the west, on the other bank of the river Danube, the outcrops at Arnhofen (in the Abensberg-Pullacher Wanne) supplied a very fine-grained, banded grey tabular chert, as well as high-quality light grey striped nodules (Binsteiner 1990a). Both nodules and tablets were smallish in size, the average length of LBK cores in the region lies between 40-65 mm (Grillo 1997, 115).

Meindling, in contrast to Hienheim, is situated in an area without chert-bearing layers in its subsoil. The nearest outcrops occur at a distance of some seventeen kilometres to the north-west, on the north bank of the Danube, where small residual outcrops of Jurassic (more specifically Malm beta) chalks at the Buchberg and the Helmberg near Münster (Ldkr, Straubing-Bogen) contain nodular cherts (Weissmüller 1991). Similar exposures occur c. 35 and c. 50 km to the south-east at Flintsbach-Hardt (Ldkr. Deggendorf) and in the Ortenburg (Ldkr. Vilshofen) region (Binsteiner 1990b, Röhling 1987, Weissmüller 1991). Following Weissmüller's suggestion (1991, 35) in this paper the name 'Ortenburger Jurassic chert' (*Ortenburger Jurahornstein*) will be used for this type of raw material. At present, exploitation of the Münster outcrops can only be presumed (Binsteiner 1990b), but at both Flintsbach and Maierhof/Weng (Ldkr. Vilshofen) systematic exploitation of residual deposits of this type of chert has been documented (Moser 1980/1999, 450; Weissmüller 1991). Here, too, the nodules are small-sized, with an average core length between 40-50 mm (Grillo 1997, 116). Approximately 50% of the cherts found at Meindling came from these outcrops of Ortenburger chert and c. 35% from the Franconian Alb. The remainder may stem either from river gravels or from the residual loams of the Franconian Alb (de Grooth 1992).

For a more detailed analysis of the procurement strategies prevailing at Meindling one must first determine whether or not both groups of raw material were treated in different ways and whether the situation in Meindling differs in this respect from that in Hienheim. The reference material from Hienheim used in this study consists of a sample of 754 artefacts stemming from 16 Early and Middle LBK refuse pits and made of nodular cherts from the Franconian Alb (de

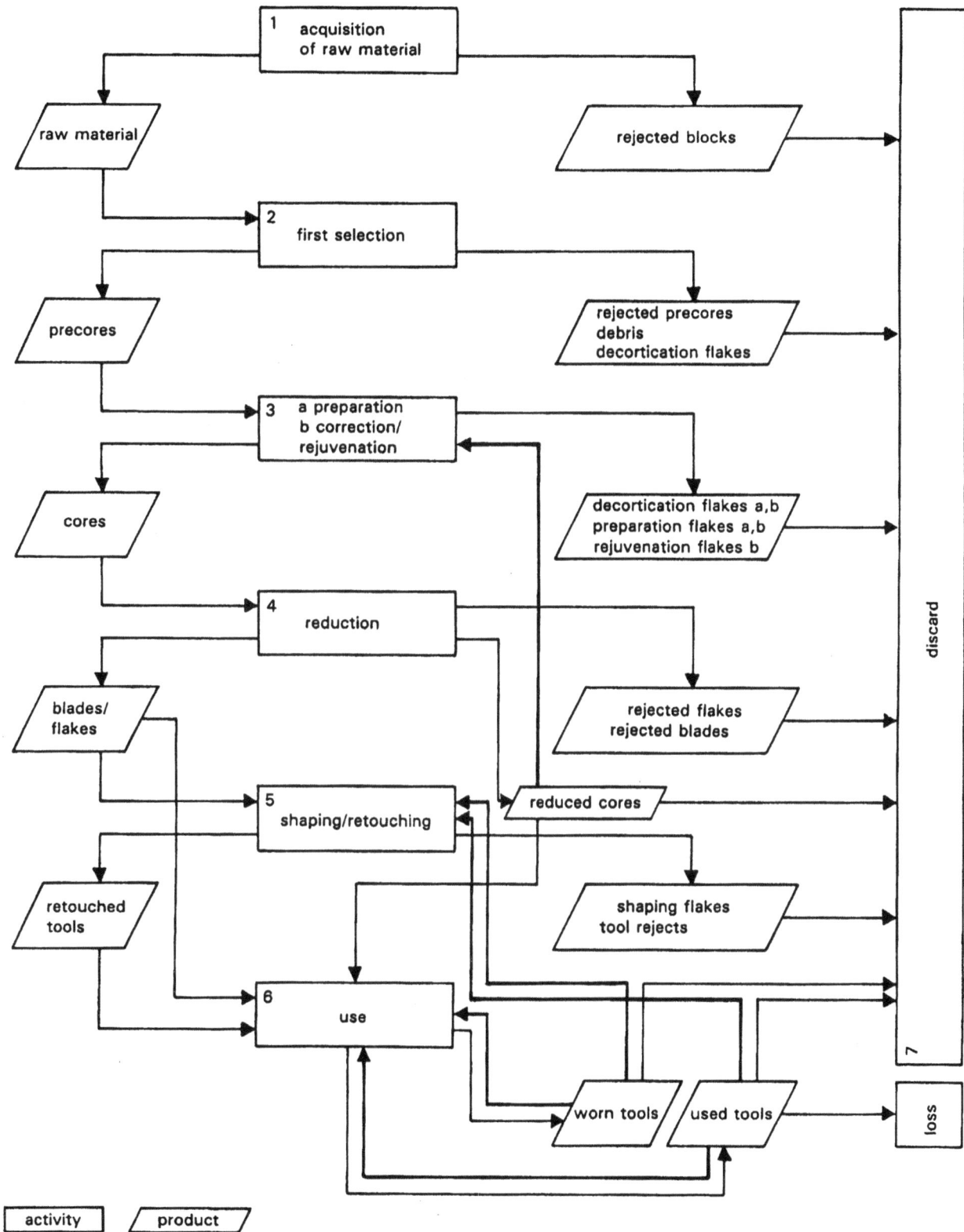

Figure 2. Flow model for Bandkeramik chert working.

Grooth 1994). The assemblages from Meindling and Hienheim do not differ as regards the average dimensions of blades and flakes), indicating that similar knapping techniques were used at both sites (table 1).

Between the samples, however, marked differences are found in the frequency of the various categories of artefacts. Thus, we find in Hienheim for every nodular core/hammerstone twice as many blades, and almost four times as many flakes as in Meindling (table 2). In Meindling the proportion of flakes is identical for both types of raw material, but the Ortenburg chert has even fewer blades for every core. In this respect the Meindling figures are comparable to those from LBK settlements in the Lower Vils Valley, situated some 20-30 km to the south-east, where Ortenburger Jurassic cherts were the predominant raw material (Schötz 1988). This could mean that the cherts were transported to Meindling at a later stage of the reduction sequence than that at which they reached Hienheim, i.e. not as unprepared blocks or initially prepared cores, but as completely prepared or even partially reduced cores.

This idea was supported through a detailed comparison of technological variables (table 3) : the Meindling assemblage contained fewer artefacts with cortex and fewer blanks with striking platforms consisting of cortex and/or natural surfaces. Moreover, there were more blanks with a primary or secondary facetted platform, the result either of more careful platform preparation or of a more frequent use of exhausted core faces as striking platforms, indicating that at Meindling cores were also worked more intensively than at Hienheim. Core rejuvenation also seems to have been practised slightly more frequently at Meindling.

Thus, the analysis of technological variables confirmed that both types of chert arrived in Meindling in a later stage of the reduction sequence than did the cores in Hienheim. No indications for a more intensive working of cores were found, however: the average number of striking platforms and core faces on the cores does not really differ, and the average size of the exhausted cores is higher at Meindling than at Hienheim. In combination with the higher proportion of facetted platforms and core rejuvenation, this could mean that at Meindling cores were not actually worked more intensively, but that a higher proportion of blanks derive from later stages in the reduction sequence, when platforms generally were prepared more carefully (Cahen 1984; de Grooth 1987; 1988).

The tools may offer additional information on the availability of raw material. In Meindling an astonishing 50.2% of the assemblage show intentional retouch or macroscopically visible traces of use-wear. Their relative frequencies are rather remarkable, too, with sickle-blades being by far the most frequent type (table 4). However, the intensity of tool maintenance and recycling, as estimated on the basis of the average number of modifications visible on the main tool types, turned out to be very similar to that in Hienheim (table

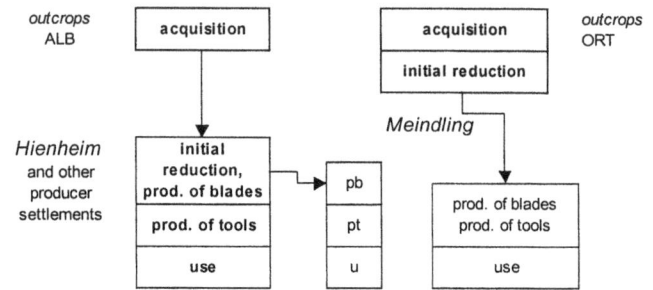

Figure 3. Procurement strategy and distribution mechanism prevailing at Meindling. Narrow arrows: within-group transport. Broad arrow: exchange. ALB: cherts form Franconian Alb. ORT: Ortenburger Jurassic cherts.

5). Thus, the tools do not support the idea of constrained availability of raw material either.

As a final step one should ascertain how the acquisition of both types of raw material was organised in terms of lithic procurement strategies and distribution mechanisms. For this purpose the model presented above may be compressed, focussing on four main stages in the production process, and emphasising the importance of transport between them (fig. 3; de Grooth 1991; cf. Torrence 1986).

During the LBK Hienheim's inhabitants exploited all available chert resources, seemingly in a rather haphazard way, but showing an initial preference for the nodular varieties. All material was brought into the settlement in an early stage of the reduction sequence, as precores or as initially prepared cores. In other words, at the various extraction sites the raw material was only tested for suitability : the production of blanks and tools and the use thereof took place in the settlements (fig. 4a). They apparently had unrestricted access to all regional resources, and the exchange of chert occurred over relatively short distances, not exceeding c. 80-100 km. In socio-economic terms, this procurement strategy corresponds to a *domestic mode of production*, in which the family, living in a single household, is the main unit of production and consumption (de Grooth 1987, van de Velde 1979).

Both of the Meindling assemblages could be the result of several procurement strategies :

1. If the inhabitants of Meindling had direct and open access to the sources of raw material, they themselves would have completely prepared the cores at the extraction sites, bringing them home for further reduction;
2. In the case of an indirect supply system, two distribution mechanisms would be possible :
- People having direct access to the resources worked according to the system described above and subsequently exchanged some of the prepared cores.
- The producers transported selected, unworked nodules to their settlements for further reduction, and exchanged some of the cores after preparation, or possibly even after an initial

series of blanks was produced.

This last seems the most plausible interpretation for the cherts from the Franconian Alb region, as it is compatible with the procurement strategy practised by the inhabitants of settlements such as Hienheim, who took unworked nodules home for further reduction and thus could conceivably distribute prepared or initially reduced cores through down-the-line exchange networks.

For Meindling's Ortenburger cherts, direct acquisition would be more probable than the two possibilities involving exchange. At Straubing-Lerchenhaid, the only excavated LBK site located closer to the outcrops at Münster, only a very small number of cherts were found (Grillo 1997, 94) so this settlement certainly did not serve as a regional distribution centre. This interpretation is supported by data from the Lower Vils Valley indicating that people there, living at a distance of 10-15 km from extraction sites, also adhered to the strategy of performing the initial stages of core reduction elsewhere (Schötz 1988). A group of interconnected pits documented during a rescue excavation at Künzing-Bruck, for example, contained a total of 359 chert artefacts, with a core:flake ratio 1:4 – and a baffling core:blade ratio of 1:1– (Grillo 1997, 58-60). Moreover, the debris excavated at the Flintsbach mines shows that a substantial amount of core preparation and blank production was indeed performed in the extraction area, whilst the discarded cores are very similar in type to the cores at Meindling (Weissmüller 1991). The considerable distance between settlements and exploitation areas (as well as other factor such as difficulties crossing the Danube or the unpredictability of raw material quality) may have led to the practice of performing the first stages of the reduction sequence at the mining site, thus reducing the risk of transporting substantial amounts of unsuitable/worthless nodules. A similar strategy was described for the LBK exploitation at the Tomaszów 'chocolate-flint' mines in Poland, located at a distance of more than one day's walk form the nearest settlements (Lech 1989).

This would mean that at Meindling two types of raw material, even though arriving at the site at the same stage of reduction, were procured through different strategies, based on direct acquisition for the regionally available Ortenburger cherts, and on down-the-line exchange for the material from the distant Franconian Alb (fig. 3).

Whilst the basic spatial organisation of chert production in the Kelheim region remained the same during the Middle Neolithic, important changes occurred as regards both the acquisition of raw material and the regional distribution mechanism. The initial preference for nodular chert changed gradually, and in the Middle Neolithic tabular chert was used almost exclusively. The main technological advantages of tabular chert are twofold: cores need little preparation and it is easy to produce standardised naturally backed blades. An increase in the number of settlements was combined with a decrease in the number of extraction sites. At Arnhofen, a

large mining complex with shafts up to 8 m deep, dates from this period (Binsteiner 1990a). The tablets at Baiersdorf were probably exploited by open cast mining at this time (Binsteiner 1989).

The regional distribution mechanism changed as well: unworked cores and substantial amounts of debitage (production waste) of Arnhofen chert are present mainly in settlements located at a distance of less than 20 km from the mines. Outside this area, Arnhofen striped tabular chert occurs mainly, although not exclusively (Grillo 1997), as blades and finished tools (de Grooth 1994). Extraction at Arnhofen may be seen as a short-term, seasonal activity, performed jointly by inhabitants of all the small settlements located in the vicinity of the mine. The distribution outside this 'production area' was partly directed at immediate neighbours, i.e. at immediate kin. An important structural long-distance circulation, however, was clearly present as well, as the material was transported as far as Eastern Bohemia and Lower Silesia to the Northeast (250-350 km, Lech 1987), Thuringia to the North (c. 200 km), and Hesse and Westphalia to the Northwest (over 200 km, Binsteiner 1990a; Zimmermann 1995). This type of exploitation can be practised under a *lineage mode of production*, where the unit of production and consumption is formed by a group of related families belonging to the same lineage or and temporarily aggregated into a larger workforce (de Grooth 1987, van de Velde 1979).

The benefit of the spatial and temporal concentration and intensification of mining activities may not only be regarded in terms of minimising expenditure of time and energy, but also of stimulating inter-group activities, controlled sharing of scarce resources and intensification of both regional and long-distance communication. In other words, the change in procurement strategy may be understood in terms of social reproduction and ideology rather than in terms of purely economic behaviour. To achieve this, one must place deep shaft mining and the creation and maintenance of long-distance distribution networks in a broader context, combining them with other characteristics of the societies involved (de Grooth 1997).

These are : first, the marked increase of Middle Neolithic settlement sites compared with the number of LBK sites in the whole of South-eastern Bavaria. Secondly, at about the same time, all over South-eastern Bavaria and adjacent regions, a whole series of impressive enclosures was erected (Petrasch 1990). In several cases they are situated at regular intervals, and they seemed to have functioned as a focus point for groups of small settlements in the area. As their construction as well as their regular renewal necessitated the combined efforts of several settlements, they may be seen as examples of episodic, institutionalised, and in this case clearly ritually inspired collective efforts of normally segregated groups. Thirdly, the originally very uniform LBK pot decorations, which probably served as social and cultural markers (Van de Velde 1979, 1997), had diversified into completely separate, idiosyncratic regional traditions. In this case, the archaeological distinctions of different 'groups' may well correspond to past expressions of group identity.

There does not seem to be any compelling technological reason for the extremely laborious –an estimated 160 person-hours were needed for the extraction of 2,7 kg high-quality tablets – deep-shaft mining of striped Arnhofen chert. It is, however, highly characteristic and attractive. As such, it may have served as a means to express the extractors' group identity in their communications with the outside world. On the other hand, internally, its controlled extraction would offer a means of maintaining communication, and of regulated social relations between kin groups which had to reconcile the need to uphold a settled way of life in distinct, isolated territories with the need to maintain shared unrestricted rights of access to localised resources, while at the same time strengthening traditional kinship ties. Thus, enclosures, systematic mining and structured long-distance exchange may all be regarded as efforts to re-define and re-emphasise group identity both internally and externally after a period of rapid change and upheaval visible in large parts of the Bandkeramik world (de Grooth 1997).

In conclusion, this study is not simply another example of 'lithomania', looking at lithics for their own sake. Rather, perceiving material culture as representing the products and consequences of actions and ideas, it documents how two LBK groups showing marked similarities in their material culture and even communicating through the exchange of chert artefacts, nevertheless developed different strategies for dealing with raw material procurement. Thus, it helps to refute the often expressed idea of the 'almost pathological conventionality' (Keeley 1992, 82) of LBK farmers, whose 'archaeological remains point to a rather rigid system, in which, in a sense, they lived with their backs to natural diversity' (Louwe Kooijmans 1998), in favour of seeing Bandkeramik lifestyle characterised by 'diversity in uniformity' (Modderman 1988).

Bibliography

BAKELS, C.C., 1978, Four Linearbandkeramik settlements and their environment. A palaeoecological study of Sittard, Stein, Elsloo and Hienheim, *Analecta Praehistorica Leidensia* 11.

BAYERLEIN, P., 1985, *Die Oberlauterbacher Gruppe in Niederbayern*. Kallmünz/Opf : Michael Lassleben. (Materialhefte zur Bayerischen Vorgeschichte A 53).

BINSTEINER, A., 1989, Der neolithische Abbau auf Jurahornsteine von Baiersdorf in der südlichen Frankenalb. *Archäologisches Korrespondenzblatt* 19, p. 331-339.

BINSTEINER, A., 1990a, Das neolithische Feuersteinbergwerk von Arnhofen, Ldkr. Kelheim. Ein Abbau auf Jurahornsteine in der Südlichen Frankenalb (mit Beiträgen von J. Riederer und B. Engelhardt). *Bayerische Vorgeschichtsblätter* 55, p.1-57.

BINSTEINER, A., 1990b, Die Feuersteinlagerstätten Südbayerns und ihre vorgeschichtliche Nutzung. *Der Anschnitt* 42, p.162-168.

CAHEN, D., 1984, Technologie du débitage laminaire. In: Otte, M., *Les Fouilles de la Place Saint-Lambert à Liège 1*. (Etudes et Recherches Archéologiques de l'Université de Liège 18), p. 171-197.

COLLINS, M. B., 1975, Lithic Technology as a Means of Processual Inference. In *Lithic Technology, Making and Using Stone Tools* edited by E.H. Swanson. The Hague: Mouton, p. 15-35.

GRILLO, A., 1997, *Hornsteinnutzung und –Handel im Neolithikum Südostbayerns*. Weissbach: Beier & Beran. (Beiträge zur Ur- und Frühgeschichte Mitteleuropas 12).

GROOTH, M.E.Th., de, 1977, Silex der Bandkeramik. In: Modderman, P.J.R., *Die neolithische Besiedlung bei Hienheim, Ldkr. Kelheim. I. Die Ausgrabungen am Weinberg 1965 bis 1970*. Kallmünz/Opf.: Michael Lassleben (Materialhefte zur bayerischen Vorgeschichte Reihe A, Bd. 33) p. 59-71.

GROOTH, M.E.Th., de, 1987, The Organisation of Flint Tool Manufacture in the Dutch Bandkeramik. *Analecta Praehistorica Leidensia* 20, p. 27-52.

GROOTH, M.E.Th., de, 1988, Zusammensetzungen von Silexartefakten. In: Boelicke U., Brandt, D. von, Lüning, J., Stehli P. & Zimmermann, A., *Der bandkeramische Siedlungsplatz Langweiler 8, Gemeinde Aldenhoven, Kreis Düren*. Bonn: Habelt. (Rheinische Ausgrabungen 28,) p. 787-794.

GROOTH, M.E.Th., de, 1991, Socio-economic aspects of neolithic flint mining: A preliminary study. *Helinium* 31, p. 153-190.

GROOTH, M.E.Th., de, 1992, Chert Procurement Strategies in the Linearbandkeramik Settlement of Meindling, Bavaria. *Analecta Praehistorica Leidensia* 25, p. 43-55.

GROOTH, M.E.Th., de, 1994, Die Versorgung mit Silex in der bandkeramischen Siedlung Hienheim 'Am Weinberg' (Ldkr. Kelheim) und die Organisation des Abbaus auf gebänderte Plattenhornsteine im Revier Arnhofen (Ldkr. Kelheim). *Germania* 72, p. 355-407.

GROOTH, M. E. Th,. de, 1995, The organization of chert exploitation in Southeastern Bavaria during the Neolithic. *Archaeologia Polona* 33, p. 163-172.

GROOTH, M.E.Th., de, 1997, Social and economic interpretations of the chert procurement strategies of the Bandkeramik settlement at Hienheim, Bavaria. *Analecta Praehistorica Leidensia* 29, p. 91-98.

KEELEY, L. H., 1992, The introduction of agriculture to the western north European plain. In: *Transitions to Agriculture in Prehistory*, edited by A.B.Gebauer, & T.D. Price. Madison: Prehistory Press, p. 81-95.

LECH, J., 1989, A Danubian raw material exchange network: a case study from Bylany. In: *Bylany Seminar 1987, Collected Papers*, edited by J. Rulf. Prag,: Archaeological Institute of the Czechoslovak Academy of Sciences, p. 111-121.

LOUWE KOOIJMANS, L.P., 1998, Understanding the Mesolithic/Neolithic Frontier in the Lower Rhine Basin, 5300-4300 cal. BC. In: *Understanding the Neolithic of north-western Europe* edited by M. Edmonds & C. Richards. Glasgow: Cruithne Press, p. 407-428.

MODDERMAN, P.J.R., 1977, *Die neolithische Besiedlung bei Hienheim, Ldkr. Kelheim. I. Die Ausgrabungen am Weinberg 1965 bis 1970.* Kallmünz/Opf: Michael Lassleben (Materialhefte zur bayerischen Vorgeschichte Reihe A, Bd. 33).

MODDERMAN, P.J.R., 1986, *Die neolithische Besiedlung bei Hienheim, Ldkr. Kelheim. II. Die Ausgrabungen am Weinberg 1971 bis 1974. III. Die Ausgrabungen im Fuchsloch 1975. IV. Landschaft und Besiedlung des Hienheimer Lössgebietes.* Kallmünz/Opf: Michael Lassleben (Materialhefte zur Bayerischen Vorgeschichte A 57).

MODDERMAN, P.J.R., 1988, The Linear Pottery Culture: Diversity in Uniformity. *Berichten van de Rijksdienst voor het Oudheidkundig Bodemonderzoek* 38, p. 63-139.

MODDERMAN, P.J.R., 1992, Linearbandkeramik aus Meindling, Gem. Oberschneiding, Ldkr. Straubing-Bogen. *Analecta Praehistorica Leidensia* 25, p. 25-43.

MOSER, M., 1980/1999. In: *5000 Jahre Feuersteinbergbau. Die Suche nach dem Stahl der Steinzeit.* Edited by G. Weisgerber, R. Slotta & J. Weiner. Veröffentlichungen aus dem Deutschen Bergbau-Museum Bochum 22, 446-448; 451-454. (3rd revised edition 1999).

NADLER, M., A. ZEEB, et al., 1994, Südbayern zwischen Linearkeramik und Altheim, ein neuer Gliederungsvorschlag. In: *Der Rössener Horizont in Mitteleuropa* edited by H.-J. Beier. Wilkau-Hasslau: Beier & Beran (Beiträge zur Ur- und Frühgeschichte Mitteleuropas 6), p. 127-190.

PETRASCH, J., 1990, Mittelneolithische Kreisgrabenanlagen in Mitteleuropa. 71. *Bericht der Römisch-Germanischen Kommission*, p. 407-565.

RÖHLING, K., 1987, Die Hornsteinvorkommen der "Ortenburger Schichten" (Malm Beta) in Ost-Niederbayern. In: *Proceedings of the first international conference on prehistoric flint mining and lithic raw material identification in the Carpathian Basin, Budapest-Sümeg, 20-22 May, 1986* edited by K. Biró. Budapest: Magyar Nemzeti Muzum, p. 129-130.

SCHÖTZ, M., 1988, Zwei unterschiedliche Silexabsatzgebiete im Neolithikum des Vilstals. *Bayerische Vorgeschichtsblätter* 53, p. 1-16.

TORRENCE, R., 1986, *Production and exchange of stone tools. Prehistoric obsidian in the Aegean.* Cambridge etc.: Cambridge University Press (New Studies in Archaeology).

VELDE, P., van de, 1979, On Bandkeramik Social Structure. An analysis of pot decoration and hut distributions from the Central European neolithic communities of Elsloo and Hienheim. *Analecta Praehistorica Leidensia* 12.

VELDE, P., van de, 1997, Much ado about nothing: Bandkeramik funerary ritual. *Analecta Praehistorica Leidensia* 29, p. 83-91.

WEISSMÜLLER, W., 1991, Der Silexabbau von Flintsbach-Hardt, Lkr. Deggendorf. Eine bedeutende Rohmateriallagerstätte für die Steinzeit. *Vorträge des 9. Niederbayerischen Archäologentages*, p. 11-40.

ZIMMERMANN, A., 1995, *Austauschsysteme von Silexartefakten in der Bandkeramik Mitteleuropas.* Bonn: Habelt (Universitätsforschungen zur prähistorischen Archäologie 26).

	M-ORT Flakes	M-ORT blades	M-ALB flakes	M-ALB Blades	H-ALB flakes	H-ALB blades
Width (when complete) [mm]	x = 24.5 s = 6.0 N = 28	x = 17.6 s = 3.8 N = 43	x = 24.9 s = 6.7 N = 16	x = 16.8 s = 3.7 N = 32	x = 27.3 s = 12.7 N = 203	x = 16.7 s = 5.1 N = 153
Thickness (when complete) [mm]	x = 6.4 s = 2.3 N= 48	x = 4.9 s = 1.6 N = 54	x = 7.5 s = 4.1 N = 27	x = 5.4 s = 2.1 N = 44	x = 7.9 s = 5.1 N = 326	x = 5.3 s = 2.0 N = 301
Platform width (when complete) [mm]	x = 13.9 s = 7.4 N = 39	x = 9.0 s = 2.6 N = 25	x = 12.7 s = 7.8 N = 23	x = 9.4 s = 2.7 N = 21	x = 14.0 s = 9.4 N =223	x = 9.4 s =3.2 N= 151
Platform thickness (when complete) [mm]	x = 4.6 s = 2.6 N = 39	x = 3.5 s = 1.5 N = 25	x = 4.3 s = 3.0 N = 23	x = 4.0 s = 1.8 N = 21	x = 5.4 s = 3.8 N = 225	x = 4.2 s = 1.7 N = 151
Length (fragments included) [mm]	x = 26.9 s = 7.6 N = 48	x = 29.6 s = 9.3 N = 54	x = 27.1 s = 9.3 N = 27	x = 31.6 s = 11.6 N = 44	x = 30.6 s = 12.9 N = 323	x = 33.4 s = 12.1 N = 302

Table 1. Measurements of blanks in Meindling (M) and Hienheim (H). ALB: Franconian Alb cherts; ORT: Ortenburger Jurassic cherts.

	M-ORT	M-ALB	H-ALB
Core : flake	1:4	1:4	1:15
Core : blade	1:4	1:6	1:14

Table 2. Proportions of cores, flakes and blades at Meindling and Hienheim.

	M-ORT	M-ALB	H-ALB
Artefacts with cortex (%)	49.2	49.4	66.7
Striking platforms on blanks (%)			
– cortex	17.4	16.0	23.6
– smooth	39.1	43.0	45.7
– facetted	37.7	42.0	22.6
– other	5.8	8.0	8.2
Dorsal scars (blanks)	x = 1.9	x = 2.0	x = 2.0
	s = 1.1	s = 1.2	s = 1.1
	N = 83	N = 54	N = 496
Rejuvenation blanks (%)	6.9	7.0	5.1
Weight of cores (gr)	x = 88.6	x = 111.7	x = 77.6
	N = 13	N = 7	N = 15
Negatives on cores	x = 5.8	(x = 7.0	x = 7.2
	s = 3.1		s = 3.8
	N = 9	N = 2)	N = 15
Core faces/striking platforms	x = 3.2	(x = 5.5	x = 3.8
	s = 1.0		s = 1.2
	N = 9	N = 2)	N = 16

Table 3. Comparison of technological data for Meindling and Hienheim nodular chert.

	Meindling N	Meindling %	Hienheim N	Hienheim %
Arrow heads / borers / burins	2	1.8	23	9.6
End-scrapers	18	15.2	28	11.7
Sickle blades	29	24.6	27	11.3
End-retouched	14	11.9	19	7.9
Side-retouched	13	11.0	48	20.0
Utilised	20	16.9	27	11.3
Splintered pieces / hammerstones	22	18.7	68	28.3
N	118	100.1	240	100.1

Table 4. Tools frequencies in Meindling compared to those in a sample of 240 LBK tools from sixteen dated pits in Hienheim.

	Meindling			Hienheim		
Tool type	x	s	N	x	s	N
Sickle blades	4.1	1.6	29	4.0	0.9	26
End-scrapers	3.2	1.2	18	2.6	0.8	23
End-retouched blades	2.5	1.2	14	2.8	1.4	18
Side-retouched blades	3.1	1.3	13	2.8	0.9	44

Table 5. Average number of modifications on main tool types in Meindling and Hienheim.

44

LITHIC RAW MATERIAL DISTRIBUTION NETWORKS AND THE NEOLITHIZATION OF CENTRAL EUROPE

Detlef GRONENBORN*

The Linear Pottery Culture (LBK) is traditionally viewed as the earliest fully developed Neolithic culture in Central Europe. Contemporaneous pottery traditions such as La Hoguette or Limburg might to a certain degree have been associated with farming or horticultural practices, but the economy still should have been largely based on hunting and gathering (Erny-Rodmann *et al*. 1997; Kalis *et al*. 2001). According to the 14C-dates from traditional archaeological sites but also from palaeobotanical studies where human impact was dated, LBK should have made its appearance along the Rhine river by 5500 cal BC (Schweizer 2001) and should begin 100 to 150 years earlier in eastern Austria, western Hungary and Slovakia. These early manifestations of LBK have been termed "earliest" (Germ. *älteste*) LBK and are stylistically, technologically and economically distinguishable from later phases (Quitta 1960; Meier-Arendt 1966; Gronenborn 1999). Despite repeated postulations, that LBK evolved out of local Late Mesolithic traditions throughout Central Europe (Tillmann 1993; Otte and Noiret 2001), a more complex scenario of farmers migrating from the western Carpathian Basin and the acculturation of local groups into the newly founded settlements seems more plausible (Gronenborn 1997 ; 1999 ; Price *et al*. 2001). The combination of migration and local adaptation is visible in the lithic industry of the earliest LBK.

During Earliest LBK times all of the raw materials utilized at any of the sites have been manufactured into the complete tool range. Production has taken place locally as all major raw materials are represented by discarded waste flakes. Hence, during Earliest LBK none of the siliceous raw materials seem to have had a role as prestige items. The exchange of siliceous rocks and the manufacture of tools were part of ordinary economic activities. Earliest LBK craftsmen obtained the raw-materials for their tools from a variety of sources. Apart from several long distance networks many

(*) Seminar für Vor- und Frühgeschichte, Johann Wolfgang Goethe-Universität, Grüneburgplatz 1, D-60323 Frankfurt am Main, *gronenborn@em.uni-frankfurt.de*

local or regional systems existed (Gronenborn 1997, 105-119). Generally these exchange networks, local, regional, or supra-regional have operated either internally or externally. Internally operating networks were those which were maintained by the LBK communities themselves, while external networks incorporated individuals or groups which were not part of the Earliest LBK societies. In order to understand the multiple and diverse social processes underlying these networks it is helpful to take a closer look at four long distance distribution systems. Two of these are based on internal connections:. that of radiolarite from the Bakony Mountains in Transdanubia and that of chert from Wittlingen on the Swabian Alb (fig. 2). The other two are based on external contacts, that of flints from the Maas Valley region and that of obsidian from Tokaj in the east Hungarian Bükk mountains (fig.1).

Obsidian was used widely during the sixth and seventh millennium B.C. in the eastern Carpathian Basin (Willms 1983). The beginnings of this distribution network go back as far as the Paleolithic (Radovanovic 1981, 100 ; Biró 1984) but a first peak was reached with the onset of an agrarian subsistence, during the Proto- Starcevo Culture (Vlassa 1972, 185-186). At this time obsidian was already taken north across the Carpathian ridge as it was found in Polish Late Mesolithic sites (Kozlowski 1989, 202). During the following centuries the amount rarely rises above 10 % at Starcevo-Körös sites but increases at the times of the early AVK (Kalicz and Makkay 1976) near the outcrop (fig. 1a). At Earliest LBK sites the presence of this material indicates external contacts, in this case to late Körös and early AVK.

External contacts are also evidenced on the western margins of Earliest LBK distribution range. At several sites in Hesse flint varieties from the Maas valley sources were found in different percentages, among which flint from the Vetschau/Lousberg outcrops near Aachen, Germany, seems to have been of considerable importance for the initial phases (Gronenborn 1997 b, 261). Rijckholt-flint from a source in the southern Netherlands is of major importance for the transitional periods to phase II. The outcrop at Rijckholt conti-

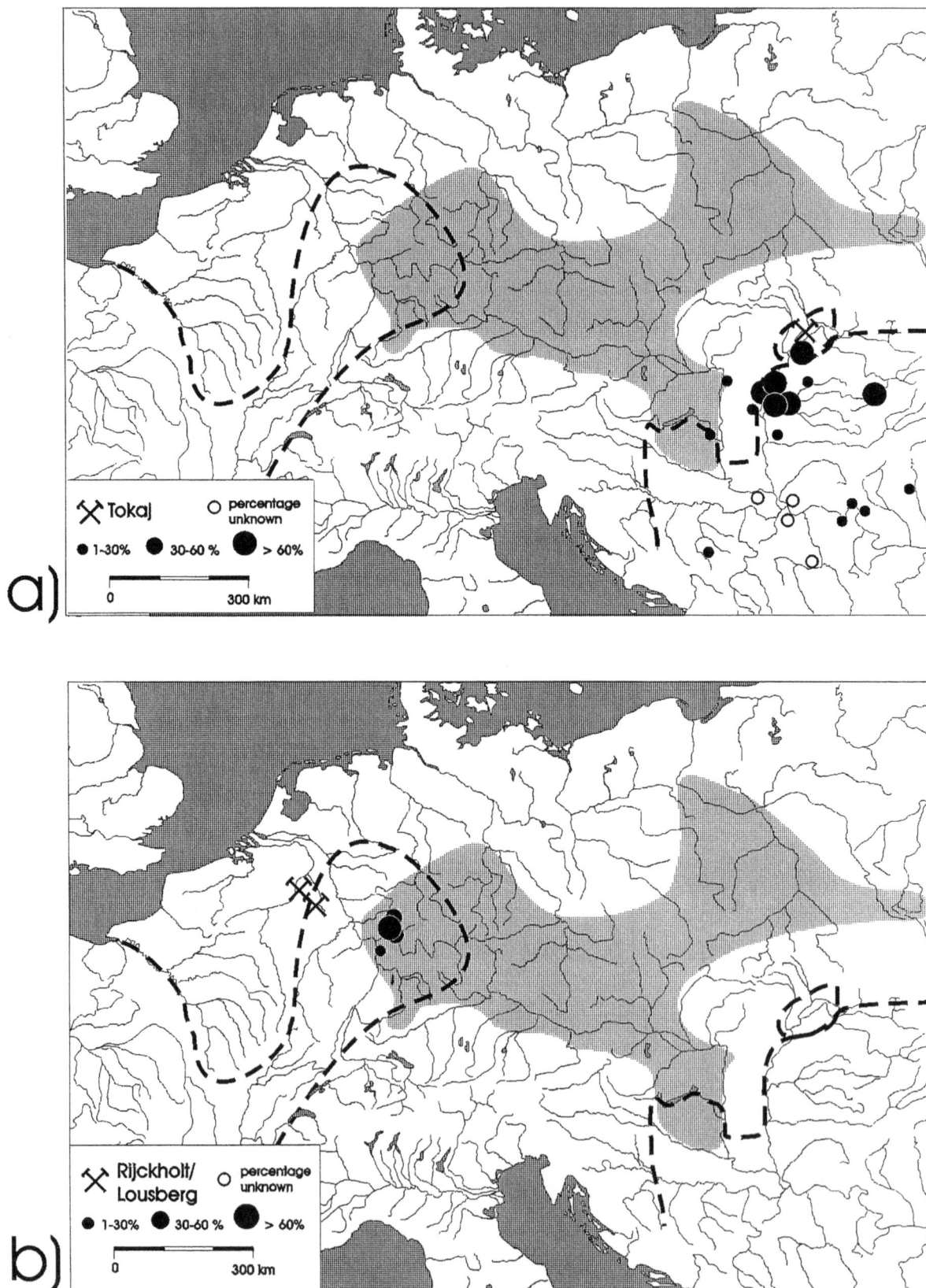

Figure 1. External lithic distribution network systems of Earliest LBK. Mapped are the distribution areas of La Hoguette, earliest LBK, Szatmár, and Stacrevo-Körös-Cris cultures. a) Obsidian; b) Mass-valley flints (after GRONENBORN 1997, 1999).

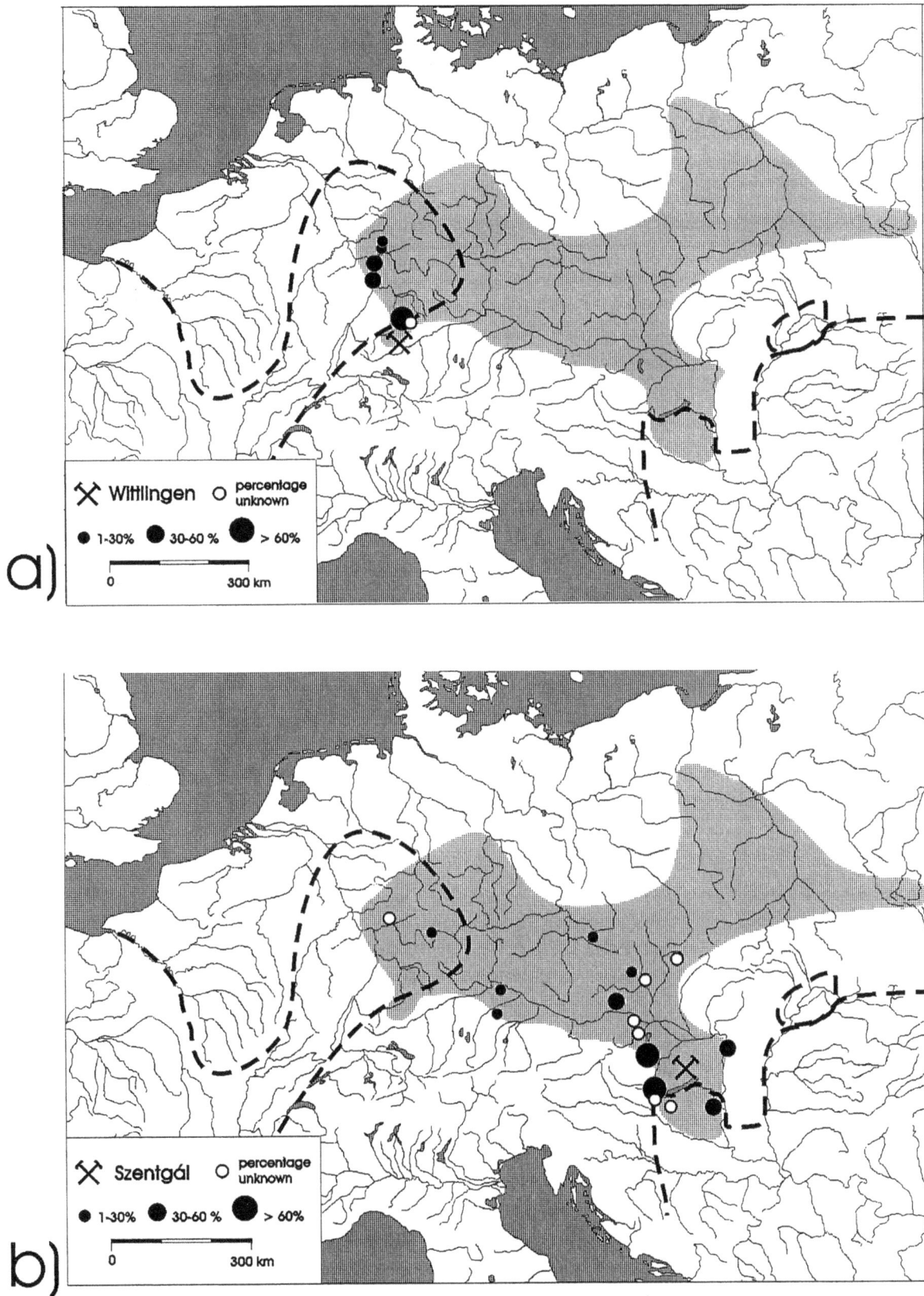

Figure 2. Internal lithic distribution network systems of Earliest LBK. a) Wittlingen chert; b) Szentgál radiolarite in earliest LBK and late Starcevo (after GRONENBORN 1997, 1999; KIND in prep.; MATEICIUCOVA 2001).

nued to be exploited during later LBK times (Zimmermann 1995, 110-115) and was mined extensively during the Aeneolithic (de Grooth 1991). The origins of the distribution system of Maas valley flint antedates the Neolithic period by millennia (Gronenborn 1997 a). Another Mesolithic raw material distribution system that has been incorporated into LBK society is that of chert from Wittlingen on the Swabian Alb (Abb. 2a). It was utilized in Mesolithic times and transported over considerable distances during the Late Mesolithic (see above), but later incorporated in the LBK networks. Such cherts have been found on several sites in Hesse and along the Upper Neckar. A contact network is indicated which reached down to the Rhine River and further to the Rhine-Main confluence area (fig. 1b).

A most notable raw material distribution system indicating supra-regional internal contacts is the one of radiolarite from the Bakony Mountains in Transdanubia, particularly the so called Szentgál variety. During the Earliest LBK Szentgál type radiolarite is distributed widely within the Carpathian basin (fig. 2b). The flaked stone assemblage from Pityerdomb, a site with Late Starcevo and earliest LBK components at the eastern margins of Transdanubia is exclusively composed out of Szentgál material (Bánffy 2000a, 377 ; 2000b, 179) and at the site of Neckenmarkt it still dominates the spectrum with about 90 % (Gronenborn 1997a, 20). The rate decreases further away from the outcrops and reaches about 30 % at the site of Brunn II (Gronenborn 1997a, 60; Mateiciucová 2001). But Szentgál type radiolarite was distributed much further west, as far as a site in the Rhine-Main confluence region where it is present with about 1 % (Gronenborn 1999, 169). This is at a distance of about 800 km from the source. Thus the distribution system of Szentgál radiolarites is certainly among the most extensive distribution networks of siliceous rocks during the Early Neolithic in Central Europe (Gronenborn 1994a, 138). The origins of this impressive network lie in the regional Mesolithic cultures of the Carpathian Basin. The material was used during Mesolithic times (Biró and Regenye 1991, 348-349 ; Biró 1991 ; Kertész 1994, I. Mateiciucová, personal communication) in eastern Hungary. Also it is found in considerable amounts on Starcàevo sites (Kalicz et al. 1998, 167). But presently there is no evidence that either during the Early or Late Mesolithic Szentgál type radiolarite was used in Bavaria or Lower Austria, although admittedly sites dating to the latter period are extremely scarce. It thus seems quite likely that the rapid and far reaching expansion of the distribution system to the west was ignited by the onset of the Earliest LBK. But the network did not continue for any greater length of time and seems to have collapsed with the beginning of phase II of the LBK (Gronenborn 1999, 169). From then on Szentgál type radiolarites continued to be distributed regionally within the later LBK in Transdanubia and remain of considerable importance in the Carpathian Basin up to the Aeneolithic (Biró and Regenye 1991, 348-349 ; Biró 1998).

Lithic technology in Earliest LBK times clearly derives from general Late Mesolithic traditions. It is based on the production of regular blades out of which a large proportion of tool types were manufactured, notably trapezes (fig. 3, 3). Apart from the trapeze other microlith types were used in various sub-regions of the overall distribution area of Earliest LBK, often indicating external contacts. One of these are triangular points at the western margin of Earliest LBK, the above mentioned so-called "Danubian points". Examples of these have been found at two sites in Hesse, associated with La Hoguette pottery and Maas Valley flints (fig. 3, 1-2). Several sites in southern Germany produced so-called asymmetric trapezes (fig. 3, 5). These are regionally limited and do not occur further east and are also considered to be a local Mesolithic component. A lunate was found at the site of Neckenmarkt in Austria (fig. 3, 6). In Central Europe such microliths have disappeared with the beginning of the Late Mesolithic, however they have remained regularly in use in southeastern Europe and are equally found in other Early Neolithic assemblages. Thus lunates in southeastern Earliest LBK assemblages demonstrate that the Transdanubian LBK lithic industry was influenced by surrounding groups and was well rooted in regional traditions. This is also becoming apparent in the ceramic assemblage of Pityerdomb where stylistic elements of earliest LBK pottery are associated with the late Starcevo tradition (Bánffy 2000).

Apart from microliths, scrapers, borers, and various cutting tools complemented the range of the Earliest LBK tool-kits. Of particular interest is a certain type of borer at the site of Schwanfeld in Frankonia (fig. 3,4). These borers resemble the so-called *mèches de forêt* of the late Early Mesolithic Sauveterrien of south-western France and northern Italy, a tradition which might have spread to Bavaria during the Late Mesolithic (Heinen 1998, 144; Street *et al.* 2001, 408 ff.). Hence stylistic resemblances to local traditions are evident in the complete tool range of Earliest LBK sites. Summing up all observations on lithic technology, typology and raw material distribution systems, it is presently possible to forward the general hypothesis that Earliest LBK lithic assemblages are composed of both surpa-regional as well as local traditions in raw material distribution, typology and technology (Gronenborn 1997a). Supra-regional traditions partly go back to a general Mesolithic heritage observed in all Early Neolithic lithic assemblages in Europe, but as in the case of Szentgál radiolarites some supra-regional phenomena can be attributed to the rapid spread of the Neolithic of Danubian tradition from its core zone in Transdanubia towards the west. Because of its rapidity this spread would have to be attributed to human migration (Gronenborn 1999 ; Petrasch 2001). Local traditions are interpreted as evidence for contact between Earliest LBK settlers and surrounding non-LBK groups (Gronenborn 1994a, 145-147).

Bibliography

BANFFY, E., 2000, Neue Daten zur Entstehung der Bandkeramik. In Karanovo Band III. Beiträge zum Neolithikum in Südosteuropa, edited by S. Hiller u. V. Nikolov. Wien: Phoibos, p. 375-382.

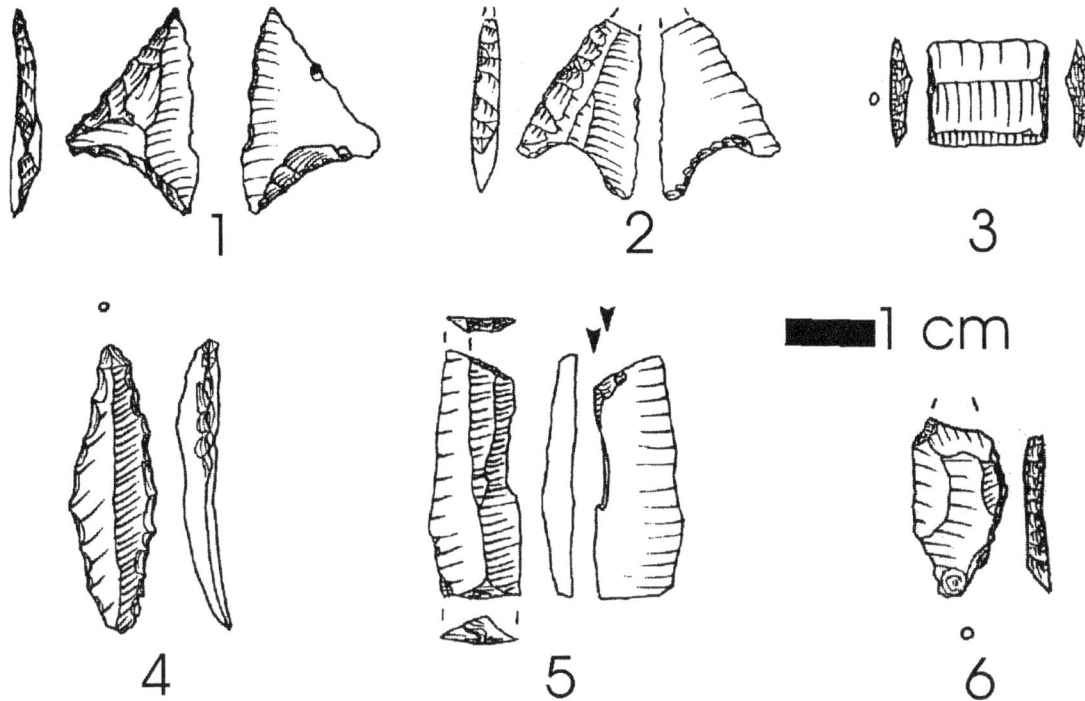

Figure 3. Earliest LBK tools and microliths (all after GRONENBORN 1997). 1-2 So-called pointe danubien (1. Bruchenbrücken, 2. Goddelau, Hessia, Germany); 3 trapeze (Enkingen, Bavaria, Germany); 4 mèche de forêt (Schwanfeld, Austria); 5 asymmetric trapeze (Mintraching, Bavaria, Germany); 6 lunate (Neckenmarkt, Austria).

BANFFY, E., 2000, The Late Starcevo and the Earliest Linear Pottery Groups in Western Transdanubia. In 7th Neolithic Studies. Documenta Praehistorica XXVII. Oddelek za Archeologijo Univerza v Ljubljani: Lubljana, p. 173-186.

BIRÓ, K., 1984, Distribution of obsidian from the Carpathian sources in Central European palaeolithic and mesolithic sites. *Acta Archaeologia Carpathica* 22, p. 5-42.

BIRÓ, K, 1991, Lithic industries in Hungary during the existence of Vinca culture. *Banatica* 11, p. 33-36.

BIRÓ, K.T., & REGENYE, J., 1991, Prehistoric workshop and exploitation site at Szentgál-Tüsköveshegy. *Acta Archaeologia Hungaricae* 43, p. 387-410.

BIRÓ, K. T., 1998, *Lithic Implements and the Circulation of Raw Materials in the Great Hungarian Plain during the Late Neolithic Period*. Hungarian National Museum (Budapest 1998).

ERNY-RODMANN, CH., GROSS-KLEE, E., HAAS, J. N., JACOMET, ST., & ZOLLER, H., 1997, Früher "human impact" und Ackerbau im Übergangsbereich Spätmesolithikum-Frühneolithikum im schweizerischen Mitteland. *Jahrbuch der Schweizerischen Gesellschaft für Ur- und Frühgeschichte* 80, p. 27-56.

GRONENBORN, D., 1994, Überlegungen zur Ausbreitung der bäuerlichen Wirtschaft in Mitteleuropa - Versuch einer kulturhistorischen Interpretation ältestbandkeramischer Silexinventare. Praehistorische Zeitschrift 69/2, p. 135-151.

GRONENBORN, D., 1997a, Silexartefakte der ältestbandkeramischen Kultur. Mit einem Beitrag von Jean-Paul Caspar. *Universitäts-forschungen zur prähistorischen Archäologie* 37. Bonn: Habelt.

GRONENBORN, D., 1997b, Die Steinartefakte. In Ein Siedlungsplatz der Ältesten Bandkeramik in Bruchenbrücken, Stadt Friedberg/Hessen, edited by J. Lüning. *Universitätsforschungen zur prähistorischen Archäologie* 39. Bonn: Habelt, p. 257-332.

GRONENBORN, D., 1999, A variation on a basic theme: The transition to farming in southern Central Europe. *Journal of World Prehistory* 13, p. 123-210.

GROOTH, M. E. TH. de, 1991, Socio-economic aspects of Neolithic Flint mining : a preliminary study. *Helinium* 31/2, p. 153-189.

HEINEN, M., 1998, *Mèche de Forêt* - eine charakteristische aber weitgehend unbekannte Werkzeugform des Mesolithikums. In *Aktuelle Forschungen zum Mesolithikum*, edited by N. J. Conard & C.-J. Kind. Urgeschichtliche Materialhefte 12. Tübingen : Mo Vince, p. 133-146.

KALICZ, N., & MAKKAY, J., 1976, Frühneolithische Siedlung in Méhtelek-Nádas. *Mitteilungen des Archäologischen Instituts Budapest* 6, 13-24.

KALICZ, N., VIRAG, Z. M., & BIRO, K. T., 1998, The northern Periphery of the Early Neolithic Starcevo Culture in Southwestern Hungary - a case study of an excavation at the Lake Balaton. In Neolithic Studies, edited by M. Budja. *Documenta Praehistorica* 25. Univerza v Ljubljani, Filozofska Fakulteta (Ljubljana 1998), p. 151-188.

KALIS, A. J., MEURERS-BALKE, J., VAN DER BORG, K., VON DEN DRIESCH, A., RÄHLE, W., TEGTMEIER, U., & THIEMEY-ER, H., 2001, Der La-Hoguette-Fundhorizont in der Wilhelma von

Stuttgart-Bad Cannstatt. Anthrakologische, archäopalynologische, bodenkundliche, malakozoologische, radiometrische und säugetierkundliche Untersuchungen. In Zeit-Räume. Gedenkschrift für Wolfgang Taute Band 2, edited by B. Gehlen, M. Heinen & A. Tillmann. Deutsche Gesellschaft für Ur- und Frühgeschichte / Rudolf Habelt (Bonn 2001), p. 649-672.

KERTÉSZ, R., 1994, Late Mesolithic chipped Stone industry from the site Jástelek I (Hungary). In A Kökortól a Középkorig - Tanulmányok Trogmayer Ottó 60. Születésnapjára/ Von der Steinzeit bis zum Mittelalter - Studien zum 60. Geburtstag von Ottó Trogmayer, edited by L. Gábor. Szeged, p. 23-39.

KIND, C.-J., in prep., Die Steinartefakte aus der Siedlung der ältesten Bandkeramik von Rottenburg-Fröbelweg.

KOZLOWSKI, S. K., 1989, Mesolithic in Poland. A new Approach. Warszawa: Wydownictwa Universytetu Warszawskiego.

MATEICIUCOVA, I., 2001, Silexindustrie in der ältesten Linearbandkeramik-Kultur in Mähren und Niederösterreich auf der Basis des Silexindustire des Lokalmesolithikums. In From the Mesolithic to the Neolithic. Proceedings of the International Archaeological Conference held in the Damjanich Museum of Szolnok, September 22-27, 1996, edited by R. Kertész & J. Makkay. Archaeolingua 11, p. 283-300.

MEIER-ARENDT, W., 1966, Die bandkeramische Kultur im Untermaingebiet. Veröffentlichungen des Amtes für Bodendenkmalpflege im Regierungsbezirk Darmstadt Heft 3. Bonn: Habelt.

OTTE, M., & NOIRET, P., 2001, Le Mésolithique du Bassin Pannonien et la formation du Rubané. L'Anthropologie 105, p. 409-419.

PETRASCH, J., 2001, "Seid fruchtbar und mehret euch und füllet die Erde und macht sie euch untertan": Überlegungen zur demographischen Situation der bandkeramischen Landnahme. Archäologisches Korrespondenzblatt 31, p. 13-26.

QUITTA, H., 1960, Zur Frage der ältesten Bandkeramik in Mitteleuropa. Prähistorische Zeitschrift 38, 1-38.

RADOVANOVIC, I., 1981, Padina - Early Holocene flint industry from the site of Padina in the Iron Gates. Archeologicke Institute Belgrade Materialiae Vol. 4. Belgrade.

STREET, M., BAALES, M., CZIESLA, E., HARTZ, S., HEINEN, M., JÖRIS, O., PASDA, CL., TERBERGER, TH. & VOLLBRECHT, J., 2001, Final Palaeolithic and Mesolithic Research in Reunified Germany. Journal of World Prehistory 15/4, p. 365-453.

TILLMANN, A., 1993, Kontinuität oder Diskontinuität? Zur Frage einer bandkeramischen Landnahme im südlichen Mitteleuropa. Archäologische Informationen 16/2, p. 157-187.

VLASSA, N., 1972, Eine frühneolithische Kultur mit bemalter Keramik der Vor-Starcevo-Körös-Zeit in Cluj-Gura Baciului, Siebenbürgen. Prähistorische Zeitschrift 47, p. 174-197.

WILLMS, CHR., 1983, Obsidian im Neolithikum und Äneolithikum Europas. Ein Überblick. Germania 61/2, p. 327-351.

ZIMMERMANN, A., 1995, Austauschsysteme von Silexartefakten in der Bandkeramik Mitteleuropas. Universitätsforschungen zur Prähistorischen Archäologie 26. Bonn: Rudolf Habelt.

GESTION DES MATÉRIAUX SILICEUX DANS LES PREMIÈRES COMMUNAUTÉS DANUBIENNES (CULTURE À CÉRAMIQUE LINEAIRE ET GROUPE DE BLICQUY-VILLENEUVE-SAINT-GERMAIN) À VAUX-ET-BORSET (HESBAYE, BELGIQUE)

Jean-Paul CASPAR & Laurence BURNEZ-LANOTTE*

Résumé

Le site de Vaux-et-Borset (Hesbaye liégeoise, Belgique) a livré deux villages mitoyens : l'un de la Culture à Céramique rubanée et l'autre du Groupe de Blicquy-Villeneuve-Saint-Germain. Les fouilles menées dans ces occupations ont été d'une importance primordiale pour l'intelligibilité des rapports chronologiques et culturels de ces deux cultures archéologiques en Hesbaye. Cette présentation résume les premiers résultats des analyses typologiques et fonctionnelles des industries lithiques des deux villages. Les études indiquent, contrairement à l'idée habituellement acceptée, une dichotomie qui concerne l'économie et la gestion des matières siliceuses de part et d'autre. Ces résultats montrent des différences pertinentes de comportement.

Abstract

The site of Vaux-et-Borset (Hesbaye liégeoise, Belgium) comprises two neighbouring villages, one of the Linear Pottery Culture, the other one of the Blicquy-Villeneuve-Saint-Germain group. The investigation of this site has been of major importance for our understanding of chronological and cultural connections between the two cultures involved in Hesbaye. This paper will summarize results of the extensive typological and use-wear analysis of the lithic industry of both villages. These clearly indicate, contrary to accepted ideas, a dichotomy with regard to raw material management, to all stages of the reduction sequences and to original utilisations and specific hafting methods for certain tool classes. The results show clear differences of behaviour.

Présentation du site

Le site s'insère dans une zone riche en occupations de la culture à Céramique Linéaire régionale ou Rubané dit "Omalien". L'origine de nos travaux y est due aux découvertes de J. Docquier (Cercle archéologique Hesbaye-Condroz). Les installations sont implantées sur le sommet et sur la pente méridionale de la crête en faible relief d'un plateau limoneux de la Hesbaye. L'occupation rubanée s'étend sur la pente méridionale du plateau. 6 680 m² ont été fouillés (de 1989 à 1995, dont 2 950 m² en 1989 et 1990). Les principales structures mises au jour sont : une enceinte délimitée par un fossé interrompu dont le tracé forme un quadrilatère irrégulier délimitant une superficie de 4,5 ha et un village dont 3 habitations, leurs fosses de construction et une batterie de silos ont été explorés. Au moins deux phases d'habitat ont été reconnues par les recoupements de ces structures. Au nord-ouest et au sud-ouest de cette occupation, les vestiges du Groupe de

Blicquy/Villeneuve-Saint-Germain (BQ/VSG) ont été étudiés sur 8 450 m² (1989-1990) répartis en deux secteurs : l'un sur la crête et sur le haut de la pente méridionale et l'autre, plus à l'ouest, sur une pente également orientée au sud (fig. 1). Une

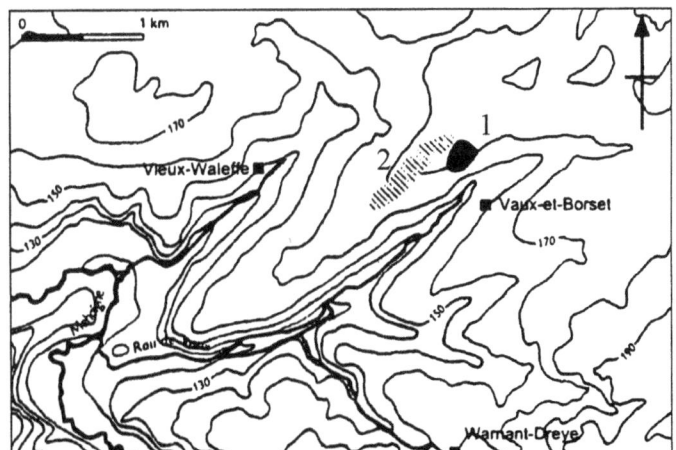

Figure 1. Vaux-et-Borset : implantations des deux villages. 1 : Rubané. 2 : Groupe de Blicquy.

(*) Université de Namur et associé à l'UMR 7041 (CNRS - France) "Protohistoire européenne", 13 rue de l'Arsenal, B-5000 Namur - Belgique laurence.burnez@fundp.ac.be

51

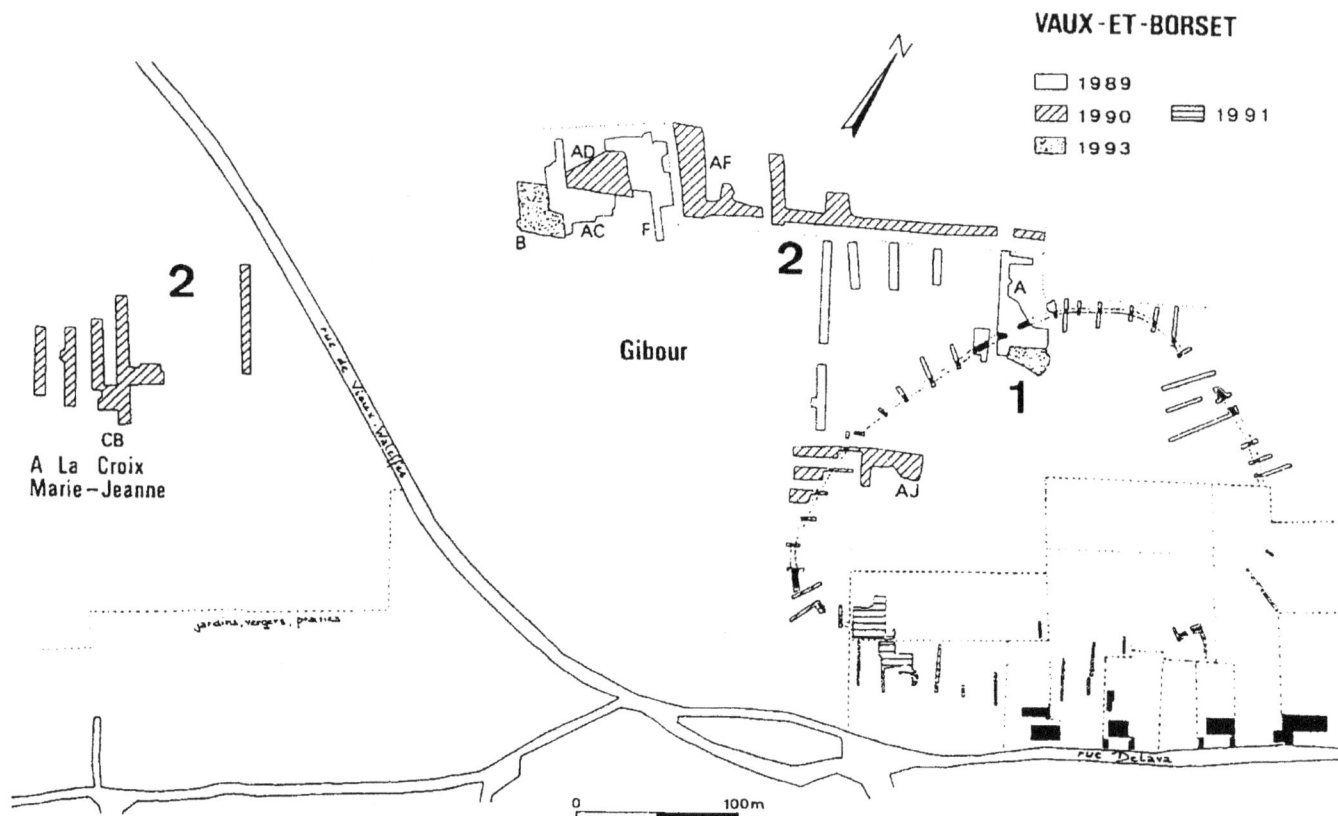

Figure 2. Vaux-et-Borset : plan général des fouilles des deux villages. 1 : Rubané. 2 : Groupe de Blicquy.

campagne de fouille réalisée en 1998 dans le secteur occidental du site (Caspar *et al.* 1999) sur une surface de 3 000 m² a montré les limites occidentales de l'extension du village du Groupe de Blicquy-Villeneuve-Saint-Germain et la présence de quelques structures détritiques particulièrement riches. A ce jour, trois habitations blicquiennes érodées ont été mises au jour (Burnez-Lanotte *et al.* 1993). Les structures rubanées et blicquiennes les plus proches sont distantes de 36 m. Aucun recoupement n'a été observé entre structures des deux villages mitoyens qui s'excluent mutuellement (fig. 2).

Industries lithiques

Pour ce qui est des industries lithiques rubanée et blicquienne de Moyenne Belgique (Cahen *et al.* 1986), on a surestimé leur parenté. Nous avons pu montrer qu'à Vaux, c'est une situation très contrastée qui prévaut dans l'économie et la gestion des matières siliceuses de part et d'autre (Caspar et Burnez-Lanotte 1994 et 1998). Les différences portent sur toutes les étapes du traitement et de l'usage de la matière première.

Matières premières

A Vaux, les Rubanés exploitent un matériau d'origine exclusivement locale, issu de la craie, par opposition aux Blicquiens que caractérise la diversité des sources et des processus d'acquisition des matériaux siliceux. Si les variétés d'origine locale (silex fin - SFH - et grenu - SGH - de Hesbaye) sont enco-

re largement majoritaires avec 95 % des effectifs (Caspar et Burnez-Lanotte 1994), elles proviennent en priorité de contextes remaniés (poches de dissolution). Une catégorie mineure (4% des pièces) concerne deux types de silex exogènes : l'un, gris-éléphant (SGM), dont l'origine a été attribuée au Crétacé du Hainaut (Ghlin-les-Mons en Hainaut ; Hubert 1970, 1982), l'autre, un silex marron-beige à grain très fin, issu des bancs tertiaires du Bassin parisien (SMB). Cette circulation de matières siliceuses sur de longues distances individualise à Vaux le Groupe de Blicquy-Villeneuve-Saint-Germain (importations d'artefacts en silex extra-régionaux), par rapport au Rubané (silex exclusivement local).

Débitage d'éclats et exploitation de blocs ou de débris

Pour le Rubané, le débitage d'éclats n'est pas objectivement attesté (Caspar & Burnez-Lanotte 1998), alors que pour le Blicquien, l'échantillon de pièces numériquement le plus important témoigne d'une gestion opportuniste de matériaux directement accessibles, aboutissant à des outils sur éclat, bloc et débris peu élaborés.

Productions laminaires

Description

Manifestement, l'importance des productions laminaires respectives est un caractère de différenciation des deux indus-

52

tries. Dans le Rubané, le débitage est représenté par tous les éléments de la chaîne opératoire d'une production laminaire dominante en silex local : nucléus (6) et pièces techniques (89) tels que des bords de nucléus, des tablettes, des lames à crête et des flancs. Le débitage laminaire est également attesté par 15 nucléus à lames recyclés en percuteur (14) ou en pièce martelée (1). Les lames brutes, soit 304 spécimens en silex local, représentent 12% du débitage (304 pièces sur 2 534, non compris les débris et l'outillage) et offrent des caractéristiques très homogènes du point de vue morphologique, technique et dimensionnel. Leur extrémité proximale est caractérisée par un talon large et lisse, quasi systématiquement sans préparation, une corniche surplombante formée par les contrebulbes très prononcés des enlèvements antérieurs et un bulbe de percussion large et proéminent. D'un point de vue dimensionnel, les pièces complètes excèdent très rarement les 8 cm.

La composante laminaire (Caspar & Burnez-Lanotte 1994, p. 10) représente dans le Blicquien 2,3% du débitage (607 pièces sur un total de 26 443, non compris les débris ni l'outillage) dont les deux tiers sont en silex locaux (53% en SFH et 13% en SGH), 32% en silex exogènes (25% en SGM, 7% en SMB) et 2% d'origine indéterminée (compte non tenu des pièces ayant subi une altération thermique). Les caractéristiques morphotechniques des lames en silex local sont rigoureusement identiques à celles retrouvées dans les contextes détritiques du village rubané. Par contre, les éléments en silex exogènes témoignent d'une grande régularité et présentent des talons généralement étroits, lisses ou préparés, avec une corniche aménagée et un bulbe de percussion soit diffus, soit court et net (Caspar & Burnez-Lanotte 1997). D'un point de vue dimensionnel, certaines pièces entières peuvent atteindre de 12 à 16 cm de long.

Lieu de production

Pour le Rubané, les éléments de la chaîne opératoire de production laminaire en silex local existent (cfr. supra) et attestent d'un débitage intra-muros.

Pour le Blicquien, les seuls témoins d'une production locale (parmi lesquels les premiers remontages) concernent l'outillage sur bloc, sur éclat ou sur débris issu de dépôts remaniés, selon toute vraisemblance les poches de dissolution qui jouxtent la bordure sud-occidentale de l'occupation. Les indices d'un débitage laminaire, silex de toutes origines confondues, font quasiment défaut dans les inventaires blicquiens. Aucun nucléus à lames n'a été découvert, même réemployé comme percuteur. Au niveau des enlèvements particuliers, soit 43 éléments répartis en nombre décroissant de fréquence en lames à crête, tablettes et flancs de ravivage, plus de la moitié (26) sont en silex exogènes. Pratiquement tous attribués au silex dit de Ghlin (23) qui a pu être acheminé sur le site à l'état de nucléus préformés et de supports semi-finis à finis. Ce fait est attesté par l'absence d'éclats de décorticage dans ce matériau et la présence d'un nombre important d'éclats minces, arqués, typiques de la préparation

des crêtes. Le silex tertiaire a également fait l'objet d'un débitage intra-muros (2 pièces techniques et des éclats de façonnage de lame à crête) mais proportionnellement nettement moins fréquent. Il est intrusif dans la plupart des cas sous forme de produits laminaires semi finis à finis.

Les pièces techniques blicquiennes en silex locaux (16 en SFH et 1 en SGH) comprennent seulement 13 lames à crête et 4 tablettes qui ne constituent pas en soit, au vu de leur rareté, une preuve d'une mise en oeuvre de l'ensemble de la chaîne opératoire de la production des supports laminaires bruts dans les contextes détritiques de cette culture, alors que ces produits en silex local dominent (377 contre 182 en silex exogène). La quasi absence caractérisée du débitage laminaire en silex local dans le village blicquien confrontée à la fréquence des lames en ce matériau pose le problème de la localisation de ces productions : extra-muros ou dans un secteur encore non étudié du site (bien qu'il ait été exploré par tranchées larges sur sa quasi totalité). Résultent-elles d'un débitage moins soigné, par opposition à une technologie plus élaborée (silex exogènes) comme ce qui a été proposé dans le VSG du Bassin parisien (Bostyn 1994) ? Parmi les paramètres qui pourraient expliquer la présence en contexte blicquien de lames en silex local, à l'hypothèse de la perduration d'une tradition technologique, on préfèrerait celle d'un processus de récupération plus ou moins étendu de spécimens rubanés par les Blicquiens. Cependant, à l'heure actuelle, cette théorie appliquée aux lames brutes en silex local ne bénéficie pas de preuves irréfutables comme, par exemple, le remontage de certains de ces éléments issus des contextes blicquiens avec des vestiges de la chaîne de production laminaire rubanée. Ce type de recherche n'a pas encore été mené.

Outillages

Les outillages blicquiens (Caspar & Burnez-Lanotte 1994, tableau 5) et rubanés (Caspar & Burnez-Lanotte 1998, tableau 6) se distinguent clairement dans les quantités relatives d'outils sur lame et sur support d'éclat ou de bloc : les outils sur support laminaire représentent un peu moins d'un cinquième du total (19%) des outils dans le Blicquien et 68% dans le Rubané (non compris les fragments d'outils indéterminés, de percuteurs, ainsi que les chutes de burin). Exclusivement local dans le Rubané, l'outillage laminaire blicquien reste dominé par les deux variantes hesbignonnes (46% en SFH, 6,5% en SGH) et comprend des effectifs importants en matériaux exogènes (25% en SGM et 14% en SMB) ; le restant étant de provenance indéterminée. Les caractéristiques morphotechniques des produits laminaires retouchés, qu'ils soient rubanés ou blicquiens, sont identiques à celles distinguées sur les spécimens bruts en relation avec l'origine de la matière première. Les valeurs dimensionnelles affichent le même contraste que pour les produits bruts entre les variantes siliceuses locales d'une part et celles d'origines exogènes d'autre part.

L'outillage non laminaire rubané représente 31% de l'effectif. Il se répartit en outils sur bloc (percuteurs) et sur

Jean-Paul CASPAR & Laurence BURNEZ-LANOTTE

éclat (denticulés, pièces esquillées et/ou martelées, éclats retouchés....) issus de la mise en forme des rognons dans le cadre du débitage de lames, à l'instar des sites rubanés de Hesbaye (Cahen et *al.* 1986). Pour le Blicquien, l'outillage sur bloc (polyèdres) ou sur éclat et débris (denticulés, grattoirs, pièces esquillées et/ou martelées, racloirs, pièces retouchées...) domine largement les inventaires (80 %, non compris les fragments d'outils indéterminés et les éclats de retouche ; Caspar & Burnez-Lanotte 1994, tableau 5).

Hypothèse d'une corrélation entre technologie lithique, dispositif instrumental et économie des matières siliceuses

Outillage laminaire

Dans l'outillage blicquien sur lame en silex local se pose à nouveau le problème de l'origine culturelle du support. Une étude en cours montre que son appartenance culturelle ressortit à une explication plus complexe qu'il ne semble en première analyse. L'approche se réfère à des caractères stylistiques et fonctionnels propres à chacune des cultures. En effet, il apparaît clairement que les outils sur lame qui présentent des caractéristiques typiques du BQ/VSG sont réalisés exclusivement en silex exogènes.

Dans la catégorie des grattoirs (51% en silex locaux, 47% en silex exogènes et 2% en silex d'origine indéterminée), seuls les spécimens dont le front présente une convexité prononcée (front en arc brisé ou ogival) et qui du point de vue morpho-métrique et du style ne peuvent être attribués qu'au Blicquien, sont tous réalisés sur support laminaire en silex exogènes. Les grattoirs en silex locaux et quelques exemplaires en silex exogènes sont à front faiblement arqué et correspondent aux modèles classiques rubanés (Caspar & Burnez-Lanotte 1998 p. 231). Les premières analyses fonctionnelles confirment une différenciation des traces d'usure en rapport avec ces deux ensembles qui, dans l'état actuel des observations, indiquent de part et d'autre des usages et des dispositif instrumentaux distincts (Caspar, étude en cours).

De manière équivalente, seules les faucilles de morphologie et de style exclusivement BQ/VSG sont en silex exogènes, à savoir : les petits éléments à bord ou dos convexe des faucilles composites (fig. 4 : 4) et les grandes lames qui sont des couteaux de récolte simples fig. 4 : 1), vraisemblablement liés à de nouveaux modes de récolte des végétaux non ligneux, domestiques ou non (Caspar & Burnez-Lanotte 1994). Les éléments de faucille en silex locaux sont, par contre, des pièces typiques du Rubané : fragments de lames bruts ou retouchés par troncature rectiligne, droite ou oblique et/ou par retouches abruptes d'un bord latéral ou d'un cran. De plus, une analyse tracéologique systématique des objets (fig. 4) révèle une prépondérance de leur réemploi sur des matériaux autres que les plantes non ligneuses tels qu'ils affectent les faucilles rubanées (Caspar 1988 ; Vaughan 1994). Ce type de réemploi est inexistant dans les éléments lustrés du BQ/VSG (Allard *et al.* à par.).

Les burins se répartissent en 39 % en silex locaux et 53 % en silex exogènes (8% en silex autres). Au sens strict, les burins n'appartiennent pas aux inventaires typologiques du Rubané européen à l'exception du Rubané Récent du Bassin parisien, si l'on exclut quelques nucléus sur tranche d'éclat diminutifs erronément interprétés. Manifestement, le débitage sur tranche d'éclat, attesté uniquement dans l'aire hesbignonne de répartition du Rubané en Moyenne Belgique est orienté vers la production de lames épaisses, de section le plus souvent quadrangulaire, assimilables à de grossières chutes de burin, nommées "frites". En réalité, nous sommes en présence de burins blicquiens en silex local opposé à une absence de burins dans les séries rubanées. Or, les supports présentent des caractéristiques morpho-techniques rubanées qui tranchent nettement avec les stigmates présents sur les supports en silex exogènes typiques du Blicquien. La production du coup de burin qui constitue une technique originale de réfection d'un bord (et non pas une mise en forme destinée à obtenir un biseau ou une dent comme c'est le cas par exemple pour certains burins du Paléolithique supérieur) est assurément BQ/VSG. Mais la production du support de l'outil reste hypothétique, en l'absence, toujours, de vestiges liés aux chaînes opératoires d'une production laminaire en silex local dans les contextes blicquiens du site. S'agit-il de phénomènes de récupération de lames brutes par les Blicquiens dans l'entité rubanée, recyclées en burin pour un usage lié au raclage des matières végétales dures non ligneuses, tel qu'il transparaît des premières études fonctionnelles faites à Vaux et qui est généralisé pour ce type d'outil dans tout le VSG du Bassin parisien (Allard *et al.* à par.) ?

Les lames retouchées et les troncatures sont stylistiquement rattachables sans partage aux deux cultures. Seul le style de débitage les différencie à nouveau en fonction de la matière première. Une étude est en cours afin d'évaluer les types et techniques de retouche des produits laminaires retouchés afin de déterminer d'éventuelles différences en regard de l'origine des matériaux lithiques.

Les perçoirs et pièces associées (alésoirs, pièces appointées) dans le Blicquien de Vaux se répartissent comme suit : 75% en silex locaux, 19% en silex exogènes et 6% en silex d'origine indéterminée. La plupart, quelle que soit la provenance de leur matériau, peuvent stylistiquement être attribués aux deux cultures en présence. Ce qui peut les différencier, pour deux cas d'entre eux, réside dans la longueur des supports, soit deux lames respectivement de 16 et 11 cm de long en l'état de leur découverte, gabarit inexistant dans le Rubané de Vaux. Ces deux pièces sont réalisées en silex exogènes. Elles divergent aussi des prototypes rubanés par la morphologie des extrémités retouchées agissantes. L'une d'elles est appointée distalement par petites retouches alternes (Caspar & Burnez-Lanotte 1994, fig. 11 n°1), l'autre par un petit museau mousse (fig. 3 : 2). L'étude fonctionnelle de cette dernière nous a permis d'attester la présence d'un foret à arc utilisé pour le percement mécanique des palets en schiste (Caspar & Burnez-Lanotte 1996). L'usage par rotation mécanique des mèches en pierre est inexistant au Rubané

54

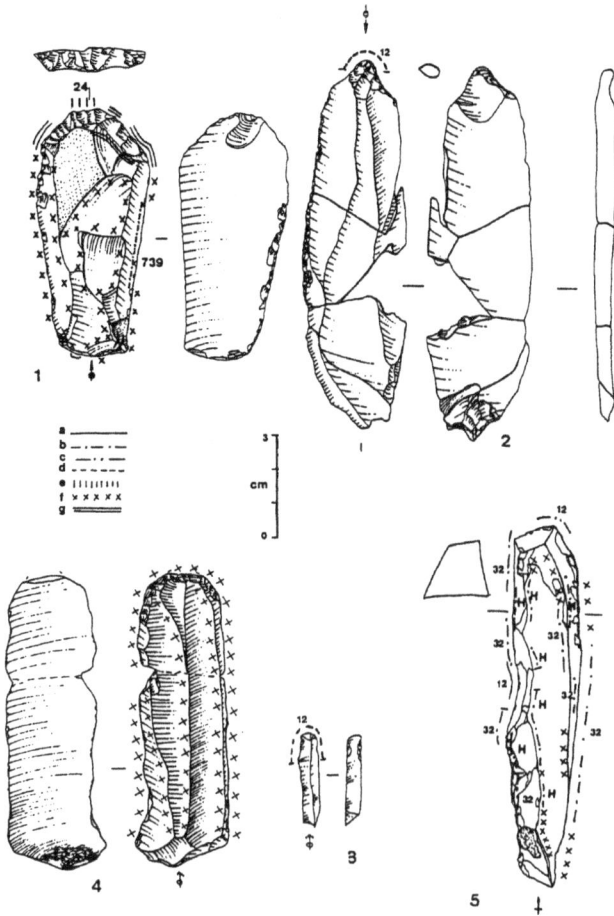

Figure 3. 1 : grattoir-herminette ; 2 : alésoir ; 3 : chute de burin ; 4 : pièce à extrémité martelée ; 5 : quartier d'orange. a : action longitudinale ; b : action transversale ; c : rainurage ; d : action rotative ; e : action transversale en percussion lancée ; f : préhension, emmanchement ; g : abrasion intentionnelle. 24 : bois ; 739 ou H : matériau dur à l'état indéterminé ; 32 : peau ; 12 : pierre tendre. 1 : SGM ; 2 : SMB ; 3 : SGM ; 4 : SMB ; 5 : SFH.

Figure 4. 1 à 10 : pièces à luisant. a : lustre végétal. 1 : action longitudinale. 2 : action transversale. 3222 : peau à l'état sec, sale. 3223 : peau à l'état sec avec abrasif. 1 : SMB. 2, 3, 4, 6, 7, 10 et 11 : SFH. 4 et 8 : SGM. 9 : SBT.

(Caspar 1988, Vaughan 1981, Van Gijn 1990). Une fois de plus, lorsqu'une empreinte BQ/VSG est formellement attestée, en l'occurrence des microtraces résultant d'une mécanisation de l'outil au sein d'un dispositif intrumental original, le silex est d'origine exogène. A Vaux, les seuls autres cas relevés de ce mode de travail concernent une chute de burin (fig. 3 : 3) et un burin sur éclat simple sur troncature très oblique (Caspar & Burnez-Lanotte 1994, fig. 14 n°3 et fig. 18 n°8), tous les deux en silex exogène.

Ce qui nous interpelle au vu de ces observations c'est que, dans les inventaires typologiques en silex local retrouvés dans les contextes détritiques blicquiens à Vaux, mis à part les burins (dont l'appartenance aux corpus rubanés de Hesbaye est douteuse), aucun trait spécifique à la typologie, à la stylistique ou à la techno-fonctionnologie blicquienne n'existe. Pour tout ce qui touche le support laminaire, ce qui est typique de l'identité technique blicquienne n'est identifié que sur les pièces en silex exogène à savoir : les lames de faucille, grattoirs

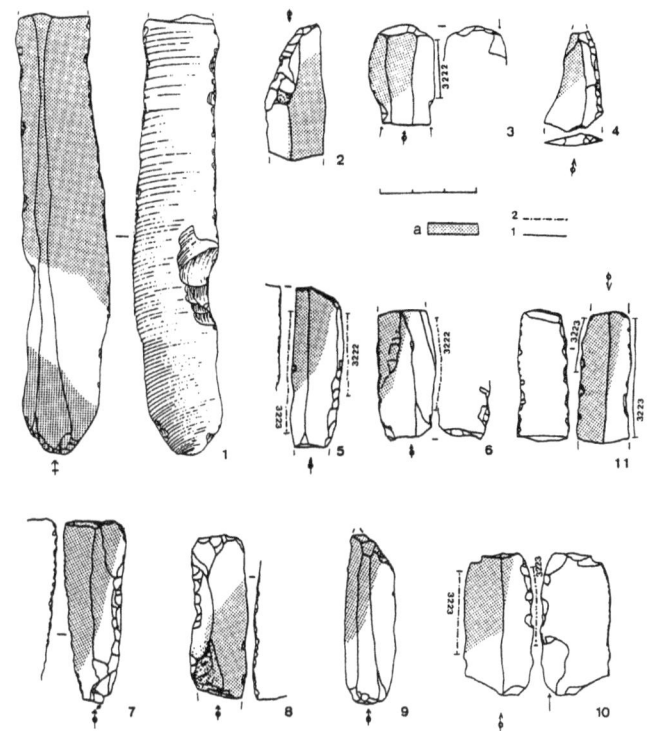

museaux, forets, à l'exclusion des burins. En revanche, les grattoirs à front légèrement convexe, les troncatures, les perçoirs, les lames retouchées qui pour la plupart existent dans les deux ensembles sous la forme d'outils conventionnels sont réalisés exclusivement dans le silex local pour le Rubané et dans les formes locales ou exogènes pour le Blicquien. Dans le cas où, ce qui ne peut être bien sûr exclu, les Blicquiens auraient débités des lames en silex local, la question se pose de savoir pourquoi ils n'auraient pas façonné des produits typiquement blicquiens en ce matériau. Quelle que soit l'hypothèse retenue sur la paternité de ce débitage, il ne fait aucun doute qu'une certaine forme d'exclusion existe entre ces produits laminaires en silex local et le répertoire de l'outillage spécifiquement blicquien.

Analyse tracéologique de produits laminaires bruts en silex local

Au sein de la série des lames brutes en silex local de Vaux dont les stigmates technologiques sont rigoureusement identiques

55

aux séries rubanées hesbignonnes (comme celles qui ont été bien étudiées dans le site proche de Verlaine fouillé par l'un de nous : Burnez-Lanotte et Allard ce volume; Allard 2002), vingt fragments proximaux ont été portés à l'analyse microscopique. Celle-ci atteste d'un recyclage systématique, quasi ubiquiste, dans le travail du schiste par rainurage/sciage des palets à l'aide des angles de chasse proéminents et des angles formés par le talon et les portions adjacentes des bords latéraux. L'expérimentation a par ailleurs prouvé l'efficience de ces éléments pour la découpe centrale des palets et pour le sciage/rainurage de plaques brutes en vue de leur fragmentation (Burnez-Lanotte & Caspar à par.). A Vaux, cet usage de parties spécifiques des extrémités proximales des lames est exclusivement blicquien et n'a jamais été diagnostiqué dans aucune série rubanée qui depuis 1985 font l'objet d'examens systématiques des parties réputées non actives des outils dans la recherche des microtraces liées à l'emmanchement (Caspar 1988) ou au mode de production (Caspar recherches dans le cadre du projet "Microwear analysis of non-active parts of a diachronic serie of lithic artefact" 1998-2001, K.U.Leuven). De surcroît, aucune étude tracéologique à l'heure actuelle n'atteste du rôle du silex pour le travail des matières minérales tendres au Rubané (Caspar op. cit., Vaughan op. cit., Van Gijn op. cit.). Ici, il s'agit bien d'un choix délibéré et non anecdotique de pièces destinées à l'artisanat du schiste. Enfin, aucune des lames brutes analysées (15) issues des contextes rubanés de Vaux ne présente un usage quelconque sur une matière minérale tendre.

Si l'on peut encore considérer pour l'heure qu'il peut y avoir doute sur l'origine rubanée de ces lames et donc qu'une production laminaire locale hypothétique par les Blicquiens reste possible à Vaux, il n'en est pas de même des trois éléments de débitage sur tranche d'éclat (SFH) spécifiquement rubanés retrouvés en contexte blicquien à savoir : 2 frites et 1 quartier d'orange (fig. 3 : 5) recyclés dans l'artisanat du schiste (Caspar & Burnez-Lanotte 1994). L'analyse microscopique de ces spécimens apporte les preuves formelles d'une récupération et d'un recyclage par les Blicquiens de pièces issues des ruines du village rubané voisin. On ignore bien sûr l'ampleur du phénomène, mais il peut être très important à l'instar des ramassages aléatoires dans les poches de dissolution. Les proportions de cette pratique pourraient par hypothèse s'étendre, comme nous le supposons, à des séries numériquement très conséquentes et dont pourraient faire partie les lames brutes en silex local ainsi qu'une pléthore d'éclats qui présentent de petits émoussés limités généralement à une portion de bord inférieure à un centimètre. Ces derniers sont réalisés dans un silex local issu des poches de dissolution exploitées au Groupe de Blicquy - l'utilisation de ce matériau est quant à elle non attestée dans les séries du village rubané - générateur d'éclats de petites dimensions auxquels s'ajoutent des éclats de plus grandes dimensions qui, au stade actuel de l'étude, pourraient être issus de blocs provenant de la craie, correspondant au mode d'approvisionnement typique des Rubanés.

Outillage blicquien sur éclat et bloc

L'origine des matières premières des outils sur éclat ou bloc présente une situation tout à fait différente de celle des outils sur produits laminaires. Toutes catégories typologiques confondues, le matériau dominant est local (95 % en SFH et SGH), les classes en silex exogènes (SGM et SMB) bien identifiées ne représentent que 3% des effectifs (Caspar & Burnez-Lanotte 1994, tableau 5). Cette répartition prévaut tant pour les types spécifiquement blicquiens que pour ceux qui sont présents indifféremment dans les inventaires des cultures rubanée et blicquienne. Le premier groupe comprend essentiellement les polyèdres, les éclats à retouches écailleuses envahissantes inverses, les burins et les grattoirs à esquilles inverses (grattoir-herminette, fig. 3 : 1 ; Caspar et Burnez-Lanotte 1996) ou à museau simple ou multiples, adjacents ou non (sur le pourtour d'un grattoir en éventail ou périphérique), destinés au travail du schiste (Burnez-Lanotte & Caspar à par.) qui recouvrent la totalité de la classe des grattoirs sur éclat à l'exclusion de tout spécimen comparable aux types rubanés. Le second ensemble d'outils, qui appartiennent indistinctement aux inventaires des deux cultures, compte principalement les denticulés, les pièces encochées, les éclats à retouches marginales à moyennes, les pièces à stigmates macroscopiques d'utilisation et les perçoirs. Le silex local aux dépends duquel sont façonnés les outils sur éclat et bloc blicquiens est issu en majorité des poches de dissolution (pièces à surfaces gélifractées, patinées ou au cortex lisse altéré). A cela s'ajoute un certain nombre de spécimens, qu'une étude en cours permettra de quantifier avec précision, caractérisés par la présence d'un cortex crayeux résultant d'un prélèvement de nodules en position géologique originale. La présence de ce silex résulte t-elle d'un approvisionnement par les Blicquiens directement dans les bancs de craie ou provient-elle d'une récupération dans les amas de débitage des ruines du village rubané mitoyen ? Nos recherches actuelles évaluent l'hypothèse, à nos yeux la plus convaincante, selon laquelle les supports d'outils sur éclat et bloc blicquiens concernés sont issus, dans des proportions qui restent à établir, d'une part du recyclage de produits rubanés et d'autre part, de petits blocs issus de la craie, qui se distinguent par leur dimension réduite des rognons prélevés par les Rubanés pour leur débitage laminaire spécifique.

Transferts d'éléments rubanés et blicquiens

Les positions stratigraphiques des éléments, très peu nombreux, clairement diagnostiques de chaque culture qui sont déplacés d'un village à l'autre montrent une opposition entre deux situations récurrentes (Burnez-Lanotte, Caspar, Constantin 2001). Les pièces retouchées de typologie rubanée au sens strict retrouvées dans les structures blicquiennes sont peu nombreuses, réparties dans toute l'épaisseur des stratigraphies concernées et témoignent d'une récolte volontaire des Blicquiens dans les ruines du village rubané mitoyen. Par contre, les vestiges blicquiens dans le village rubané proviennent exclusivement des phases terminales des remplissages. Ces faits témoignent d'une part, d'un télescopage involontaire des pièces blicquiennes en contexte rubané à la suite de l'érosion des parties sommitales des fosses blicquiennes situées plus haut sur la crête à proximité du village rubané et/ou d'autre part, des rejets sporadiques dans des fosses rubanées incomplètement comblées qui résulteraient d'activités blicquiennes. Ces dernières ont pu être réalisées en dehors du village rubané (déplacements longs) ou à l'intérieur (déplacements courts) de ce dernier, comme c'est par exemple le cas pour les grattoirs à esquilles inverses utilisés en percussion lancée de Vaux et de Darion (grattoir fosse 83003 : activité de fouille des rejets rubanés pour y retrouver les vestiges récupérables ?). Ces observations montrent un déplacement dans les deux sens : l'un volontaire, l'autre volontaire et involontaire.

Artisanat du schiste

L'exclusivité et l'importance de l'artisanat du schiste dans l'économie blicquienne apparaît nettement à Vaux. Les ateliers de fabrication d'anneaux et de bagues nous ont en effet permis de reconstituer la quasi totalité des phases de cette production, depuis la mise en forme des plaques jusqu'à la finition des pièces (Caspar & Burnez-Lanotte 1994). On insistera sur le fait que le travail du schiste ne requiert pratiquement pas l'usage d'objets standardisés, ni de savoir-faire et de technique élaborée. Mis à part deux pièces utilisées par un procédé mécanique de forage au foret à arc ou à pompe qui constitue un dispositif instrumental extrêmement novateur, la totalité des pièces investies dans la chaîne technique de fabrication des anneaux en schiste répond à la recherche d'une morphologie particulière de bord actif, généralement limité (angle de chasse, éperon proéminent sur un bord brut, épine sur les fronts de grattoir, etc...), sur des supports du tout venant (fragments proximaux de lames à corniche non préparée, éclats retouchés en grattoir au front non régularisé, éclats divers, supports gélifractés, etc...) tenus à main nue. L'expérimentation a montré le peu d'investissement technique nécessaire à la réalisation de l'ensemble de la chaîne technique liée au travail du schiste (Burnez-Lanotte & Caspar à par.).

Conclusion

Au vu de ces résultats, les industries des deux villages rubané et blicquien de Vaux témoignent de distinctions nettes vis à vis de la gestion des matériaux lithiques de part et d'autre. En ce qui concerne les silex locaux, la chaîne de production depuis l'approvisionnement jusqu'à la fabrication des produits finis répond à des schémas clairement plus contraignants pour les Rubanés (approvisionnement dans les bancs crétacés en place, standardisation des produits bruts et, dans une mesure qui reste à préciser, des modes de fragmentation, des modes de retouche et peut-être des modes d'emmanchement) que pour les Blicquiens. Pour ces derniers, l'ensemble de la production locale est opportuniste (accompagnée d'une récolte de petits blocs dans les bancs de craie) : récolte au sein des poches de dissolution, récupération des produits dans les contextes détritiques rubanés et leur recyclage dans les activités liées majoritairement au travail du schiste. Les seuls éléments répondant à un modèle technologique élaboré typique du BQ/VSG sont réalisés aux dépens des silex exogènes et appartiennent à des catégories d'usages et/ou à des dispositifs intrumentaux originaux de cette culture, en particulier dans le cadre de certaines

techniques de forage du schiste comme c'est le cas avec le foret mécanique qui représente une innovation technique majeure. Cette situation originale n'est peut-être pas liée au seul fait que les Blicquiens de Vaux soient, en Hesbaye, quelque peu isolés aux marges de répartition de leur territoire originel. Les recherches en cours permettent de faire l'hypothèse que ce phénomène pourrait s'étendre sur l'entièreté de leur domaine de distribution. Si cela était confirmé, on pourrait alors qualifier les silex d'origines exogènes et plus particulièrement le silex tertiaire, comme de véritables marqueurs identitaires du BQ/VSG.

Enfin, la présence de matériaux exogènes dans les villages rubané et blicquien de Vaux est un élément également pertinent à distinguer deux comportements culturels. On sait que les Rubanés de Hesbaye ont eu recours à des approvisionnements externes pour certaines herminettes en roches tenaces (amphibolites, roches magmatiques et métamorphiques). Parallèlement, le village rubané de Verlaine (à 3 km de Vaux) a livré les témoins d'une production laminaire en silex fin de Hesbaye excédentaire par rapport aux besoins du seul village dont les produits ont été nécessairement exportés (Burnez-Lanotte & Allard ce volume). Les tenants et aboutissants de ces déplacements, la gestion de cette circulation tant au niveau régional qu'extra régional, son importance relative et sa signification relèvent d'une problématique complexe. L'extension de l'aire géographique concernée par cette distribution du silex fin de Hesbaye indique des relations intra-culturelles orientées vers les autres centres de peuplement rubanés, par ordre de fréquence décroissant : vers l'ouest (Hainaut) et le sud (Lorraine) d'une part, vers le nord (Limbourg hollandaise) et l'est (Rhénanie) d'autre part (Allard, 2002 et Allard, ce volume). Du point de vue des circulations extra-régionales, nous avons vu que les Blicquiens de Vaux disposent manifestement de matériaux siliceux exogènes (silex de Ghlin du Hainaut et, dans une proportion mineure, silex Bartonien du Bassin parisien). Par contre, si leurs ateliers de fabrication d'anneaux en schiste local témoignent d'une production conséquente, l'importance numérique des produits finis (anneaux et bagues) retrouvés plaiderait en faveur d'un usage le plus vraisemblablement interne. L'existence d'une redistribution externe éventuelle d'une proportion de ces artefacts en schiste, qu'elle soit régionale ou extra régionale, reste à prouver (sur base de la comparaison avec des situations d'échanges dans le Groupe de Villeneuve-Saint-Germain : Plateaux 1990, Constantin 1985, Constantin et al. 2001, Bostyn 1994, Fromont 2001). D'autant qu'en Hesbaye, tant pour le Rubané (à l'exclusion des travaux encore inédits menés par P. Allard sur les matières siliceuses : Allard 2002) que pour le Groupe de Blicquy, la problématique des mouvements de matériaux et de produits (semi-finis ou finis), de leur distribution géographique (locale, régionale, extra-régionale), ainsi que du statut des sites qui y sont impliqués (producteur et/ou distributeur, receveur, consommateur, etc..) n'en est actuellement qu'à l'état de documentation très partiel.

Remerciements

Nous remercions vivement Mike Ilett (Université of Paris I

Panthéon-Sorbonne and UMR 7041 CNRS) pour la traduction anglaise du résumé.

Bibliographie

ALLARD, P., 2002, *Matières premières, technologie lithique et identité culturelle des premiers agriculteurs du nord-est de la France et de la Belgique*. Nouveau doctorat d'archéologie, anthropologie et ethnologie, Université de Paris I Panthéon-Sorbonne.

ALLARD, P., AUGEREAU, A., BEUGNIER, V., BURNEZ-LANOTTE, L., BOSTYN, F., CASPAR, J.-P., GILIGNY, F., HAMARD, D., MARTIAL, E., PHILIBERT, S., (à paraître), Fonction des outillages lithiques dans le Bassin parisien au Néolithique. In : *Actes du 25ème Congrès Préhistorique de France*, Nanterre, novembre 2000.

BOSTYN, F., 1994, *Caractérisation des productions et de la diffusion des industries lithiques du groupe de Villeneuve-Saint-Germain*, Mémoire de Doctorat, Université de Paris X, 2 vol.

BURNEZ-LANOTTE, L., ALLARD, P., 1998, Mode de production laminaire dans le Rubané de Hesbaye au "Petit Paradis" à Harduémont (Verlaine, Lg.) : premiers résultats. In: Organisation néolithique de l'espace en Europe du Nord-Ouest, Actes du XXIIIe Colloque Interrégional sur le Néolithique, *Anthropologie et Préhistoire* 109, p. 15-26.

BURNEZ-LANOTTE, L., CASPAR, J.-P., (à paraître), Technologie des anneaux en schiste dans le Groupe de Blicquy à Vaux-et-Borset (Hesbaye, Belgique) : l'apport de l'expérimentation.

BURNEZ-LANOTTE, L., CASPAR, J.-P., CONSTANTIN, C., 1993, I. Introduction, *In*: CASPAR, J.P., *et al.*, Nouveaux éléments dans le groupe de Blicquy en Belgique: le site de Vaux-et-Borset "Gibour" et "A la Croix Marie-Jeanne", *Helinium*, XXXIII, 1, 1993, p. 67-79.

BURNEZ-LANOTTE, L., CASPAR, J.-P., CONSTANTIN, C., 2001, Rapports chronologiques et culturels entre Rubané et Groupe de Blicquy à Vaux-et-Borset (Hesbaye, Belgique). *Bulletin de la Société Préhistorique Française* 98, n°1, p. 53-76.

CAHEN, D., CASPAR, J.P., OTTE, M., 1986, *Industries lithiques danubiennes de Belgique*, Etudes et Recherches Archéologiques de l'Université de Liège, 21, Liège, 88 p.

CASPAR, J.P., 1988, *Contribution à la tracéologie de l'industrie lithique du Néolithique ancien dans l'Europe nord-occidentale*, Dissertation pour l'obtention du grade de Docteur en Philosophie et Lettres, Université de Louvain, 3 vol.

CASPAR, J.-P., & BURNEZ-LANOTTE, L., 1994, III. Le matériel lithique, *In* : CASPAR J.P. *et al.*, Nouveaux éléments dans le groupe de Blicquy en Belgique: le site de Vaux-et-Borset "Gibour" et "A la Croix Marie-Jeanne", *Helinium*, XXXIV, 1, 1994, p. 3-93.

CASPAR, J.-P., & BURNEZ-LANOTTE, L., 1996, Groupe de Blicquy-Villeneuve-Saint-Germain, nouveaux outils: le grattoir-her-

minette et le foret, *Bulletin de la Société Préhistorique Française*, 93, 2, p. 235-240.

CASPAR, J.-P., & BURNEZ-LANOTTE, L., 1997, L'industrie lithique de Vaux-et-Borset (Hesbaye liégeoise): nouveaux éléments dans le groupe de Blicquy (Belgique), *In : Le Néolithique danubien et ses marges entre Rhin et Seine*, Actes du XXIIe colloque interrégional sur le Néolithique, Strasbourg, 1995, p. 411-429.

CASPAR, J.-P., & BURNEZ-LANOTTE, L., 1998, L'industrie lithique du Rubané récent de Hesbaye à Vaux-et-Borset "Gibour" (Villers-le-Bouillet) dans le contexte de la problématique des rapports chrono-culturels entre Rubané et Groupe de Blicquy en Hesbaye liégeoise (Belgique), *In : Organisation néolithique de l'espace en Europe du Nord-Ouest*, Actes du XXIIIe colloque interrégional sur le Néolithique, Bruxelles 1997, *Bulletin de la Société Royale belge d'Anthropologie et de Préhistoire*, t. 109, p. 217-236.

CASPAR, J.-P., CONSTANTIN, C., HAUZEUR, A., BURNEZ-LANOTTE, L., 1993-1994, Nouveaux éléments dans le groupe de Blicquy en Belgique : le site de Vaux-et-Borset "Gibour" et "A la Croix Marie-Jeanne", *Helinium*, XXXIII, 1, 1993, p. 67-79; XXXIII, 2, 1993, p. 168-252; XXXIV, 1, 1994, p. 3-93.

CASPAR, J.-P., DELYE, E., ROTS, V., et ROCHUS, N., 1999, Villers-le-Bouillet/Vaux-et-Borset : Campagne de fouilles "A la Croix Marie-Jeanne", *Chronique de l'Archéologie Wallonne*, 7, p. 79.

CONSTANTIN, C., 1985, *Fin du Rubané, Céramique du Limbourg et Post-Rubané*. Oxford, BAR International Series, vol. 273.

CONSTANTIN, C., HANCE, L., et VACHARD, D., 2001, Un réseau d'échange de calcaire utilisé pour la fabrication d'anneaux pendant le groupe de Villeneuve-Saint-Germain. *Bulletin de la Société Préhistorique Française* 98, n°2, p. 245-253.

FROMONT, N., 2001, *Caractérisation de la production et de la diffusion des anneaux en matériaux lithiques dans le Nord de la France et l'Ouest de la Belgique au Néolithique ancien*. Mémoire de D.E.A. Université de Paris I Panthéon-Sorbonne, 2 vol., 95 p., 71 fig.

HUBERT, F., 1970, Ellignies-Ste-Anne (Ht.) : un site de la civilisation de Roessen, *Archéologie*, 1, p. 17-21.

HUBERT, F., 1982, Quelques traces du passage des danubiens dans la région de Nivelles, Actes du *Congrès de la Fédération Archéologique et Historique de Belgique*, XLV, fasc. 2, p. 141-148.

PLATEAUX, M., 1990, Quelques données sur l'évolution des industries du Néolithique danubien de la Vallée de l'Aisne, in : *Rubané et Cardial*, Actes du colloque de Liège, 1988, p. 239-255.

VAN GIJN, A., 1990, The wear and tear of flint. Principles of functional analysis applied to dutch neolithic assemblages, *Analecta Praehistorica Leidensia*, 22.

VAUGHAN, P., 1994, Microwear analysis on flints from the Bandkeramik sites of Langweiler 8 and Laurenzberg 7, *in*: LÜNING, J, & STEHLI, P., Die Bandkeramik im Merzbachtal auf der Aldenhovener Platte, *Rheinische Ausgrabungen*, 36, p. 535-552.

SURPLUS PRODUCTION IN THE BELGIAN LINEARBANDKERAMIK : BLADE DEBITAGE AT VERLAINE "PETIT PARADIS" (HESBAYE, BELGIUM)

Laurence BURNEZ-LANOTTE* & Pierre ALLARD**

Résumé

Depuis 1996, L. Burnez-Lanotte a entrepris la fouille programmée du site du "Petit Paradis" à Verlaine en Hesbaye liégeoise. Les structures sont datées du début du Rubané récent. Il s'agit d'un habitat rubané de type classique dont l'originalité tient à la découverte de nombreux rejets de débitage laminaire du silex fin de Hesbaye disponible localement, dans des proportions inconnues jusqu'ici dans ces contextes. On estime que l'amas de débitage de la première structure découverte (structure 01) a livré un nombre de 770 nucléus pour un poids total d'une demi tonne. Ces données témoignent clairement d'une surproduction laminaire qui dépasse les besoins d'un simple village.

Abstract

Fieldwork has been undertaken since 1996 by L. Burnez-Lanotte on the "le Petit Paradis" site at Verlaine, located in Hesbaye near Liège and dated to the beginning of the late Linearbandkeramik. This classic domestic settlement has produced previously unequalled quantities of flint blade production waste. One feature contained almost half a ton of flint, including 770 cores and at least 20 000 other items. These data clearly indicate surplus blade production beyond the needs of a single village.

As part of a project on early sedentary societies in Middle Belgium (attached to the C.N.R.S programme "U.M.R. 7041/ European protohistory"), over the last five years Laurence Burnez-Lanotte has carried out a research excavation on the "Omalian" Linearbandkeramik (LBK) site of Verlaine "Petit Paradis" (Hesbaye liégeoise). The site, which we are still excavating, was discovered by E. Vanderhoeft. He found a single pit of modest size, containing an extremely dense and compact mass of waste resulting from blade debitage of Hesbaye light grey flint. The quantity of lithic finds was exceptionally high for the LBK in Hesbaye. The major contribution is that, for the first time in Belgium, surplus production of blades has been revealed in a LBK context.

The south-east Hesbaye region, in the loess zone of Middle Belgium, includes over 200 LBK "sites". Unfortunately less than 20 have been excavated on a large scale and very few are completely published. The "Petit Paradis" at Verlaine is situated in a concentration with the highest density of sites : within a radius of 3 km, 18 settlements have been discovered. Information here is very sparse, mainly consisting of old and incompletely published data, with the exception of Donceel "Ferme de l'Abbaye" which recently produced 16 pits over an area of 3 500 m² (Frébutte & Marchal 1998).

The "Petit Paradis" LBK occupation, north-west of the village of Verlaine, is situated on a gently sloping loess plateau (Burnez-Lanotte & Allard 1998), 300 m from the river Yerne which flows from the south to join the river Geer 12 km to the north. The settlement lies on the limit between the upper Cretaceous (Nouvelles layer; white chalk with black flint) and the lower Tongrian (clayey sand and grey clay). On the sides of a gully which crosses the site, weathering of the chalk has led to formation of clay-with-flint, beneath a thin layer of loess.

The primary research objective was to find out if the first pit discovered with the huge concentration of flint waste (feature 01) belonged to an occasional knapping site nearby

(*) Université de Namur and UMR 7041 CNRS, rue de l'Arsenal 13, B-5000 Namur Belgique, laurence.burnez@fundp.ac.be
(**) UMR 7041 CNRS, Maison de l'archéologie et de l'ethnologie, 21 allée de l'Université, F-92023 Nanterre cedex, auxiette.allard@wanadoo.fr

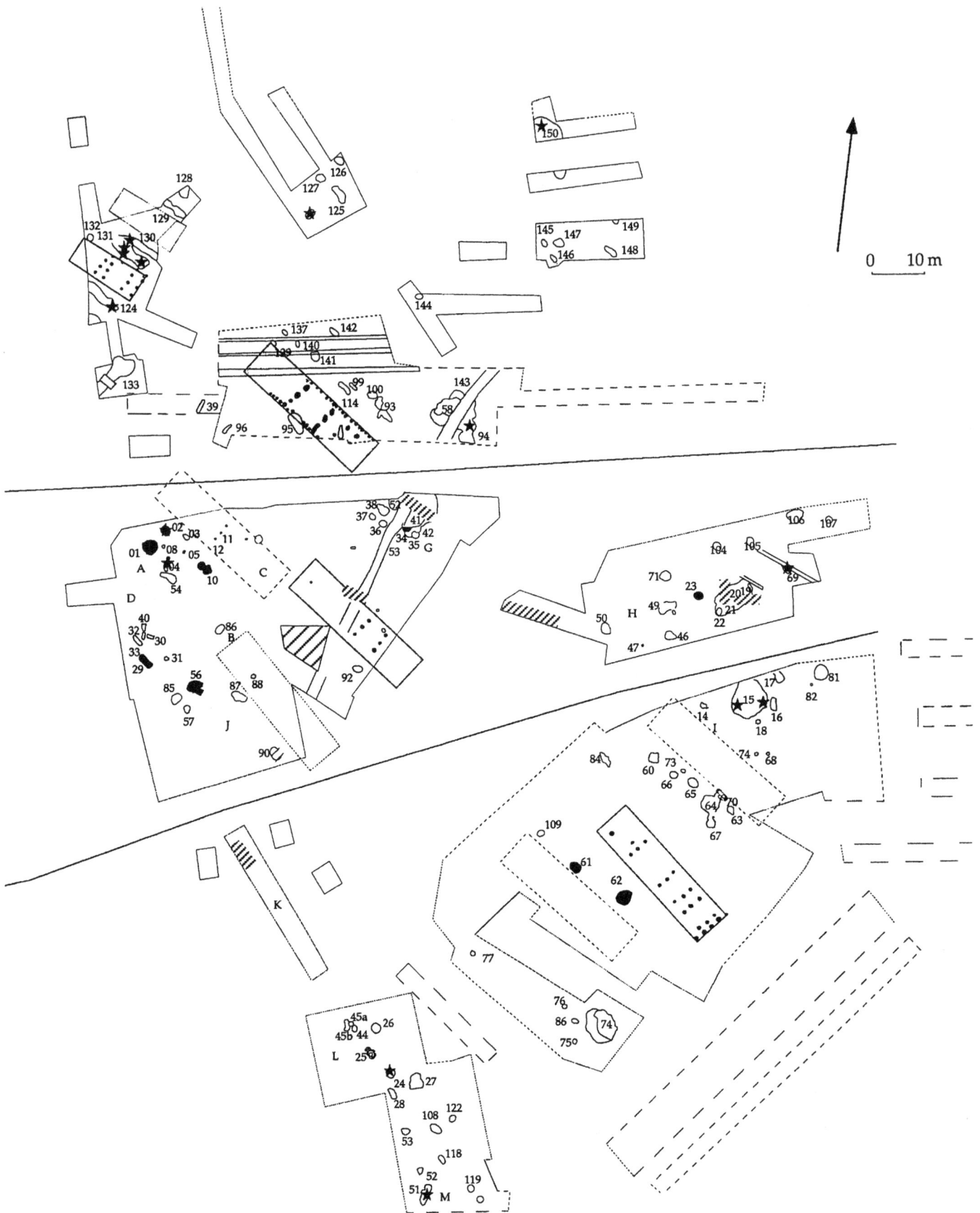

Figure 1. Verlaine "Petit Paradis" : general plan of the site (1996-2001). ✦ : concentration of debitage waste.

flint outcrops or to a classic domestic settlement. Our excavation has in fact uncovered a classic, densely occupied domestic settlement, the size of which can be currently estimated at 3 ha. The surface area investigated is 11.800 m² (fig. 1). The edge of the settlement has been defined to the south-west, south and west, due respectively to a complete absence of loess, a break in the topography and a lack of archaeological features. However, the settlement could well extend further north-west and this will be checked in future campaigns. Altogether, 130 LBK features and between 6 and 10 houses have so far been identified. As a working hypothesis, we think that the houses were set in parallel rows. A total of 17 debitage concentrations have now been found (fig. 2).

There are currently no radiocarbon dates available for the site. For the relative dating of the occupation, stratigraphic relations are scarce. So far, at least two occupation phases have been identified and relative dating can be obtained through seriation of pottery decoration (Burnez-Lanotte forthcoming). It can be noted that although the "Petit Paradis" has particularly substantial evidence for flint blade production, pottery is also quite well represented. A preliminary analysis of decoration techniques, from a sample of 137 vessels from 9 pits, indicates (table 1) that the majority (90%) was decorated with a single-pointed instrument used to make, in decreasing order of frequency, separate impressions (65%), incisions (14%) and dragged impressions (11%) (Allard & Burnez-Lanotte in press). Use of combs is rare (10%), and combs with two or three teeth predominate. The pivoted impression technique is absent. We can put forward the hypothesis that the site was occupied during the late LBK : period II c and the beginning of period II d of P.J.R. Modderman (Modderman 1970). A count of band filling types using Stehli's typological system (Stehli 1994) strengthens the hypothesis that the pottery from Verlaine belongs to a late phase of the LBK (phase 4b of the Merzbach sequence). Confirmation of these observations will have to await the complete study of pottery from the whole site (Burnez-Lanotte in progress).

Analysis of lithic finds is in progress (Allard 2002). The aims are to characterize blade production technology, reconstruct the knapping operative scheme, offer an initial evaluation of the numbers of blades produced and examine the context of these activities at site level, by comparing the massive debitage concentrations with lithic finds from other areas on the site which show evidence for more diversified domestic activities.

The predominant raw material at Verlaine (98,4% of the flint finds) is known as "fine Hesbaye flint" (*silex fin de Hesbaye*), or "light grey Hesbaye flint". The major debitage concentrations are almost exclusively made up of this kind of flint, which originates from the Senonian formations of the local Cretaceous. This flint is easily accessible in the beds of chalk which outcrop on the slopes bordering the site, as well as in the weathered chalk present in the clay deposits of gully crossing the site. The presence in the pits of small rough blocks,

Figure 2. Verlaine "Petit Paradis" : concentration of debitage waste (feature 56).

some of which are frost-damaged, and others showing visible cracks prior to debitage, shows that there was no selection during collecting. The sources were therefore close to the settlement. A second and much less common variety of raw material is the "granular Hesbaye flint", which also comes from the immediate vicinity of the site (less than 500 m). The frequency of granular flint varies considerably between features. It seems relatively common in pits close to certain buildings, but is practically absent in the debitage concentrations (table 2).

Feature 01 is of modest size and it contained blade production waste in huge quantities : between 25.000 and 30.000 objects, for an estimated weight of half a ton. Observations made on the fill of the pit during our excavation indicate that its content represents a homogeneous find group (confirmed by refitting), although the mode, or modes, of deposition could not be recorded. The analysis of a sample of 24.800 artefacts (more than 2.500 blades) and 450 cores (that is all the complete cores available out of an estimated total of 770) shows that:
- this discard only contains blade debitage waste including the first sequences of the *chaîne opératoire* as well as the actual debitage maintenance phases; there is no debitage of flakes or flake edges ;

61

Laurence BURNEZ-LANOTTE & Pierre ALLARD

- there are extremely few tools (only seven blade tools) ;
- the material is in excellent condition and was abandoned after debitage ; out of 450 cores, only 15 were re-used as hammers (table 3).
The tendency is for the debitage to produce a standard form of blade with parallel, regular edges, and a straight profile. (blades 80-120 mm long, 15-25 mm wide and 4-8 mm thick are the most common). The complexity of the shaping out of blocks is determined by the natural morphology of the initial block (we recognize two main variants of blade debitage). Generally speaking, the shaping out is as simple as possible, taking maximum advantage of the natural angles of the flint nodules. The estimated total of 770 cores in the pit must have produced a minimum number of 5.000 to 7.500 blades.

Eight pits with sizeable lithic assemblages (13.660 flint artefacts) distributed amongst the various sectors so far investigated, were selected for comparison with the discard in feature 01. Some of them contain concentrations of debitage waste (56 and also several pits not included in this article), the remainder being storage pits (34, 23), pits related to a house (61, 62), and various pits whose fills contain relatively large amounts of lithic finds (02, 10, 29). The technological inventory shows three distinct groups which can be distinguished by the varying presence of the differents phases of shaping out or preparation of the blocks, in opposition to tools and waste (tool debris or thermally altered flakes).
1. The first group includes features (02 and 56) whose lithic finds have the same technological characteristics as pit 01, leaving aside the quantitative aspect. These pits are characterised by blade debitage waste (fig. 2) in which the various phases of the chaîne opératoire are proportionally represented, with very few regular blades, tools or other kinds of refuse from domestic activities.
2. The second group corresponds to 2 pits close to a house (61 and 62). They clearly differ from the first group : the phases of shaping out are poorly represented (twice as few flakes for each sequence) whilst tools and domestic waste (utilised flakes and burnt flakes) account for more than a third of the lithic finds. Characteristic elements of the chaîne opératoire are anecdotal and there are no refits. On the other hand, there is a high percentage of regular blades, and cores are frequently re-used as hammers (table 3).
3. The third group is heterogeneous with an under-representation of the shaping out phases and a higher rate of tools.
An important observation is that pit 01, although an unique feature from a quantitative point of view, is identical to other features in the settlement in its distribution of different sequences of the blade debitage chaîne opératoire. Thus not all the waste related to the knapping activities of the village was discarded in this pit. This must be confirmed by the study of all the lithic artefacts on the site. In particular, new information should emerge from analysis of finds from 2 houses we are digging at the moment in the west part of the settlement. Their lateral pits contain at least 5 concentrations of debitage waste, reflecting knapping activities that took place close to the houses.

The huge quantity of lithic material in the concentrations at Verlaine raises the question of surplus production of blades in relation to the needs of the community. In order to evaluate and define surplus production in this context, the data from other sites in Belgium must be examined for comparative purposes. The first complete publication concerns the Place Saint-Lambert in Liège (Otte 1984), where a small excavation uncovered a flint concentration and 6 pits with classic domestic refuse. The concentration contains 17.800 flakes, 59 cores and 2 148 blades. This assemblage appears similar in size to feature 01 at Verlaine but is in fact overestimated, as the count included splinters (esquilles) and other small fragments which constitute 73% of the total. Using our descriptive criteria, this concentration contains just under 5.000 objects. All the characteristics of the Verlaine concentration are found here : complete regular blades are absent, the percentage of tools is low and the finds almost entirely consist of blade knapping waste.

For comparative purposes, the site of Darion-Colia offers the only published large-scale excavation of a LBK settlement in Hesbaye. On this site it has been suggested that there was a specialized mode of debitage, called "excess" production, the products of which circulated, like pottery, in a regional and extra-regional exchange network (Cahen 1985 ; Jadin 1990 ; Cahen & Jadin 1996). However, there are only 2 to 4 pits with concentrations of flint working waste at Darion, improperly termed "workshops" and containing on average 3.000 finds. The total number of flint finds from the site is 86.211, including 122 blade cores (of which 73 are re-used as hammers). Furthermore, qualitative comparison is not possible because data on the representation of the sequences of the blade debitage chaîne opératoire from features at Darion is not available. So, from a purely quantitative point of view, the waste concentrations at Verlaine offer a very much larger corpus, with a current estimation of over 1 200 blade cores (610 cores in the nine pits studied) for the 17 concentrations of flint working waste. As far as we are concerned, the hypothesis of surplus and even specialized production of blades at Darion has yet to be proven.

As has been mentioned above, the site of Verlaine is located in a tight cluster of 18 LBK settlements. Between 4 and 6 of these sites have produced comparable debitage concentrations. They include the famous Dommartin sites, located 1 km to the south-east. Unfortunately with one exception these are old, small-scale excavations and the general data on the features is no longer available. Nevertheless, the concentration of sites around the "Petit Paradis" at Verlaine implies a more complex mode of raw material procurement than simple surface collection. In this area, the number of debitage concentrations excavated, and the geographical and probable chronological proximity of the sites, point to the early emergence, at least for this region, of actual working of flint beds. Without going as far as imagining mine-shafts, one could suggest extraction in opencast pits or along the steeper slopes where the chalk layer is exposed under the loess. This may be confirmed by future research in the close vicinity of the site at Verlaine.

62

The LBK site of Verlaine provides new evidence for understanding modes of flint exploitation in LBK populations. While a number of "workshops" (a term which we propose to replace by debitage or waste concentrations) are already known from this area which is rich in flint beds, the quantities of lithic finds from a number of features are very much higher than on other sites in Hesbaye. These concentrations, associated with other pits containing identical waste (though discarded in a different manner), raise two issues. The first is the probable existence of surplus production of blades. The second is the nature of the distribution system, in a cultural and chronological context which shows clear evidence for the circulation of artefacts in Hesbaye flint well outside the region (Allard 2002). Reconstruction of the socio-economic context of production will only be possible after complete excavation of the site, exhaustive study of all the categories of finds, and spatial analysis of all activities through the various settlement phases (Burnez-Lanotte in progress).

Ackowledgements

The research presented in this paper was carried out as part of the "Mission archéologique en Hainaut" from the "Ministère français des Affaires étrangères" directed by L. Burnez-Lanotte and C. Constantin. We should like to thank Mike Ilett (University of Paris I Panthéon-Sorbonne and UMR 7041 CNRS) for helpful comments and for improving the english text. Of course, he cannot be held responsible for any rubbish still left.

Bibliography

ALLARD, P., 2002, *Matières premières, technologie lithique et identité culturelle des premiers agriculteurs du nord-est de la France et de la Belgique*. Nouveau doctorat d'archéologie, anthropologie et ethnologie, Université de Paris I Panthéon-Sorbonne.

ALLARD, P., & BURNEZ-LANOTTE, L., in press, Workshops and flint exploitation on the Linearbandkeramik site of Verlaine "Petit Paradis" (Hesbaye liégeoise, Belgium). In *Actes du VII International Flint Symposium*, Bochum, 13-17 septembre 1999.

BURNEZ-LANOTTE, L., & ALLARD, P., 1998, Mode de production laminaire dans le Rubané de Hesbaye au "Petit Paradis" à Harduémont (Verlaine, Lg.): premiers résultats. In Organisation néolithique de l'espace en Europe du Nord-Ouest, Actes du XXIIIe Colloque Interrégional sur le Néolithique. *Anthropologie et Préhistoire* 109, p 15-26.

CAHEN, D., 1985, Interprétations nouvelles du site de Darion. *Bulletin de la Société royale belge d'Anthropologie et de Préhistoire* 96, p. 75-86.

CAHEN, D., et JADIN, I., 1996, Economie et société dans le Rubané récent de Belgique. *Bulletin de la Société Préhistorique Française* 93, 1, p. 55-62.

FREBUTTE, C., & MARCHAL, J.-PH., 1998, Implantation du Rubané récent au lieu-dit "Ferme de l'Abbaye" à Donceel (province de Liège). *Notae praehistoricae* 18, p. 141-148.

JADIN, I., 1990, Economie de production dans le Rubané récent de Belgique. Approche comparative des industries lithiques de trois villages. In: D. Cahen et M. Otte (ed.), *Rubané et Cardial*, Actes du Colloque de Liège, nov. 1998, E.R.A.U.L. 39, p. 147-154.

MODDERMAN, P.J.R., 1970, Linearbandkeramik aus Elsloo und Stein. *Analecta Praehistorica Leidensia* 3, 2 vol.

OTTE, M., (ed.), 1984, *Les fouilles de la Place Saint-Lambert à Liège*. I. Etudes et Recherches Archéologiques de l'Université de Liège, 18, Liège.

STEHLI, P., 1994, Chronologie der Bandkeramik im Merzbachtal. In J. Lüning & P. Stehli (ed.). *Die Bandkeramik im Merzbachtal auf der Aldenhovener Platte*. Beitr. Neolith. Besiedlung Aldenhovener Platte. V. Rheinische Ausgrabungen 36, p. 79-191.

structure/technique	01	02	56	61	62	34	10	23	29	Total	%
single-pointed instrument: separate impressions	-	3	2	56	38	13	4	7	2	138	64,8
single-pointed instrument: draged impressions	6	1	1	1	7	5	-	2	-	23	10,8
single-pointed instrument: incised lines	2	1	1	2	5	11	4	4	1	31	14,5
2 tooth comb: separate impressions	-	-	-	-	1	2	-	-	-	3	1,4
2 tooth comb: dragged impressions	-	2	-	-	-	-	2	-	-	4	2
2 tooth comb: incised lines	-	-	-	-	-	1	-	-	-	1	0,5
comb with 3 or more teeth: separate impressions	-	-	-	-	-	4	-	1	-	5	2,3
comb with 3 or more teeth: dragged impressions	-	-	-	-	2	-	-	1	-	3	1,4
comb with 3 or more teeth: incised lines	2	-	-	-	3	-	-	-	-	5	2,3

Table 1. Verlaine "Petit Paradis" : pottery decoration techniques.

	9856	9602	9729	9610	9723	9734	9861	9862
■ granular	0.81	0.95	0	0	0.66	0.42	41.83	33.16
☐ fine	99.19	99.05	100	100	99.34	99.58	58.17	66.84

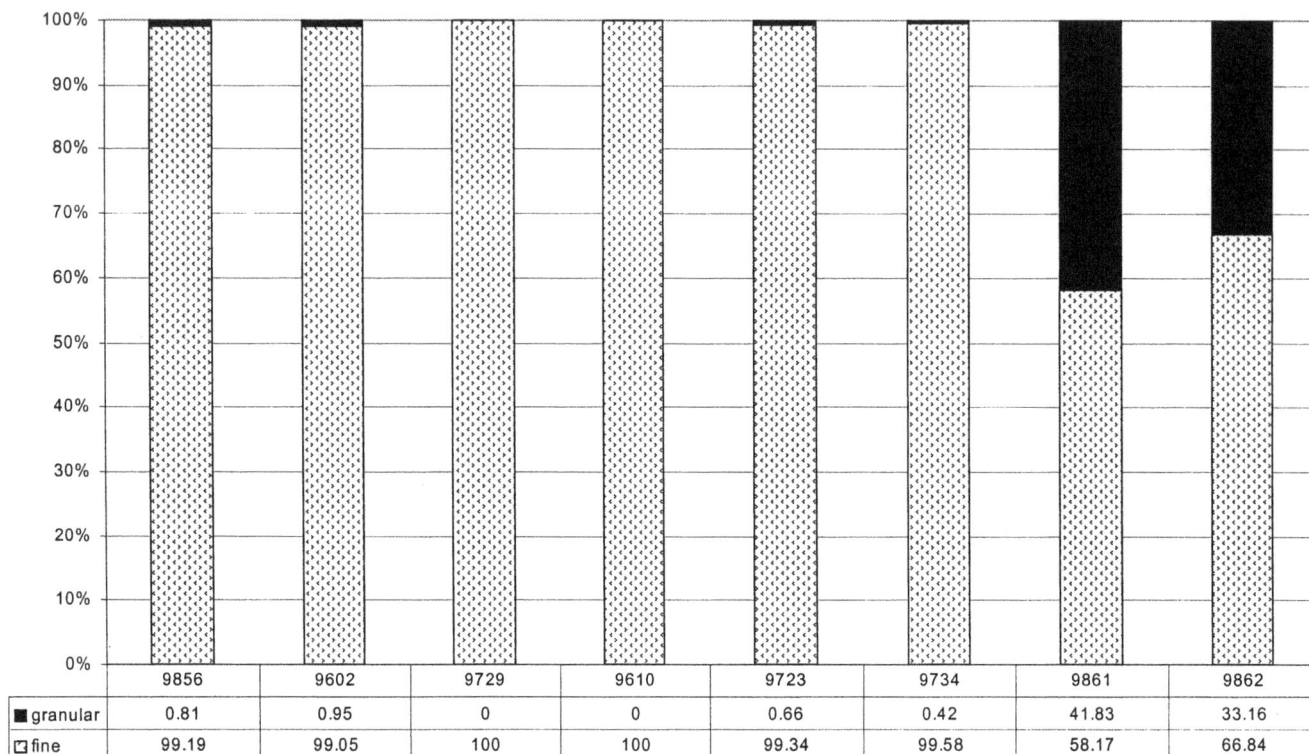

Table 2. Verlaine "Petit Paradis" : frequency of fine Hesbaye flint and granular Hesbaye flint.

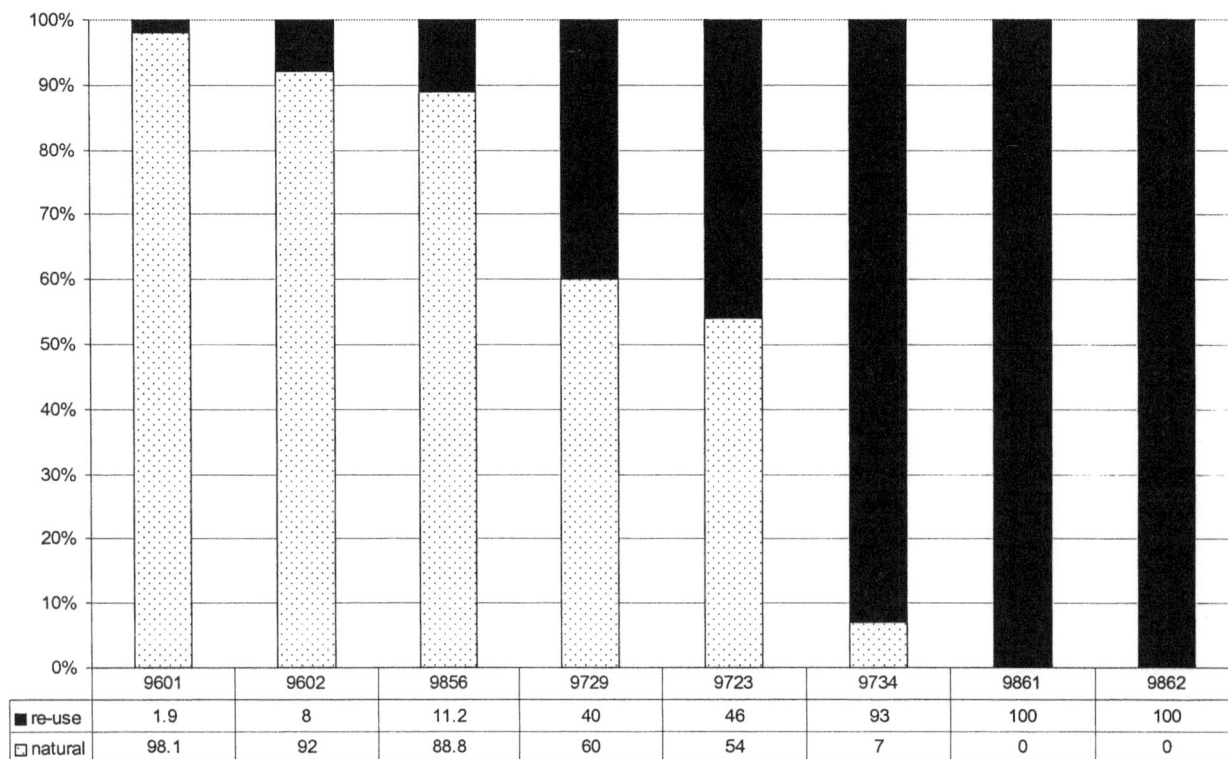

	9601	9602	9856	9729	9723	9734	9861	9862
■ re-use	1.9	8	11.2	40	46	93	100	100
☐ natural	98.1	92	88.8	60	54	7	0	0

Table 3. Verlaine "Petit Paradis" : rate of cores re-used as hammers.

64

MODALITÈS D'APPROVISIONNEMENT ET RÉSEAUX DE CIRCULATION DES PRODUITS SILICEUX DANS LA CÉRAMIQUE LINÉAIRE DU NORD-EST DE LA FRANCE ET DE LA BELGIQUE

Pierre ALLARD*

Résumé

L'essor considérable des travaux sur l'identification et la caractérisation des silex depuis les années quatre-vingt permet de dresser un premier panorama des principales matières premières exploitées par les populations rubanées. La comparaison entre les différentes régions permet de reconnaître des comportements récurrents dans l'acquisition des matériaux et de circonscrire les voies de circulation des produits siliceux. Il apparaît que les communications dans la région étudiée sont intensives et multidirectionnelles, ce qui ouvre des perspectives nouvelles pour la reconnaissance des influences ou des liens entre les différentes zones d'implantation rubanées.

Abstract

This paper presents a preliminary synthesis of supply and distribution of siliceous rocks during the late LBK in northern France et Belgium. The circulation of raw materials shows the close interaction between all LBK settlement regions.

Introduction

Les découvertes archéologiques des sites du Néolithique ancien dans le nord de la France sont principalement liées aux grandes zones de surveillance de l'archéologie préventive. Ainsi, la distribution des villages rubanés n'est pas homogène mais concentrée en quelques régions plus ou moins bien documentées. La chronologie et l'origine de ces différentes zones d'implantation n'est pas encore parfaitement établie. La néolithisation se développant d'est en ouest, les sites de la plaine alsacienne et de la moyenne vallée de la Moselle sont, à l'heure actuelle, les plus anciens. L'étape suivante dans le Bassin parisien est représentée par les villages de la plaine du Perthois dans la moyenne vallée de la Marne (Rubané moyen champenois). La fin de la séquence rubanée du Bassin parisien correspond au Rubané récent (RRBP) et final (RFBP, Constantin et Ilett 1997), principalement documentée dans les vallées de l'Aisne, de l'Yonne et de l'Oise. Cet état de la recherche, met en évidence de grandes zones vierges de découvertes danubiennes. Quelques "jalons" sont connus

comme Marainville-sur-Madon (Blouet et Decker 1993) ou encore Juvigny "les Grands Traquiers" (Tappret et Villes 1996), mais cela semble bien peu au vu de la concentration reconnue dans les régions mieux documentées (la notion de site isolé n'existe probablement pas au Rubané).

L'étude et la caractérisation des matières premières des objets en silex est susceptible d'apporter des précisions sur les contacts et les liens qui unissent ces différentes zones d'implantation. Cet article résume quelques résultats d'un doctorat sur l'étude de l'industrie lithique de 14 sites rubanés répartis dans le quart nord-est de la France et de la Belgique. Le sujet concerne principalement les étapes récentes et finales de la Céramique Linéaire car les données concernant les étapes plus anciennes sont encore trop disparates et ne concernent que la partie orientale de la zone d'étude. Il s'agit donc de faire un simple bilan de la question de l'approvisionnement et de la circulation des objets siliceux pour la fin de la séquence rubanée, ce qui permettra de dresser dans un premier temps un panorama des relations entre les différentes régions concernées. Ce travail est complémentaire de la synthèse récente menée sur les sites de la Céramique Linéaire allemande (Zimmermann 1995).

(*) UMR 7041 CNRS, Maison de l'archéologie et de l'ethnologie, 21 allée de l'Université, F-92023 Nanterre cedex, auxiette.allard@wanadoo.fr

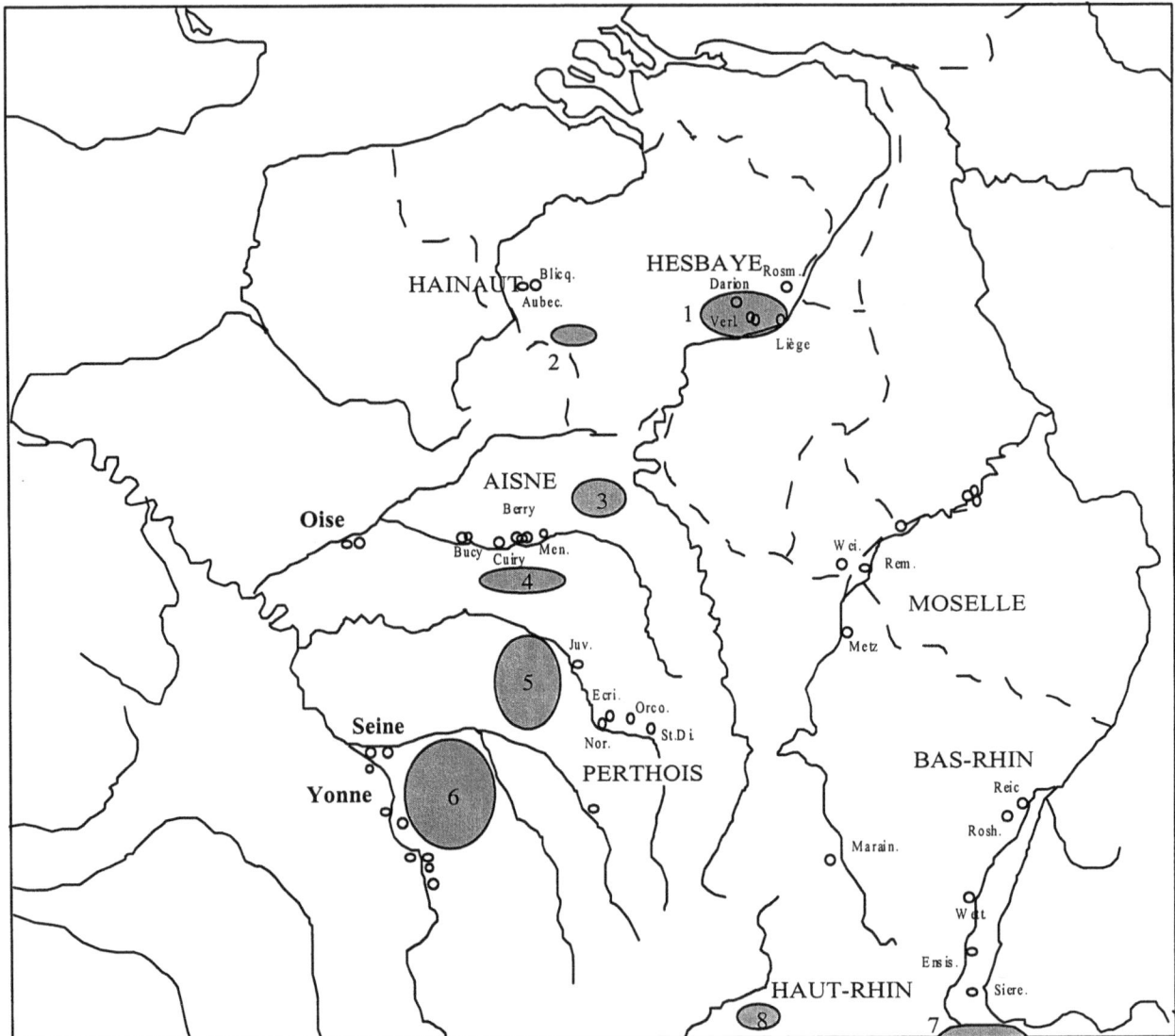

Figure 1. Localisation schématique des principaux affleurements mentionnés dans le texte. 1: silex à grain fin hesbignon (crétacé), 2: silex de Ghlin (Bassin de Mons), 3: silex turonien, 4: silex tertiaire, 5: silex sénonien (Marne), 6: silex sénonien (Seine-Yonne), 7: silex du Jura (Jurassique), 8: silex tertiaire (bassin oligocène de Vesoul).

Les ressources siliceuses

L'identification des matières premières a connu un essor considérable dans les années 80. Les silex ne sont plus considérés comme un ensemble homogène, mais décrits en fonction des possibles origines géologiques, autorisant une première approche générale des ressources offertes par le territoire. C'est par ce biais que la notion de circulation des matériaux fut présentée dans les années 80 pour le Rubané. Des produits exogènes sont signalés dans les sites lorrains (Blouet et Decker 1993), en Alsace (Mauvilly 1993) et dans la vallée de l'Aisne (Plateaux 1990, 1993). L'identification des silex est basée sur des critères macroscopiques en comparaison avec des collections de référence (lithothèques). Ce type d'approche n'est évidemment pas sans défaut et doit être présenté comme correspondant aux hypothèses les plus satisfaisantes dans l'état actuel des connaissances. Néanmoins, l'ap-

proche macroscopique présente l'avantage de pouvoir dresser un inventaire rapide sur une vaste région.

Le RRBP et RFBP de la vallée de l'Aisne

Un premier recensement des matières premières du nord de la France a été réalisé de 1986 à 1989 au cours d'une Action Thématique Programmée menée par J.C. Blanchet, C. Pommepuy et M. Plateaux (J.C. Blanchet *et al.* 1989). Les affleurements primaires peuvent être résumés en quelques grandes zones principales (fig. 1) :
- Le Crétacé de l'ouest de la Picardie livre des silex en grande quantité, du Turonien au Campanien. Néanmoins, d'après les travaux de prospection de P. Romenteau (Blanchet *et al.* 1989) et ceux de J. Fabre pour la constitution de la lithothèque du bassin versant de la Somme plus au nord (Fabre 2001), il apparaît que ces niveaux livrent des matériaux dont les carac-

téristiques communes divergent des pièces crétacées retrouvées sur les sites de la vallée (Plateaux 1993);
- Le Crétacé à l'est de la vallée (craie blanche Champenoise) est dépourvu de silex jusqu'au Turonien du Rethélois. Ce dernier contient des blocs de silex noir terne opaque, qui sont présents dans tous les sites rubanés de la vallée de l'Aisne (fig. 1, n°3);
- Le sud de l'Aisne, dans les plateaux tertiaires de l'Ile-de-France, contient des silex tertiaires bartoniens et lutétiens. Les premiers sont encore mal localisés, à l'exception de quelques affleurements ponctuels (Romigny-Lhéry par exemple), dont les habitats les plus proches sont à une vingtaine de kilomètres (fig. 1, n°4). Le Lutétien en revanche est local, il affleure le long des rebords de plateau de l'ensemble du réseau hydrographique de l'Aisne. Cette région livre également des affleurements de grès-quartzitiques;
- Plus au sud, au-delà de la vallée de la Marne, on retrouve les niveaux du Crétacé des craies blanches et grises de la Champagne. Cette craie, réputée sans silex, présente en réalité des affleurements siliceux importants le long de la Cuesta d'Ile-de-France, entre Epernay et les marais de Saint–Gond (fig. 1, n°5);
- Enfin, les alluvions de l'Aisne contiennent également divers types de matériaux des sources locales (Lutétien, grès-quartzite et galets) ainsi que des rognons du Turonien drainés depuis les formations primaires en amont.

La répartition des matériaux dans les sites de la vallée de l'Aisne montre deux situations différentes :
- Une limite est présente dans la partie orientale distinguant les sites de Berry-au-Bac "la Croix Maigret" et Menneville "Derrière le Village" (Plateaux 1993). L'approvisionnement est orienté vers un seul type de matériau qui correspond au silex turonien présent dans les alluvions de l'Aisne et en formation primaire dans le Rethelois. La qualité des silex turoniens dans ces villages suggère un accès direct aux gîtes qui sont localisés à une vingtaine de km à l'est;
- Les autres sites de la vallée, à partir de Berry-au-Bac "le Chemin de la Pêcherie" sont caractérisés par une alternance entre un approvisionnement majoritaire en silex tertiaire ou en silex secondaire sénonien. Les formations primaires de ce dernier sont à une cinquantaine de kilomètres au sud de la vallée. Les formations tertiaires affleurent en partie le long des plateaux (Lutétien) ainsi qu'à 20-25 de km au sud pour le silex bartonien (à Romigny-Lhéry par exemple).

Il semble donc que l'on ait deux directions d'approvisionnement différentes (nord-est et sud) pour des sites pourtant peu éloignés les uns des autres.

Un choix qualitatif existe dans la sélection des matières premières car les silex régionaux sont majoritaires, particulièrement dans le taux d'utilisation de l'outillage et des produits laminaires. Les matériaux lointains arrivent sous la forme de blocs préformés ou préparés (Allard à paraître). L'approvisionnement est donc considéré comme principalement régional, soit à une distance de 20 à 50 km des villages.

La plaine champenoise

Les ressources siliceuses de la Champagne sont assez abondantes, mais localisées dans les marges de la région administrative, le sous-sol crayeux du centre étant réputé sans silex. Hormis les Ardennes, les principaux affleurements reconnus se situent à l'ouest, au contact de la Cuesta d'Ile-de-France et au sud-ouest, entre les vallées de la Seine et de l'Yonne (fig. 1, n°5 et 6). Les silex présents dans les niveaux crétacés de ces deux régions sont en partie identiques, notamment pour ceux du département de l'Aube. Les affleurements répertoriés se situent entre Epernay et les Marais de Saint-Gond (fig. 1, n°5), mais l'on ne dispose d'aucune indication sur les ressources éventuelles entre la vallée du Grand-Morin et la vallée de l'Aube, à l'exception du secteur à l'ouest de Vitry-le-François (prospections V. Blouet, inédit). Les plateaux tertiaires adjacents fournissent également des silicifications très mal localisées, à l'exception du versant nord de la vallée de la Marne (par exemple Romigny-Lhéry). Localement, les alluvions de la Marne contiennent des galets de quartz et vraisemblablement des galets siliceux roulés.

Nonobstant des grands plans de village avec 12 ou 15 maisons à Orconte "les Noues" (Tappret et al. 1988) et à Écriennes "la Folie" (Tappret et Villes 1996), le mobilier est généralement pauvre, limité aux rares maisons bordées de fosses de construction. La comparaison entre les sites est donc restreinte à quelques structures, ce qui doit être considéré comme seulement indicatif et réellement susceptible d'être remanié par de nouvelles découvertes. Les silex sénoniens sont majoritairement utilisés, plus de 80% pour Juvigny, Orconte et Écriennes et 56 % à Saint-Dizier (Quenton 1999). L'identification macroscopique permet de séparer deux variétés principales qui sont difficiles à distinguer sur les éclats patinés de petite taille. L'approvisionnement est régional car les affleurements sont situés à 70 km en moyenne de la plaine du Perthois pour le silex "blond", à une trentaine de kilomètres pour le second que l'on a appelé "blond-gris". Juvigny "les Grands Traquiers" est le site le plus proche des affleurements et c'est dans cette série que les témoins du débitage sont les plus fréquents (Tappret et Villes 1996).

Dans les villages de la plaine du Perthois, si l'on peut admettre que le débitage laminaire est réalisé sur place, la forme sous laquelle arrive les blocs reste encore à préciser (notamment le silex blond).

Le silex tertiaire, probablement du Bartonien, est attesté dans tous les sites, mais il est très rare dans le Perthois (quelques pièces) et peu abondant à Juvigny (7,2%). Si l'on se réfère à la répartition des niveaux géologiques susceptibles d'en livrer, les sources potentielles ne sont pas plus éloignées que celles des niveaux sénoniens. A contrario, si les affleurements correspondent bien à ceux du nord de la vallée de la Marne, les sources sont effectivement plus lointaines que les silex crétacés, à plus de 30 km de Juvigny. Les silex tertiaires du Perthois sont considérés comme des produits exogènes car il ne s'agit que de lames ou d'outils.

Des matériaux locaux sont présents dans chaque ensemble : ce sont des silex de mauvaise qualité, gélif, et des galets de quartz. Ils apparaissent toujours sous forme d'éclats ou d'outils sur éclat. Le quartz est présent généralement sous la forme d'esquilles et rarement d'éclats (surtout à Orconte "les Noues"). L'absence d'outils en quartz dans les fosses étudiées ne permet pas de bien comprendre son utilisation, mais il ne fait pas partie des matériaux employés pour le débitage laminaire. Par comparaison avec les sites alsaciens, on peut proposer un débitage de supports destinés aux pièces esquillées (Mauvilly 1997).

Cet inventaire est complété par des matériaux présents sous la forme de lames ou d'outils sur lame, à Juvigny "les Grands Traquiers" et surtout Saint-Dizier "le Toupot Millot" (Quenton 1999). Dans ce dernier site, 9 pièces (3 fragments de lame et 6 outils sur lame) sont dans un silex translucide gris-clair, au grain fin, d'aspect savonneux au toucher. Ce matériau n'est pas identifié dans notre étude; l'hypothèse la plus convaincante, par élimination, correspond aux affleurements de silex crétacés de l'Aube et de l'Yonne. 2 fragments de lame et 8 outils sur lame correspondent à des silex issus des formations crétacées de la Belgique. 3 outils sont attribués au silex de Ghlin et 7 autres pièces au silex à grain fin de Hesbaye. Enfin, 2 fragments de lame sont apparentés soit au silex turonien du Rethelois, soit aux variétés noires du silex de Rijckholt.

Ces produits attestent d'une circulation des matériaux complexe, distinguant le site de Saint–Dizier des autres villages étudiés. Les silex tertiaires et les grès-quartzites de la plaine du Perthois et de Juvigny "les Grands Traquiers" montrent l'existence probable d'une circulation que l'on pourrait qualifier de régionale : 100 km pour le tertiaire avec la plaine du Perthois (base de référence à Romigny-Lhéry), Troyes étant à 70 km de la plaine du Perthois, et 50 km pour le grès-quartzite à Juvigny. Ces matériaux restent néanmoins secondaires dans l'approvisionnement général.

Les silex belges en revanche sont synonymes d'une circulation à grande distance. En effet, le bassin de Mons ou la Hesbaye sont situés à 220 km de Saint-Dizier (la distance des deux zones est pratiquement égale). Malgré l'éloignement des sources, ces matériaux constituent jusqu'à 9% de la série.

La vallée de la Moselle

Les découvertes et les fouilles de sites rubanés sont nombreuses dans le couloir mosellan mais, hormis des publications sur la céramique pour une périodisation de la région (Blouet et Decker 1993, Schmidgen-Hager 1993), le reste du mobilier, notamment le mobilier lithique, n'est pas encore bien connu. Les sites mosellans sont à l'écart des principales zones d'affleurements siliceux et le silex de bonne qualité fait globalement défaut. Cette région renferme néanmoins des formations exploitables (silex du Muschelkalk, parfois très bien silicifié, silex oxfordien de Saint-Mihiel par exemple), mais manifestement peu utilisées par les populations rubanées. La description de ces matériaux ne sera pas abordée ici.

Un type régulièrement présent correspond à une ou des variétés de silex dénommées "silex de type Tétange" (Löhr 1986). Dans les premières descriptions, ce silex grisâtre, plus ou moins translucide, est affilié aux formations crétacées du nord-est du Bassin parisien (Löhr 1986) puis des gisements de cette variété sont signalés dans la région de Trèves et de Luxembourg, ainsi qu'à Sarrebruck. Récemment, ce matériau est décrit comme un silex gris à gris brun foncé, évoquant une variété de silex tertiaire analogue à celle de la région de Reims (Jadin 1996) ; néanmoins les affleurements mentionnés ne livrent que des galets de taille réduite. L'origine de ces silex correspond probablement aux formations crétacées du Bassin parisien (Blouet, communication personnelle), bien attestées à Metz nord par exemple. Quelle que soit la conclusion sur l'origine de cette matière première, la mention de "type Tétange" disparaît à la frontière luxembourgeoise et française, où l'on peut penser que ces silex crétacés transluci-des sont plutôt reconnus comme des variétés du Bassin parisien. Dans les effectifs de la moyenne vallée de la Moselle allemande, le silex Tétange fait partie intégrante des matériaux couramment utilisés, son taux de représentation oscillant entre 11% et 32 % des matériaux (Schmidgen-Hager 1993, p.111). Ce matériau n'est plus mentionné à partir de la vallée du Rhin puisqu'il se confond avec une autre variété du nord de l'Allemagne, le silex "baltique" (Zimmermann 1995).

Les autres matériaux sont affiliés aux formations crétacées du Limbourg et de Hesbaye, ou au Secondaire ou Tertiaire du Bassin parisien. Tous ces matériaux sont exogènes, à des distances moyennes directes supérieures aux 100 km (fig. 1).

En détaillant la distribution des matériaux des sites du nord vers le sud, la situation varie selon le taux de représentation du silex de Rijckholt :
- Dans les villages étudiés par E. Schmidgen-Hager, établis dans un méandre de la moyenne vallée de la Moselle, ce sont les variétés du silex de Rijckholt qui prédominent dans les assemblages en composant de 47 à 67 % des séries (Schmidgen-Hager 1993 et Zimmermann 1995). Ces variétés sont essentiellement reconnues comme du silex de Rijckholt-Sint-Geertruid, les autres correspondent à des silex des alluvions de la Meuse (Schotter), quelques pièces de type Rullen et une de type Vetschau. A. Zimmermann indique également la présence du silex "baltique" (Baltischer feuerstein), entre 5 et 16 % ; ce silex n'est pas décompté dans la thèse de Schmidgen-Hager (probablement intégré dans le type Tétange). L'auteur souligne l'impossibilité de distinguer ces deux types de silex (Zimmermann 1995). Ces sites livrent également un matériau assimilé au silex à grain fin hesbignon (Hellgrau-Belgischer feuerstein), entre 1 à 6 objets, ce qui représente de 1 à 10 % du total. Pour finir, 2 pièces du type de Romigny-Lhéry sont signalées à Wengerohr et Oberbillig. Ce dernier site, qui se trouve à la frontière luxembourgeoise, se différencie des précédents par la plus faible proportion de silex de Rijckholt (30%).
- Au Grand-Duché de Luxembourg, on dispose uniquement d'indications sur les variétés siliceuses présentes. À

Remerschen "Schengerwis", les auteurs mentionnent la présence de silex maastrichiens sous la forme de produits laminaires (Hauzer et Jadin 1993). La maison de Weiler-la-Tour "Holzdreisch" , fouillée en 1990, livre quelques dizaines de pièces dont la majeure partie d'origine maastrichienne, du type Rijckholt ou de Lousberg, des pièces à grain fin hesbignonnes ainsi que du silex type "Tétange", affilié dans ce cas à du silex bartonien du Bassin parisien (Jadin 1996, p.105). À Alzingen "Grossfeld", le mobilier est abondant et comprend, en plus des matériaux locaux, une part de silex maastrichiens et d'autre part, des silex du Bassin parisien (Jadin 1996). La fouille récente menée sur l'habitat de Altwies "Op dem Boesch" n'a livré que quelques éléments siliceux, principalement du Muschelkalk et des silex d'origine maastrichienne (silex grenu et à grain fin) (Jost et al. 2000).

- En Lorraine, la série de Metz-nord que nous avons pu étudier fait pour nous office de référence. Le spectre des matériaux est composé des principales variétés rencontrées en aval. Les différents matériaux régionaux constituent 10% de la série. Les pièces en silex d'origine belgo–hollandaise sont les plus nombreuses. Néanmoins, ces silex sont à scinder en deux groupes distincts. Le premier est représenté par des silex d'aspect grenu et opaque, aux teintes grises variées, regroupés par commodité sous l'appellation "silex de Rijckholt". Les autres sont attribués avec certitude au silex à grain fin de Hesbaye tel qu'on le rencontre dans les sites hesbignons. Les variétés de type Rijckholt sont majoritaires dans la série constituant 39% de l'ensemble, les silex à grain fin hesbignons 28%. Ces silex composent donc les deux tiers de l'approvisionnement du site de Metz–nord ; la distance directe des affleurements est à peine inférieure à 200 km. La dernière part du spectre des matériaux (8%) englobe quelques objets des formations tertiaires et crétacées du Bassin parisien. 2 objets sont en silex tertiaire zoné, 10 pièces en silex translucide à grain fin, blond ou sombre, assimilables au Sénonien marnais ou de l'Aube. Enfin, 2 autres pièces sont en silex noir à grain fin opaque, totalement identique au silex crétacé du Turonien de la région de Rethel, tel que l'on peut le rencontrer dans les séries de Berry-au-Bac "la Croix Maigret" ou "le Vieux Tordoir" dans la vallée de l'Aisne. Les affleurements en position primaire de ces différents types de silex sont distants de 100 à 150 km de Metz. C'est donc un approvisionnement extra-régional qui prévaut dans cette série, où l'on peut remarquer la bipolarité des sources, les silex belgo-hollandais constituant la source majeure des matériaux siliceux (Blouet et Decker 1993).

- Marainville-sur-Madon correspond à la découverte la plus au sud des sites implantés le long de la vallée de la Moselle. La seule indication sur les matières premières concerne la diminution importante des matériaux belgo-hollandais au profit des matières crétacées du Bassin parisien, ces dernières constituant 75 % des matériaux (Blouet et Decker 1993).

L'Alsace

Le panorama des ressources est relativement simple puisque la plaine alsacienne semble dépourvue de silex de bonne qua-

lité. Les alluvions du Rhin contiennent des blocs de matériaux divers (quartz, jaspe, chailles, silex des contreforts du Jura), mais de qualité médiocre (Mauvilly 1997). C'est au sud de la région, principalement dans le nord du Jura, que sont localisés les affleurements siliceux principaux (fig. 1, n°7). Les études récentes sur les matériaux du Jura français et suisse notamment permettent d'inventorier les ressources disponibles (Cupillard et al. 1995, Honegger 2001). Les silex du Jurassique sont abondants dans la frange du Jura et la Forêt Noire sur la rive droite du Rhin, particulièrement dans les calcaires du Malm (Honnegger 2001). Ces gisements ceinturent le Sundgau, la distance entre les sites rubanés et les affleurements est de 20 à 30 km pour les plus proches. Plus à l'est, en direction du lac de Constance et du Jura Souabe, divers matériaux sont présents : des chailles du Jurassique (Forêt Noire), des silex du Muschelkalk et des silex calcédonieux (Flébot-Augustins 1992). Le territoire de Belfort et les plateaux de la Haute-Saône renferment des silex du Jurassique (Lias, Dogger), mais aussi des silex lacustres, dans le bassin Oligocène au sud de Vesoul (Cupillard et al. 1995). Ce silex tertiaire ne présente pas a priori de variations distinctes avec celui des gîtes du centre nord du Bassin parisien. Le Bas-Rhin ne renferme pas d'affleurements siliceux de bonne qualité ; les plus proches reconnus sont en moyenne à 80 km de Strasbourg avec les affleurements lorrains du Muschelkalk, les chailles du Jurassique en amont de la vallée du Neckar ou les gîtes de la Forêt Noire décrits précédemment.

L'approvisionnement des sites rubanés alsaciens est donc contraint par les possibilités régionales (Mauvilly 1997). Les spectres de répartition des ressources siliceuses par site changent en fonction de la localisation des villages, la synthèse récente de M. Mauvilly présente l'économie des matières premières en Haute et Basse-Alsace (Mauvilly 1997). Cependant, le nombre de séries est encore limité, particulièrement pour la Basse-Alsace et la durée d'occupation et la surface fouillée des sites sont extrêmement variables.

Le silex du Jura est le matériau dominant pour tous les ensembles alsaciens. Son taux décroît progressivement du sud au nord avec une rupture perceptible au niveau de Colmar (Mauvilly 1997). Dans la région de Mulhouse, ce matériau constitue l'essentiel de l'approvisionnement avec le quartz, les autres matériaux étant rares. Dans les collections étudiées dans notre travail (Sierentz et Ensisheim), on rencontre quelques objets en silex exogènes. 11 pièces à Sierentz et 3 à Ensisheim, partagées entre les silex du Crétacé supérieur et le silex tertiaire (notamment 1 éclat cortical à Sierentz). Une quarantaine d'objets en silex translucide sont également présents sans que l'on puisse les attribuer à une variété de silex précise. Ces silex translucides sont retrouvés sous forme de restes bruts de taille, de produits laminaires ou d'outils.

Les sites de la Basse-Alsace sont très pauvres et composés en grande partie de silex locaux. Le reste comprend des produits en silex du nord du Jura et du Bassin parisien (Mauvilly 2000).

La confluence Seine-Yonne

La confluence Seine-Yonne est bien documentée pour les ressources siliceuses grâce aux prospections menées par E. Mauger (plus précisément dans le Sénonais, Mauger 1985). Les niveaux du Sénonien sont très riches en silex, les affleurements sont abondants des craies du Coniacien jusqu'au Campanien supérieur (fig. 1 n°6), l'auteur mentionnant uniquement les affleurements conséquents (le Turonien semble peu fourni en rognon).

Les variétés recensées sont nombreuses, classées principalement en fonction des couleurs et du cortex. Les craies blanches renferment des silex gris, gris-brun, châtain-gris, blonds, gris-roux et noirs. Les caractéristiques sont communes aux silex sénoniens ; la matrice est translucide et, selon les variétés, contient des taches grenues grises ou des géodes crayeuses. Les critères de certains faciès sont apparemment communs (mais plus diversifiés) avec ceux rencontrés à l'ouest du département de la Marne.

L'étude de A. Augereau du secteur Seine-Yonne-Vanne et notamment des minières de l'A5 permet de documenter l'est du transept prospecté par E. Mauger. Les formations coniaciennes et santoniennes, qui affleurent le long de la Vanne, livrent des rognons de silex gris à taches grenues plus claires. Le Campanien, présent du nord de la Vanne jusqu'à la vallée de la Seine, livre également des rognons dont les affleurements sont discontinus (Augereau 1993, p. 24-25).

C'est donc l'ensemble du complexe Crétacé supérieur, de Montereau jusqu'à Troyes, qui renferme des ressources siliceuses. L'accès aux ressources est multiple : en formation primaire, en formation remaniée ou encore dans les alluvions des rivières. Il s'agit d'une région pour laquelle la matière première est facilement accessible. Les matériaux des sites rubanés de ce secteur sont quasi exclusivement des silex crétacés (Augereau 1993).

Le silex tertiaire est en revanche rare dans la région de Montereau (Mauger 1985, p.99), les quelques pièces découvertes dans les sites du Néolithique ancien sont déclarées exogènes (Augereau 1993, p. 28).

Le Hainaut

Les sites hennuyers du bassin de la Dendre sont localisés à une vingtaine de kilomètres des gisements siliceux connus. Ces affleurements correspondent à la zone du Crétacé supérieur du bassin de Mons (fig. 1, n°2). La séquence du Turonien au Maastrichien renferme plusieurs niveaux qui livrent des rognons ou des plaques de silex en quantité variable selon les assises. Le niveau basal du Tertiaire qui surmonte le Crétacé livre également des rognons remaniés au cortex verdi (Landénien). Les critères de reconnaissance sont macroscopiques et sans collection de comparaison, ni cartographie des affleurements réels. Le cadre régional reste encore à construire, les identifications reposant principalement sur les premiè-res études de la région (Cahen et van Berg 1979, Constantin 1985).

Le Rubané du Bassin de la Dendre est représenté par 3 sites bien documentés : Blicquy "la Petite Rosière" (Deramaix 1988) et "la Couture du Couvent" (Constantin et al. 1991), Aubechies "Coron Maton" (Constantin 1985), les autres n'ayant pas fait l'objet de décapages exhaustifs. La distribution des matériaux de ces 3 habitats est assez homogène, la distance entre les villages est de l'ordre d'un à deux kilomètres.

Le silex gris mat de Ghlin et les variétés de silex translucide sont les plus communs. Si les hypothèses d'affleurements sont exactes, l'approvisionnement est régional et en accès direct.

Le dernier matériau récurrent aisément reconnaissable est le silex gris translucide à grain fin de Hesbaye. Nous rejoignons l'avis de D. Cahen et P.-L. Van Berg sur l'origine hesbignonne des pièces étudiées. La quasi-absence d'éclats, le type de préparation des lames et le taux d'utilisation de ce silex confirment l'hypothèse de l'apport extérieur de ce matériau dans les sites hennuyers. Le site de Blicquy "la Petite Rosière" a livré un petit contingent de déchets de taille de ce silex (Deramaix 1988, tab.3), mais en faible proportion. Les produits laminaires constituent 27% des déchets et l'outillage sur lame presque 30% du total des silex de ce type. En conclusion, on peut admettre qu'une partie de ce silex est acheminée sous la forme de produits semi-finis, de nucléus ou/et de nucléus préparés. Néanmoins, les assises de Nouvelles sont présentes dans le Bassin de Mons (mais peu riches en silex, Robazinski 2000) ; il est donc vraisemblable que ce silex a été également récolté en position primaire, ce qui permet d'interpréter la série du site blicquien d'Irchonwelz. Cette série livre en effet un important débitage d'éclats dans un matériau similaire au silex hesbignon pour un faible taux d'outillage (Constantin et al. 1991). L'impact économique du silex hesbignon est important car sa représentation dans l'outillage est de 30 % à Blicquy "la Petite Rosière" et plus de 25% à Aubechies (Constantin 1985). C'est donc un matériau qui fait partie intégrante de l'économie des matières premières des sites rubanés hennuyers.

Les autres matériaux exogènes semblent absents, mais l'état des connaissances ne permet pas de raisonner sur les matériaux présents à quelques unités et la proximité de la frontière française n'est pas sans conséquence sur l'inventaire régional des ressources siliceuses. Étant donné que le Bassin de Mons correspond à l'extension terminale du bassin géologique de Paris, il est impossible de déterminer l'éventuelle circulation des matériaux crétacés présents dans l'Aisne, l'Oise ou la Champagne.

Il semble en outre que le silex de Spiennes soit également absent des inventaires des sites hennuyers (Cahen et van Berg 1979).

Enfin, le silex tertiaire bartonien du Bassin parisien, bien attesté dans les collections blicquiennes (Constantin

1985, Caspar et Burnez-Lanotte 1994), est quasi-absent des sites rubanés. Seul le secteur rubané d'Aubechies a livré 3 lames en silex bartonien, dans un contexte chronologique qui reste encore à préciser par l'étude du mobilier céramique (C. Constantin étude en cours).

La Hesbaye

Le panorama général des ressources siliceuses de Hesbaye est relativement simple car la zone d'implantation majeure correspond aux niveaux loessiques qui reposent sur des terrains du Crétacé supérieur (Hesbaye et pays de Herve). Les séries sont très riches en silex, l'impression générale est que l'accès aux gîtes est facile localement, bien que la cartographie des affleurements reste encore à réaliser.

Pour la Hesbaye, les matériaux siliceux se résument en 3 catégories principales :
- La variété commune est le "silex à grain fin de Hesbaye" issue, si l'on se réfère à la région de Verlaine (Burnez-Lanotte et Allard 1998), des assises de Nouvelles, dernier niveau du Campanien (Sénonien, Crétacé Supérieur).
- La seconde variété, le silex grenu, parfois silex gris grenu, est fréquente, voire majoritaire comme à Waremme "Longchamps" ou à Rosmeer (Ulrix-Closset et Rousselle 1982, Jadin 1990). Une minière du Néolithique moyen dans un silex apparenté est connue à Orp-le-Grand, dans la vallée de la Méhaigne.
- Enfin, les grès-quartzites de Wommersom peuvent être considérés comme un matériau régional ; les affleurements mentionnés sont localisés dans la frange nord-occidentale de l'occupation rubanée de Hesbaye (Cahen et al. 1986). Ce matériau, caractéristique des séries mésolithiques, est rare dans les sites rubanés. Les pièces retrouvées dans ce matériau en contexte Néolithique ancien sont généralement considérées comme des pièces mésolithiques (Jadin 1990, Caspar et Burnez-Lanotte 1994). Des variétés régionales à grain fin peu fréquentes sont parfois mentionnées (Ulrix-Closset et Rousselle 1982, p. 12, Caspar et Burnez-Lanotte 1994, p. 4-5).

Les autres matériaux sont très rares et la distance des affleurements connus n'est pas obligatoirement extra-régionale. Ainsi, des silex grenus des formations de Gulpen sont signalés à Darion, Olèye et Waremme (une dizaine de pièces par site, Jadin 1990).

Une variété de silex noir translucide est également attestée sur les sites hesbignons (Ulrix-Closset et Rousselle 1982, Otte 1984, Jadin 1990), attribuée aux formations crétacées du Bassin de Mons sous l'appellation "silex d'Obourg". Une armature en silex blond translucide est signalée à Darion, que l'auteur attribue également aux formations du Bassin de Mons (Jadin 1990).

Enfin, le silex gris mat de Ghlin est parfois présent, mais sans précisions exactes. On ne peut avoir la certitude qu'il soit réellement en contexte rubané ou intrusif dans les sites où le Blicquyen et l'Omalien se côtoient. Ce matériau est en effet retrouvé dans les structures du groupe de Blicquy de

Vaux-et-Borset "Gibour" (Caspar et Burnez 1994) et de Darion (Jadin 1999).

L'approvisionnement est souvent local, voire in situ, pour certains des sites hesbignons. Néanmoins, ce panorama simple occulte vraisemblablement un problème de reconnaissance des variétés du "silex grenu/gris grenu". Les caractéristiques macroscopiques de ce matériau le rapprochent certainement des silex de Rijckholt, Rullen, etc. À Rosmeer, sur les bords de la Meuse, implantation la plus proche des sites hollandais, le silex est associé aux formations de Gulpen qui affleurent en positions primaire et secondaire dans la région, la formation de Gulpen étant présente jusqu'à la vallée du Geer (Ulrix-Closset et Rousselle 1982, p. 12).

Le silex grenu de Hesbaye n'est pas déterminé quant à sa provenance géologique, mais il affleure en position remaniée dans la région. Il est donc fortement probable que ce matériau soit parfaitement similaire au silex de la zone crétacée du Limbourg hollandais. C'est par ailleurs ce que suggère l'étude de M. de Grooth sur les minières du Néolithique moyen de la région pour laquelle elle exprime l'impossibilité de distinguer fiablement les silex de Spiennes, Orp-le-grand et Rijckolht (de Grooth 1991, p. 161). Par conséquent, selon que les études sont menées à l'est ou à l'ouest de la Meuse, les silex du secteur Rijckholt-Rullen apparaissent ou disparaissent des décomptes. En Allemagne, le silex grenu de Hesbaye n'apparaît jamais dans les décomptes, les pièces en "hellgraue Belgischer feuerstein" semblent plutôt apparentées au silex à grain fin de Hesbaye (Zimmermann 1995, p. 26).

Modalités d'approvisionnement et circulations des produits siliceux

Bien que l'approvisionnement soit variable selon les principales zones d'implantation, il se dégage trois situations qui se résument de la manière suivante :

- La première correspond aux régions où les possibilités régionales permettent de collecter de la matière première d'une qualité satisfaisante pour le débitage laminaire. C'est le cas de la moyenne vallée de l'Aisne et de l'Oise, de la plaine du Perthois, du Haut-Rhin et du Hainaut. Dans ces habitats, il existe un choix sélectif vers des silex régionaux de bonne qualité qui auront une exploitation plus importante que les silex locaux (en général de qualité moindre). Cette sélection n'est pas toujours visible dans les décomptes bruts car ces matières sont acheminées sous la forme de blocs préparés, ce qui se concrétise par un taux d'utilisation prépondérant dans l'outillage, comme à Cuiry-lès-Chaudardes pour le silex sénonien champenois (Allard à paraître). La distance d'approvisionnement varie en moyenne de 20 à 50 km. La limite de 50 km apparaît comme représentative de l'extension du territoire des expéditions pour un accès direct, ou plutôt c'est dans cet intervalle de distance que l'on ne dénote pas de ruptures majeures dans les déchets de taille (les témoins des principales étapes du débitage sont présents dans les séries, à l'exception de la mise en forme).

71

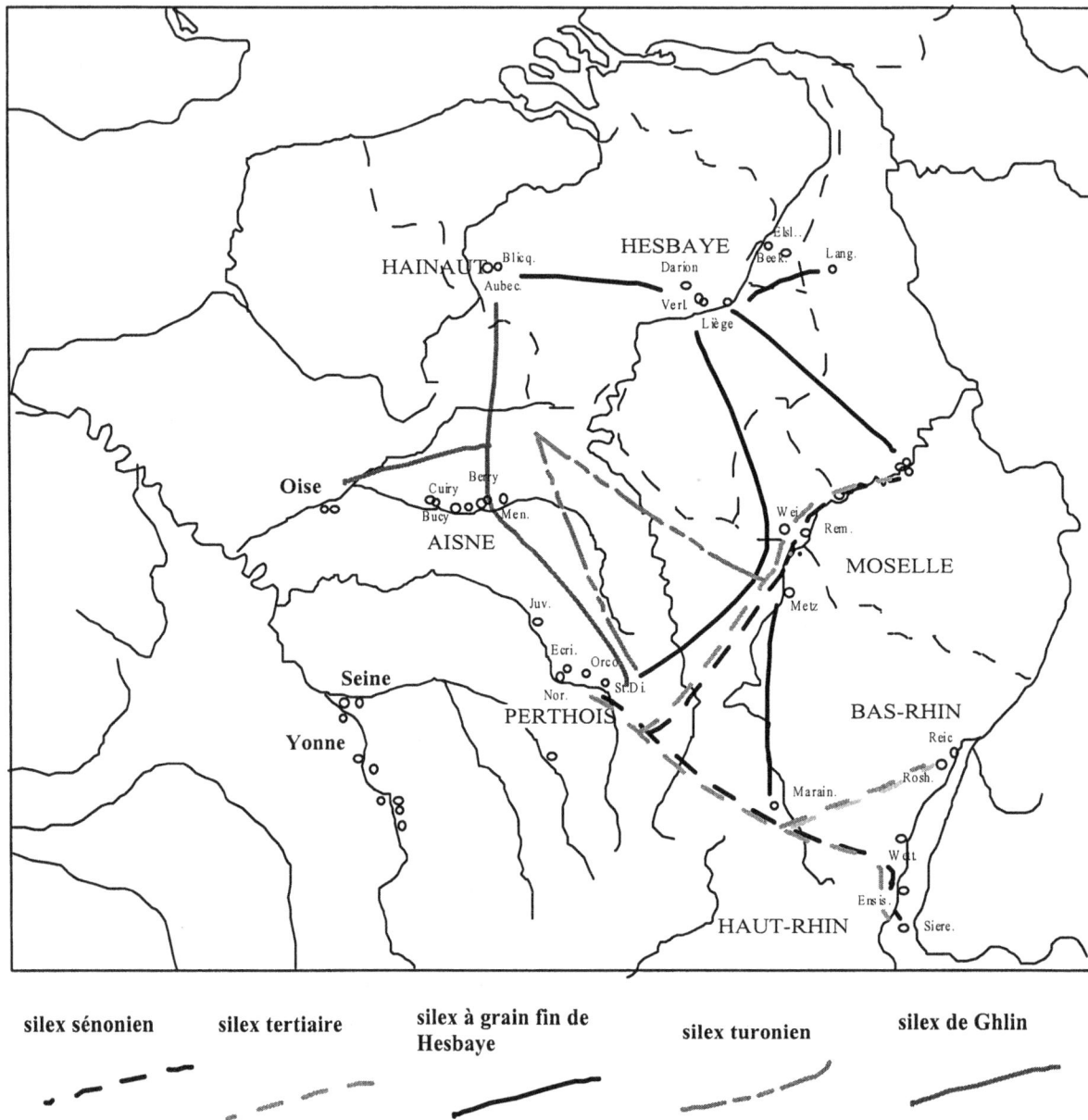

Figure 2. Carte des circulations principales des matières premières dans le Bassin parisien et les régions limitrophes au Rubané récent (sauf le silex de type Rijckholt).

Les villages de ces régions livrent quelques silex exogènes, témoins de liens avec les régions limitrophes. Ainsi, quelques pièces en silex de Ghlin du Hainaut se retrouvent dans les sites de Cuiry-lès-Chaudardes, de Pontavert et de Berry-au-Bac "le Vieux Tordoir" dans la vallée de l'Aisne. Les sites d'Ensisheim "Ratfeld" et de Sierentz "Sandgrube" ont livré des produits en silex sénonien de la Marne ou de l'Aube. Ces silex exogènes sont retrouvés en faible quantité dans les habitats, sous forme de produits finis ou semi-finis.

- Le deuxième scénario correspond aux villages dont l'environnement géologique proche et régional ne permet manifestement pas un approvisionnement de qualité satisfaisante pour le débitage laminaire. Les matériaux dominants sont alors exogènes, ce qui se manifeste par l'absence ou la rareté des déchets de taille.

Pour la Lorraine, les produits laminaires sont très majoritairement exogènes ; à Metz-nord, ce sont les silex hesbignons et de type Rijckholt qui circulent pour approvisionner les habitats. À Marainville-sur-Madon, c'est le silex sénonien de la Marne ou de l'Aube (et également le silex tertiaire) qui assure l'essentiel de l'approvisionnement (Blouet et Decker 1993). En Basse-Alsace, ce sont les silex du Bassin parisien (sénonien et tertiaire) et les silex du nord du Jura qui contribuent à l'approvisionnement des villages (en effet, ces silex sont vraisemblablement dominants dans les produits laminaires).

- Parfois, les ressources siliceuses et les lieux d'implantation des villages coïncident, ce qui est immédiatement perceptible par les quantités d'objets retrouvés dans les villages. C'est le cas de la Hesbaye et de la confluence Seine-Yonne.

Si les matières premières ne font donc certainement pas partie des critères choisis pour l'installation des villages rubanés (Cahen *et al.* 1986), ces populations recherchent néanmoins généralement des matériaux de bonne qualité. En effet, les silex régionaux ou extra-régionaux sont fréquemment employés au détriment de ressources plus proches mais de qualité moindre comme le silex Turonien ou Lutétien à cérithes dans la partie ouest de la vallée de l'Aisne ou le Muschelkalk en Lorraine. L'utilisation importante des matériaux locaux résulte parfois d'une production de supports pour les pièces esquillées comme le silex turonien de la plaine de Bucy-le-Long ou le quartz dans le Sundgau (Mauvilly 1997) et probablement le quartz dans le Perthois.

L'identification des matériaux a permis de reconnaître ou de confirmer des circulations de matières premières parfois lointaines, pour lesquelles on a pu identifier deux voies de circulations principales :
- La première concerne les variétés de silex grenus du Limbourg commodément appelés "silex de Rijckholt" et le silex à grain fin Hesbignon. Cet ensemble de matériaux bien localisés constituent assurément un des réseaux de matière première les plus "actifs". Si l'on ne sait pas encore très bien dater l'apparition de ces matières premières dans les sites hors de la zone d'approvisionnement directe (dès l'étape ancienne à Bruchenbrücken, Gronenborn 1990), les circulations sont pleinement actives pendant la majeure partie de la Céramique Linéaire dans la moyenne vallée de la Moselle allemande, luxembourgeoise et française, pour laquelle ces matériaux constituent l'essentiel ou la majorité des produits siliceux (Blouet et Decker 1993, Schmidgen-Hager 1993, Zimmermann 1995). Ces matériaux voient leurs effectifs diminuer brutalement selon les potentialités locales. Au-delà de cette zone, ces matériaux sont pour l'instant attestés en faible quantité, de l'ordre de quelques unités, à Saint-Dizier et à Marainville-sur-Madon (Blouet et Decker 1993).
- Les silex crétacés du bassin parisien constituent le second groupe de matériaux pour lesquels on peut suivre des circulations à grande échelle. La localisation précise des affleurements est complexe et les variétés restent encore à déterminer avec certitude. Ces silex sont connus dans une vaste région globalement parallèle aux plateaux tertiaires de l'Ile-de-France, d'Epernay jusqu'à Troyes. Ils composent l'approvisionnement majoritaire des phases moyenne et récente des sites champenois et de Marainville-sur-Madon. Ils sont bien attestés dans la région strasbourgeoise à Rosheim "Sainte-Odile" et encore à Wettolsheim "Ricoh" (Mauvilly 1997, 2000). Le Haut-Rhin livre également des silex crétacés similaires à ceux du Bassin parisien mais en quantité négligeable (Mauvilly 1997). Les sites du couloir mosellan sont encore mal documentés et se pose le problème du silex de type "Tétange". Si on lie ce dernier aux formations crétacées du Bassin parisien, ces silex sont alors attestés pratiquement jusqu'au Rhin, au moins dès l'étape récente.

L'apparition chronologique des silex crétacés dans les collections reste à préciser avec certitude. Ils sont manifestement présents à la phase moyenne du Rubané dans le couloir mosellan et dans la plaine alsacienne. Pour cette dernière, des pièces en "silex du Crétacé supérieur originaires de la plaine champenoise" sont signalées dès l'étape ancienne du Rubané (Mauvilly 1997, p. 333). L'avancement des travaux dans les diverses régions ne permet pas pour l'instant de préciser sur quels sites et dans quelles proportions ces pièces existent, ni de juger la qualité des contextes pris en compte. Les régions où les matériaux locaux ou régionaux sont peu exploités au profit des silex exogènes seront de précieux indicateurs pour dater l'apparition des circulations de matériaux exogènes (couloir mosellan et Basse-Alsace principalement).

Les autres circulations concernent des matériaux que l'on rencontre en petite quantité dans les habitats hors des zones d'accès direct.

La distribution du silex tertiaire reproduit fidèlement celle des silex crétacés puisqu'on le retrouve dans les mêmes sites (Lorraine, Alsace et Moselle allemande). Ce matériau est principalement utilisé à part égale avec les silex sénoniens dans le RRBP de la vallée de l'Aisne. Ailleurs, l'utilisation de cette matière chute brutalement dès la série de Juvigny, malgré le faible éloignement des sources ; les produits sont considérés comme exogènes dès la plaine du Perthois. Il faut remarquer la présence d'éléments en silex tertiaire dans le Hainaut à Aubechies (Constantin 1985).

L'identification du silex de Ghlin dans le Bassin parisien apporte également des informations pertinentes. Ces silex attestent des contacts avec le Rubané du Hainaut et on les rencontre uniquement dans des contextes RRBP et Rubané final du Bassin Parisien (également à Pont-Sainte-Maxence, hors de la vallée de l'Aisne, Françoise Bostyn étude en cours). L'incertitude chronologique demeure pour l'attribution du site de Saint-Dizier "Toupot Millot" car la céramique est peu abondante ; mais c'est une datation tardive qui fut proposée (Quenton 1999). Si l'on considère que Juvigny (Rubané récent champenois) est globalement contemporain du RRBP. C'est donc une nouvelle voie de circulation, dans l'état actuel des données, qui est attestée et circonscrite au RRBP/RFBP.

Le silex turonien du Rethelois est peu représenté hors de la vallée de l'Aisne, mais on le retrouve dans le Rubané lorrain et sur le site de Saint-Dizier.

Dans la plaine alsacienne, les silex du Jura constituent l'essentiel de l'approvisionnement des sites, même si la part de cette matière diminue dans la région strasbourgeoise (Mauvilly 1997). Néanmoins, pour cette dernière région, il s'agit de la proportion générale au sein de tous les restes. Il serait souhaitable de calculer plutôt la part de cette matière (ainsi que les matériaux exogènes du Bassin parisien) dans l'outillage et les produits laminaires car tous ces silex arrivent sous forme de produits semi-finis ou finis (Mauvilly 1997, 2000). Ils sont donc, à l'instar du Sénonien dans les sites de la vallée de l'Aisne ou du silex Hesbignon dans les sites du Hainaut, sous-représentés dans la part globale des matériaux

73

qui rassemblent l'intégralité du mobilier (déchets, débris, lames et outillage).

Les modalités de circulation des produits siliceux ne seront pas présentées ici et feront l'objet d'une autre publication (Allard et Manolakakis en cours). Pour résumer, on peut dire que les modalités de circulation sont comparables à ce que l'on connaît dans le Rubané d'Europe centrale (Lech 1987, 1990). Le type de produits (lames, outils mais également des blocs préparés) et la vocation des circulations sont en effet similaires. La présence de sites consommateurs, qui utilisent des produits exogènes au détriment du potentiel siliceux local ou régional, implique une structuration de ces circulations où, à une demande, répond une offre ; ce qui peut dans ce cas être qualifié de réseau. La nature de ces réseaux est économique (ou plutôt, elle n'est pas uniquement "sociale"), on pourrait pratiquement parler "d'importation" pour les sites du couloir mosellan par exemple. Parallèlement, la présence récurrente de produits exogènes (quelques objets) dans les régions où la matière ne fait pas défaut montre également une autre vocation, souvent qualifiée de "sociale". Ces deux types sont également identifiés dans la Céramique Linéaire d'Europe centrale (Lech 1987, 1990).

Conclusion

C'est à partir des similarités reconnues dans la céramique décorée que l'on a progressivement découpé l'aire occidentale rubanée en différents groupes régionaux. Ainsi, des liens entre le Rubané du Haut-Rhin et la Champagne sont reconnus dès la découverte des sites du Perthois (Lanchon 1992, Tappret et Villes 1996), puis entre le RRBP et le Rubané récent/final du Haut-Rhin (Ilett et Constantin 1993). Parallèlement, est isolé le RRNO (Rubané Récent du nord-ouest) qui correspond à toute la partie nord-orientale de notre région d'étude, rassemblant les étapes récentes de la Céramique Linéaire du Hainaut et des vallées de la Meuse et Moselle (Van Berg 1990). En Lorraine, les affinités avec le groupe Rhéno-Mosan sont très prononcées à la phase récente de Metz-nord (IIc), le site de Marainville dans le cours supérieur de la Moselle se distingue nettement de cet ensemble (Blouet et Decker 1993). Enfin, le Rubané alsacien est précocement divisé en deux entités dont la céramique montre des divergences importantes à l'étape récente (Jeunesse 1995). En synthétisant toutes ces observations, l'expansion occidentale de l'aire rubanée à la phase récente est subdivisée en 4 groupes régionaux pour lesquels *"la répartition des styles céramiques possède une relation directe avec l'extension des réseaux de communication"* (Jeunesse 1995 p.17).

Pourtant les réseaux de distribution qui viennent d'être présentés ne reproduisent pas les propositions des groupes régionaux. Ainsi les voies de circulation des matières premières, sensées reproduire les groupes stylistiques de la céramique, montrent au contraire des liens multiples entre toutes les différentes régions, même si la chronologie précise de ces interactions reste encore à définir. Ces réseaux dépassent donc largement les simples "contacts", ils impliquent, au-delà

des échanges de biens, des voies de circulations d'idées, de techniques et un renforcement de la cohésion sociale (Renfrew 1984). Ainsi, la vision des groupes régionaux apparaît comme bien trop statique vis-à-vis des relations mises en évidence par la circulation intensive des produits siliceux.

Cela ouvre ainsi de nouvelles perspectives pour l'étude de la genèse et des liens entre les différents groupes rubanés, pour lesquels il apparaît vraisemblable que la néolithisation s'est faite en termes d'influences réciproques et de composantes régionales multiples.

Bibliographie

ALLARD, P., à paraître, Économie des matières premières des populations rubanées de la vallée de l'Aisne. *In Les matières premières lithiques en Préhistoire.* Table ronde internationale d'Aurillac (Cantal), 20-22 juin 2002.

AUGEREAU, A., 1993, *Évolution de l'industrie du silex du Vè au IVè millénaire avant J.-C. dans le sud-est du Bassin parisien. Organisation techo-économique du Villeneuve-Saint-Germain au groupe de Noyen.* Thèse de Doctorat, Université de Paris I. 3 vol.

BLANCHET, J.C., PLATEAUX, M. & POMMEPUY, C., 1989, *Matières premières et sociétés protohistoriques dans le Nord de le France.* Action Thématique Programmée "archéologie métropolitaine", rapport d'activité, Direction des Antiquités de Picardie, 76 p.

BLOUET, V., & DECKER, E., 1993, Le Rubané en Lorraine. In *Le Néolithique du Nord-Est de la France et des régions limitrophes.* Actes du 13ème colloque sur le néolithique, Metz 1986, DAF n°41, p. 84-93.

BURNEZ-LANOTTE, L., & ALLARD, P., 1998, Production laminaire originale dans le site rubané du "Petit Paradis" à Harduémont (Verlaine, Hesbaye Liégeoise), Résultats de la campagne 1997. In Cauwe N et Van Berg P.-L. (ed.). *Organisation néolithique de l'espace en Europe du Nord-Ouest.* Actes du XXIIIème colloque interrégional sur le Néolithique. Bruxelles, octobre 1997. Anthropologie et Préhistoire, 109/1998, p. 15-26.

CAHEN, D., & VAN BERG, P.-L., 1979, Un habitat danubien à Blicquy. I - structures et industrie lithique. *Archaeologica Belgica,* n°221, Bruxelles

CAHEN, D., CASPAR, J.P., & OTTE, M., 1986, *Industries lithiques danubiennes de Belgique.* Études et Recherches Archéologiques de l'Université de Liège, n°21, Liège.

CASPAR, J.-P., & BURNEZ-LANOTTE, L., 1994, III. Le matériel lithique. in CASPAR, J.-P., CONSTANTIN C., HAUZEUR A., BURNEZ-LANOTTE L., Nouveaux éléments dans le groupe de Blicquy en Belgique : le site de Vaux-et-Borset "Gibour" et "A la Croix Marie-Jeanne". *Helinium ,* XXXIV/1, 1994, p. 3-93.

CONSTANTIN, C., 1985, *Fin du Rubané, céramique du Limbourg et post-rubané. Le néolithique le plus ancien en Bassin parisien et en Hainaut.* B.A.R., 273, Général Editors, 329 p.

CONSTANTIN, C., & ILETT, M., 1997, Une étape terminale dans le Rubané Récent du Bassin parisien. *In Le Néolithique danubien et ses marges entre Rhin et Seine.* Actes du XXIIème colloque interrégional sur le Néolithique. Strasbourg, octobtre 1995. Suppl. Cahiers de l'Association pour la Promotion de la Recherche Archéologique en Alsace, p. 281-300.

CONSTANTIN, C., FARRUGGIA, J.-P., & DEMAREZ, L., 1991, Le site rubané de Blicquy-la Couture du Couvent (Hainaut). *Bulletin des chercheurs de la Wallonie*, Tome XXXI, p. 51-78

CUPILLARD, C., AFFOLTER, J., & col. de CAMPY, M., CONTINI, D, RICHARD, H., 1995, La minière de silex néolithique de Blanc-Saule à Étrelles-et-la-Montbleuse (70) et l'exploitation du silex lacustre oligocène inférieur de Haute-Saône durant le Néolithique. In *Les mines de silex au Néolithique en Europe* . Table ronde de Vesoul, 18-19 octobre 1991. CTHS, p.179-239

DERAMAIX, I., 1988, *Etude du matériel lithique du site Rubané de Blicquy-Ormeignies "la Petite Rosière"*. Mémoire de l'Université de Liège. 1 vol.

FABRE, J., 2001, L'économie du silex dans la moyenne vallée de la Somme au Néolithique final : l'exemple de la minière d'Hallencourt et des sites périphériques. *Revue Archéologique de Picardie*, n°3/4, p. 5-80

FLÉBOT-AUGUSTINS, J., 1991, *La circulations des matières premières au Paléolithique*. Études et Recherches Archéologiques de l'Université de Liège, n°75, Liège, 2 vol.

GRONENBORN, D., 1990, Mesolithic-neolithic interactions. The lithic industry of the earliest bandkeramik site Friedberg-Bruchenbrücken, Wetteraukreis (West Germany). In Vermeesch, Van Peer. *Contribution to the Mesolithic of Europe*. Louvain 1990, p.173-182.

GROOTH, M.E.Th., de, 1991, Socio-economic aspects of neolithic flint mining - a preliminary study. *Helinium*, tome XXXI, n° 2, p. 153-189.

HAUZER, A., & JADIN, I., 1993, Le village rubané de Remerschen-Schengerwis. *Bulletin de la Société Préhitorique Luxembourgeoise*, n° 15, p. 37-71.

HONEGGER, M., 2001, *L'industrie lithique taillée du Néolithique moyen et final de Suisse*. Monographie du C.R.A n°24, CNRS, 353 p.

ILETT, M., & CONSTANTIN, C., 1993, Rubané récent du Bassin parisien et Rubané récent du Haut-Rhin. *Le Néolithique du Nord-Est de la France et des régions limitrophes. Actes du XIIIème colloque sur le Néolithique*. Metz 1986. D.A.F., n°41, p. 94-99.

JADIN, I., 1990, Économie de production dans le Rubané récent de Belgique. Approche comparative des industries lithiques de trois villages. In D. Cahen et M. Otte (eds.). *Rubané et Cardial. Actes du Colloque de Liège*, nov. 1988. Études et Recherches Archéologiques de l'Université de Liège, n° 39, p. 147-154.

JADIN, I., 1996, Le Rubané de la Moselle - trait d'union entre la Rhénanie et le Bassin parisien ? Questions et réponses après deux campagnes de fouilles au Grand-Duché de Luxembourg. In Duhamel P. (dir.). *La Bourgogne entre les bassins rhénan, rhodanien et parisien. Carrefour ou frontière ?* Actes du XVIIIe Colloque interrégional sur le Néolithique. Dijon, octobre 1991, Revue Archéologique de l'Est, suppl., n° 14, p. 101-117.

JADIN, I., 1999, *Trois petits tours et puis s'en vont... La fin de la présence danubienne en moyenne Belgique*. Thèse de Doctorat, Université de Liège. 1 vol.

JEUNESSE, C., 1995, Contribution à l'étude de la variabilité régionale au sein du Rubané. l'exemple du sud de la plaine du Rhin supérieur. *Cahiers de l'Association pour la Promotion de la Recherche Archéologique en Alsace,* tome 11, p. 1-22.

JOST, C., HAUZEUR, A., LE BRUN-RICALENS, F., & SCHOELLEN, A., 2000, Un site d'habitat rubané sur éperon à Altwies " Op dem Boesch" (Grand-Duché de Luxembourg), *internéo 3*, p. 5-11

LANCHON, Y., 1992, Le Néolithique danubien dans l'est du Bassin parisien - problèmes chronologiques et culturels. *Actes du XIème colloque interrégional sur le Néolithique, Mulhouse 1984*. Direction des Antiquités Préhistoriques d'Alsace. p. 101-117.

LECH, J., 1987, Danubian raw matériel distribution patterns in eastern central Europe. In Sievering G. de G. et Newcomer M.H. (eds.). *The human uses of flint and chert*. Cambridge, p.241-248.

LECH, J., 1990, The organization of siliceous rock supplies to the danubian early farming communities (LBK) - central european examples. In D. Cahen et M. Otte (eds.). *Rubané et Cardial*. Actes du Colloque de Liège. Novembre 1988. Études et Recherches Archéologiques de l'Université de Liège, n°39, p.51-59.

LÖHR, H., 1986, L'identification de gîtes de silex et la dispersion de leurs produits dans l'ouest de l'Allemagne et régions limitrophes pendant le Néolithique ancien. *Résumés des communications du Colloque interrégional sur le Néolithique de Metz, 10-12 octobre 1986.*

MAUGER, M., 1985, *Les matériaux siliceux utilisés au Paléolithique Supérieur en Ile-de-France*. Thèse de Doctorat à l'Université de Paris I.

MAUVILLY, M., 1993a, L'habitat Rubané récent de Sierentz "Sandgrube" (Haut-Rhin). Le matériel lithique taillé et poli de la maison 7. *Recherches et documents sur le Néolithique ancien du sud de la plaine du Rhin supérieur (5400-4800 av. J.-C.)*. Cahiers de l'Association pour la Promotion de la Recherche Archéologique en Alsace, tome 9. p. 181-203.

MAUVILLY, M., 1993b, Ensisheim "Ratfeld" (Haut-Rhin). L'habitat Rubané. Etude du matériel lithique *Recherches et documents sur le Néolithique ancien du sud de la plaine du Rhin supérieur (5400-4800 av. J.-C.)*. Cahiers de l'Association pour la Promotion de la Recherche Archéologique en Alsace, tome 9. p. 109-135.

MAUVILLY, M., 1997, L'industrie lithique de la culture à céramique linéaire de Haute et de Basse Alsace - état des recherches et bilan provisoire. *In Le Néolithique danubien et ses marges entre Rhin et Seine* Actes du XXII ème colloque interrégional sur le Néolithique. Strasbourg octobre 1995. Cahiers de l'Association pour la Promotion de la Recherche Archéologique en Alsace, p 327-358.

MAUVILLY, M., 2000, Le matériel lithique du site de Rosheim "Sainte-Odile" (Bas-Rhin). Première partie - objets en roches siliceuses et apparentées. *Cahiers de l'Association pour la Promotion de la Recherche Archéologique en Alsace*, tome 16, p. 67-81.

PLATEAUX, M., 1990, Quelques données sur l'évolution des industries du néolithique danubien de la vallée de l'Aisne. *Rubané et Cardial*. Actes du colloque de Liège, 1988. Études et Recherches Archéologiques de l'Université de Liège n°39, p.157-181.

PLATEAUX, M., 1993, Contribution à l'élaboration d'une problématique des matières premières pour le Néolithique récent dans le Bassin parisien. *Le Néolithique du Nord-Est de la France et des régions limitrophes*. Actes du XIIIème colloque sur le Néolithique. Metz 1986. D.A.F., n°41, p. 100-104.

QUENTON, P., 1999, Saint-Dizier "le Toupot Millot". *Bilan scientifique. DRAC/SRA de Champagne-Ardennes*, p. 98-100

RENFREW, C., 1984, *Approaches to social archeology*. Edinburg, University Press.

SCHMIDGEN-HAGER, E., 1993, *Bandkeramik im Moseltal*. Universitätsforschungen zur prähistorischen Archäologie. Bonn, Band 18, 236 p.

TAPPRET, E., GÉ, T., VALLOIS, V., & VILLES, A., 1988, Sauvetage d'Orconte "les Noues" (Marne)- Néolithique et protohistoire, note préliminaire. *Bulletin de la Société Archéologique Champenoise*, n°81, p. 3-29.

TAPPRET, E., & VILLES, A., 1996, Contribution de la Champagne à l'étude du Néolithique ancien. In Duhamel P. (ed.). *La Bourgogne entre les bassins rhénan, rhodanien et parisien - carrefour ou frontières ?*. Actes du XVIIIeme Colloque Interrégional sur le Néolithique. Dijon, octobre 1991. Revue Archéologique de l'Est, suppl. n°14, p. 175-256.

ULRIX-CLOSSET, M., & ROUSSELLE, R., 1982 - *L'industrie lithique du site Rubané du Staberg à Rosmeer*. Archaeologia Belgica, n° 249, 50 p., 30 fig.

VAN BERG, P.-L., 1990, La céramique du Limbourg et la néolithisation de l'Europe occidentale. In Cahen et al. (eds.). *Rubané et Cardial*. Actes du colloque de Liège, *1988*. Etudes et recherches archéologiques de l'Université de Liège, n° 39, p. 161-208.

ZIMMERMANN, A., 1995, *Austauschsysteme von Silexartefakten in der Bandkeramik Mitteleuropas*. Universitätsforschungen zur prähistorischen archäologie. Bonn, Band 37, 162 p.

EARLY NEOLITHIC SETTLEMENTS OF THE SOUTH-EAST OF THE PARIS BASIN (SEINE/YONNE SECTOR) AND THEIR FLINTWORKING INDUSTRIES : CARATERIZATION, SPECIALIZATION AND FUNCTION OF KNAPPING ACTIVITIES

Anne AUGEREAU*

Résumé

Dans la zone de confluence entre la Seine et l'Yonne, les occupations domestiques danubiennes s'étendent du Rubané final (Balloy, Barbey "Le Buisson Rond", Passy "Les Graviers") à la fin de la séquence Villeneuve-Saint-Germain (Gurgy "Les Grands Champs", Passy "La Sablonnière", Marolles "Les Près Hauts"). Les installations chronologiquement intermédiaires sont également présentes (Villeneuve-la-Guyard, Barbey "Le Chemin de Montereau", Marolles "Le Chemin de Sens"). Leurs industries lithiques se définissent par la présence d'un fond commun à l'ensemble des sites, caractéristique de la période : débitage laminaire par percussion indirecte, acquisition de matières premières exogènes ou rares sous différentes formes, débitage d'éclats par percussion dure majoritaire, abondance des grattoirs sur éclat, des denticulés, présence d'armatures de faucilles, etc. Toutefois, certaines installations se distinguent par des caractères technologiques et typologiques exceptionnels : sur-représentation des restes de taille aux dépens des produits, sur-représentation de certaines classes d'outils comme, par exemple, les armatures de faucille ou les perçoirs. Ces particularités permettent de proposer les bases de modèles sur la hiérarchisation des sites sur le plan techno-économique dans une perspective de dynamique d'occupation des sols au Néolithique ancien régional.

Abstract

In the zone of the confluence of the rivers Seine and Yonne, the danubian settlements date from the final phase of the Rubané period (Balloy, Barbey "Le Buisson Rond", Passy "Les Graviers") to the end of the Villeneuve-Saint-Germain sequence (Gurgy "Les Grands Champs", Passy "La Sablonnière", Marolles "Les Près Hauts"). Intermediate chronological installations are also to be found (Villeneuve-la-Guyard, Barbey "Le Chemin de Montereau", Marolles "Le Chemin de Sens"). The flintworking industries of all these sites have developped from the same basic techniques which caracterize the period : blade knapping by indirect percussion, acquisition of rare or imported raw materials, flake knapping mainly produced by hard percussion, the abundance of flake scrapers, denticules, presence of flint sickles. Certain settlements can be distinguished by their exceptional technological and typological characteristics : over-representation of knapping waste, over-representation of certain tool classes such as sickles or awls. From the viewpoint of the dynamics of early Neolithic settlement in the region, these various characteristics allow us to propose a hierarchical system of the sites based on their techno-economic level.

In the zone of the confluence of the rivers Seine and Yonne (fig. 1), the danubian sequence is characterized by settlements dating from the final phase of the Rubané period (Balloy "Les Réaudins", Barbey "Le Buisson Rond", Passy "Les Graviers", Mordant 1991, Renaud & Gouge 1992, Carré 1984) to the end of the Villeneuve-Saint-Germain sequence (Gurgy "Les Grands Champs", Passy "La Sablonnière", Marolles "Les Près Hauts", Meunier 2000, Carré 1984, Augereau & Gouge 1995). Intermediate chronological installations are also to be found (Villeneuve-la-Guyard, Barbey "Le Chemin de Montereau", Marolles "Le Chemin de Sens",

Prestreau 1992, Renaud & Gouge 1992, Séguier 1995, Augereau & Bonnardin 1998). These sites are mainly represented by domestic settlements where we can find typical danubian building substructures with their lateral pits. In some cases, the building substructures are not preserved, only the lateral pits.

This area of the south-east of the Paris Basin is characterized by a very abundant flint raw-material. The geological substratum is mainly formed by Cretaceous chalk, which contains numerous flint levels. The Campanian period is represented in the north of the sector, the Santonian and Coniancian periods in the south (fig. 1). The Tertiary formations, which are present in the north of the sector and only residual in the south, do not contain flint levels but only limestone (calcareous) and sand-stone.

(*) I.N.R.A.P./Direction interrégionale Centre-Ile-de-France, U.M.R. 7041 et 5594, Centre archéologique, Château de Passy, F-89510 VÉRON, baseafan.passy@wanadoo.fr

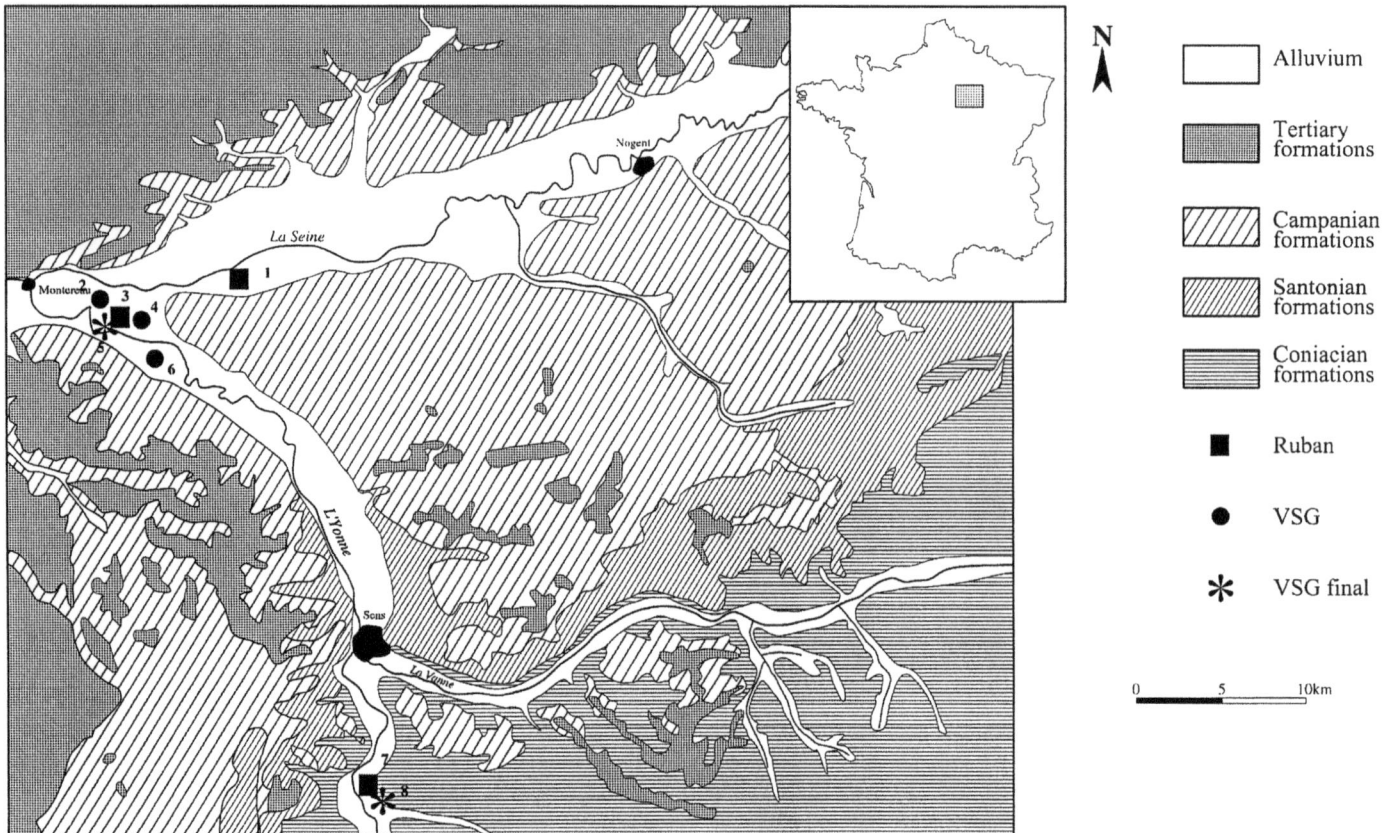

Figure 1. - Map of studied area with the implantation of the sites and the main geological formations (P. Pihuit/I.N.R.A.P., *del.*). 1, Balloy "Les Réaudins" (Seine-et-Marne); 2, Marolles "Le Chemin de Sens" (Seine-et-Marne); 3, Barbey "Le Buisson Rond" (Seine-et-Marne); 4, Barbey "Le Chemin de Montereau" (Seine-et-Marne); 5, Marolles "Les Prés Hauts" (Seine-et-Marne); 6, Villeneuve-la-Guyard "Les Falaises de Prépoux" (Yonne); 7, Passy "Les Graviers" (Yonne); 8, Passy "La Sablonnière" (Yonne). The site of Gurgy "Les Grands Champs" is located at 40 km from Passy to the south, in the Yonne valley.

Raw material distribution

The flintworking industries of these sites have developed from the same basic techniques which characterize the period. During the early Neolithic, three types of flint were used as raw material in the lithic industries. Amongst all of the artefacts (tabl. 1), the proportion of these different flints is globally constant, with the majority of artefacts manufactured in the local flint : from 81 (Gurgy) to 99 % of the totality (Balloy, Passy "Les Graviers", Villeneuve-la-Guyard, etc.). The flint comes from the Cretaceous formation, and mainly from Campanian chalk. This cretaceous flint has a black to blond matrix, a thin chalk cortex and numerous zones of bad silicification. These imperfections make it a medium quality flint. Another flint has a fine-grained matrix and is soft to the touch. Its cortex is thick (3 to 5 millimeters) and it doesn't have any zones of bad silicification. I call it "fine-grained flint". Its exact origin has still not been determined but this flint may be a particular facies of local cretaceous flint. It probably belongs to the Coniacian formations located in the south of the studied area. Its particularity is that it is rare in both archaelogical and geological contexts and the proportion of this flint in the sites is in minority : from 0,2 (Villeneuve-la-Guyard) to 18 % (Gurgy). A third type of flint is Bartonian flint, which is of very high quality, with a very homogeneous

matrix. It is not found in the sector. The closest outcrop is located at 50 km to the north, in the Marne valley, for example at Jablines (Bostyn & Lanchon 1992). In south-east of the Paris basin, this can be considered as an imported flint. It is rare in the sites, less than 0,5 % of the totality of the artefacts. Barbey "Le Chemin de Montereau" is the only site with a larger proportion which reaches 1,2 % of the artefacts : 114 pieces have been counted in this site.

The same raw material distribution pattern has been observed for tools (in other words, retouched flakes and "plein débitage" blades which are retouched and unretouched, tabl. 2). The local flint represents the majority of tool production (from 64 to 94 %). Fine-grained flint is in the minority with 5,6 (Marolles "Le Chemin de Sens") to 33,7 % (Gurgy), and Bartonian corresponds to a small pourcentage of artefacts: from 0,07 (Passy "Les Graviers") to 7 % (Marolles "Les Prés Hauts").

Raw material management

The raw material management is different according to the different types of flint. Comparing tool distribution by flint type shows that if local flint gives the majority of tools, we must distinguish (fig. 2) :

Local flint

Rubané   *VSG*   *VSG final*

□ Retouched flakes   ■ Retouched "plein débitage" blade products
▨ Unretouched "plein débitage" blade products

Fine-grained flint

Rubané   *VSG*   *VSG final*

□ Retouched flakes   ■ Retouched "plein débitage" blade products
▨ Unretouched "plein débitage" blade products

Bartonian flint

Rubané   *VSG*   *VSG final*

□ Retouched flakes   ■ Retouched "plein débitage" blade products
▨ Unretouched "plein débitage" blade products

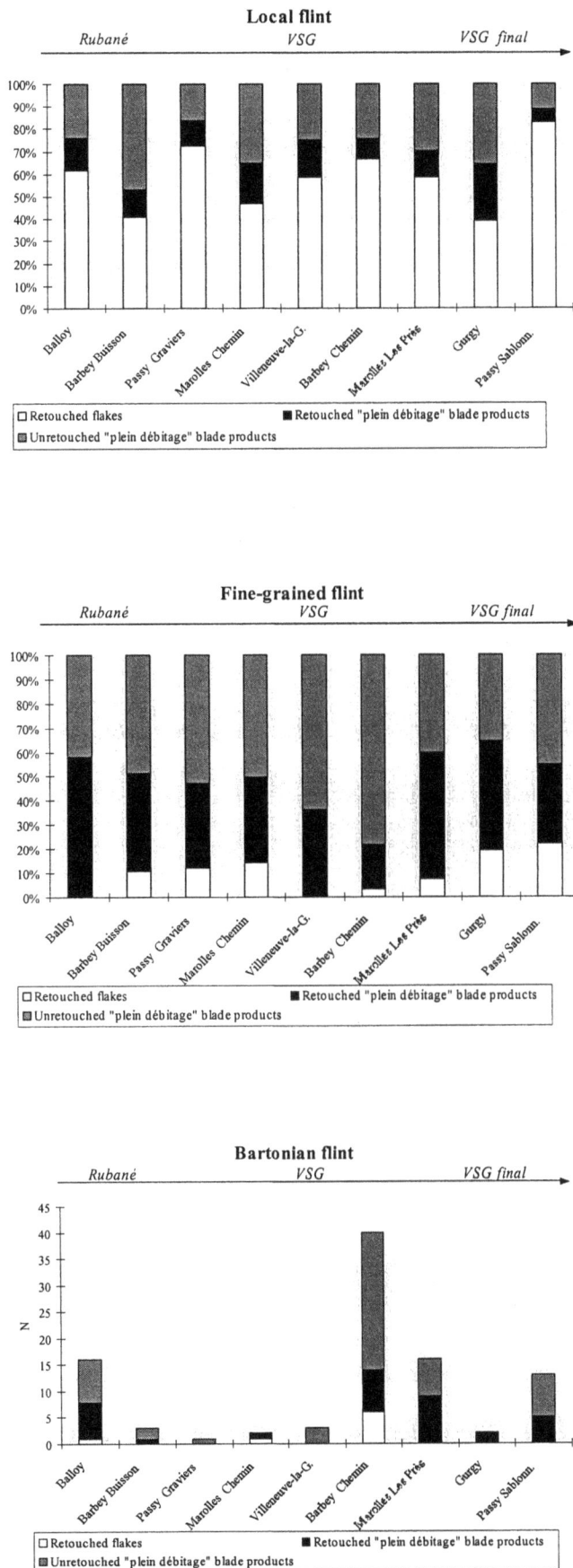

Figure 2. Products distribution by type of flint (retouched flakes,
unretouched and retouched "plein débitage" blades).

- a flake production by hard percussion which represents between 39 (Barbey "Le Buisson Rond") and 83 % (Passy "La Sablonnière") of the local flint tools. This production is characterized by no preparation of the cores : the striking platform is opened by flake removal. It is an opportunistic "débitage".
- In local flint, the blade production by indirect percussion represents 17 (Passy "La Sablonnière") to 59 % (Barbey "Le Buisson Rond"). A proportion of these are retouched.
- Fine-grained flint is mainly used for blade production, also by indirect percussion. Blades manufactured in this type of flint represent from 78 % (Passy "La Sablonnière") to the totality of the products (Balloy and Villeneuve). A very low proportion is also used for retouched flakes : from 11 to 22 % of the products.
- Bartonian flint is mainly used for blades by indirect percussion. A few flakes, from 1 in Balloy to 6 examples in Barbey "Le Chemin de Montereau", are also used for retouched tools.

The different types of flint give different blade productions (Augereau 1993). In local flint, we have the lower quality blade products : these are usually less regular than other flints blades, they have large cortical zones, and their dimensions are not strictly standardized (fig. 3, n° 1). The medium quality raw material is partly responsible for this low quality production but we also note that the preparation of the cores is slender : only one front crest, a partial crest in most of cases. The preparation with 2 crests (one on the front, one on the back) is rare. The quality of fine-grained flint blade products is better (fig. 3, n° 2, 3) : knapping technics are the same, indirect percussion, but here, the blades are regular with parallel and rectilinear edges and arris ; metric studies indicate a better control of the thickness with measurements grouped in just a few classes of thickness (between 2 and 7 millimeters). These characteristics are the consequence of higher raw material quality (without imperfections in the matrix) and better preparation of the cores : these are prepared with 2 crests (one on the front, one on the back). Three crests are made in some cases : one on the front and 2 lateral crests. Bartonian flint gives the most regular blades, especially during the Villeneuve-Saint-Germain period where we find the longest and most regular products (fig. 3, n ° 4, 5). For example, the Bartonian blades of the Villeneuve-Saint-Germain site of Passy "La Sablonnière" can reach up to 105 mm long (fig. 3, n° 5). The average length of local and fine-grained flint blades is about 66 to 67 mm. They are also knapped by indirect percussion and we find them only as finished-products. This indicates that they are imported onto the sites. Howewer, this importation seems more complicated than a simple exchange between producer sites near Bartonian outcrops in the north and domestic settlements of the south-east of the Paris basin (Bostyn 1994, 1995).

In most of settlements, the blade production waste (in others words, cores, preparation and rejuvenation flakes of blades cores, and crests) in both local and fine-grained flint is in proportion to the number of products (fig. 4). For most sites, the representation of local flint waste is between 76

Anne AUGEREAU

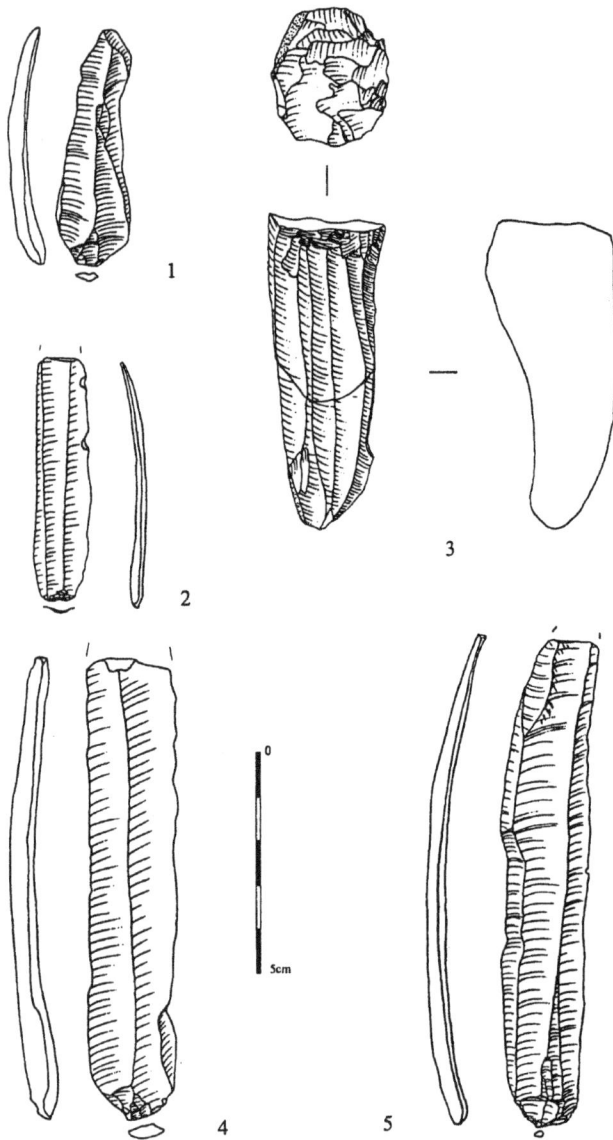

Figure 3. Flint blades production. 1, local flint blade (Passy "Les Graviers"); 2, fine-grained flint blade (Balloy "Les Réaudins"); 3, fine-grained flint core (Villeneuve-la-Guyard); 4, 5, Bartonian flint blades (4, Passy "La Sablonnière"; 5, Barbey "Le Chemin de Montereau").

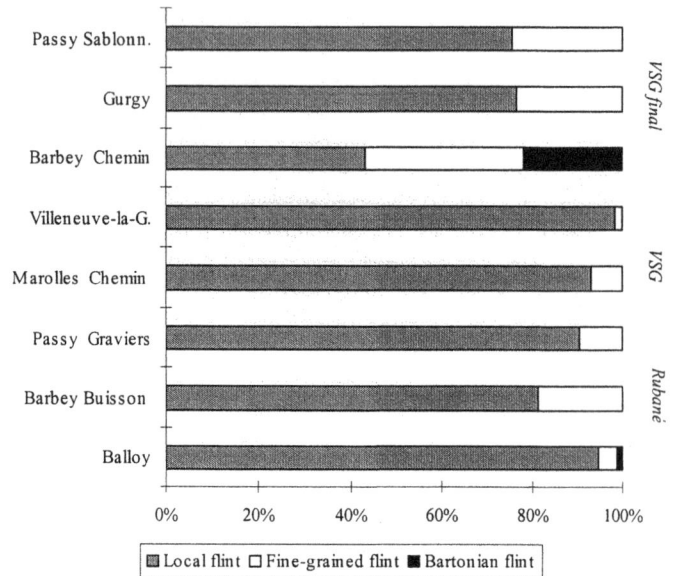

Figure 4. Flint raw material distribution amongst the waste blade production (cores, preparation and rejuvenation flakes, crests).

(Passy "La Sablonnière") and 99 % (Villeneuve-la-Guyard) of the blade production waste. For fine-grained flint, the representation of blade production waste is between 4 (Balloy) and 24 % (Passy "La Sablonnière"). In most of the settlements, waste from Bartonian flint is absent except at Balloy, for one example, and at Barbey "Le Chemin de Montereau", during the Villeneuve-Saint-Germain period. On this site, waste from Bartonian flint production is over-represented, demonstrated by 22 % of total waste products, mainly rejuvenation flakes but no cores. In this light, Barbey "Le Chemin de Montereau" is an exception and indicates that the site rejuvenated Bartonian flint cores for blade production. We can consider the hypothesis that Barbey "Le Chemin de Montereau" is a Bartonian flint workshop where itinerant knappers, coming from the Bartonian outcrops, were knap-

ping blades in pre-prepared cores for local consumption (Augereau 1997).

At Barbey "Le Chemin de Montereau", we also note a more important proportion of fine-grained flint waste in comparison with others settlements (35 %). However, this site is characterized by a low proportion of "plein debitage" blades in local, fine-grained and Bartonian flints. This site may have functioned as a blade workshop using all the flints and as a product distribution centre for the surrounding settlements.

Synthesis : organisation of flint tools procurment

The synthesis of these observations about raw material management allows to propose a provisional model of organisation of flint tool procurment. I have already developed it in an other paper and I will simply summarize it here (Augereau 1997) :
- each member of the community could have manufactured flakes and blades in local flint in domestic settlements. Inexperienced younger flint knappers would have produced the major part of the flakes, the more experienced adults the blade products.
- The blade production in fine-grained flint would have been made by the more experienced knappers, who may have been part-time specialists ; in actual fact, the "débitage" methods for this flint are neater than in local flint. This, and the identification of one of the workshops (Barbey "Le Chemin de Montereau"), could indicate that this high quality and rare raw material is reserved for the better knappers who distribute the products of their work.
- The Bartonian flint comes from 50 km to the north. At the end of early Neolithic, the procurement of the blades in this type of flint could have been realized by the intermediary of itinerant knappers coming from settlements near Bartonian

80

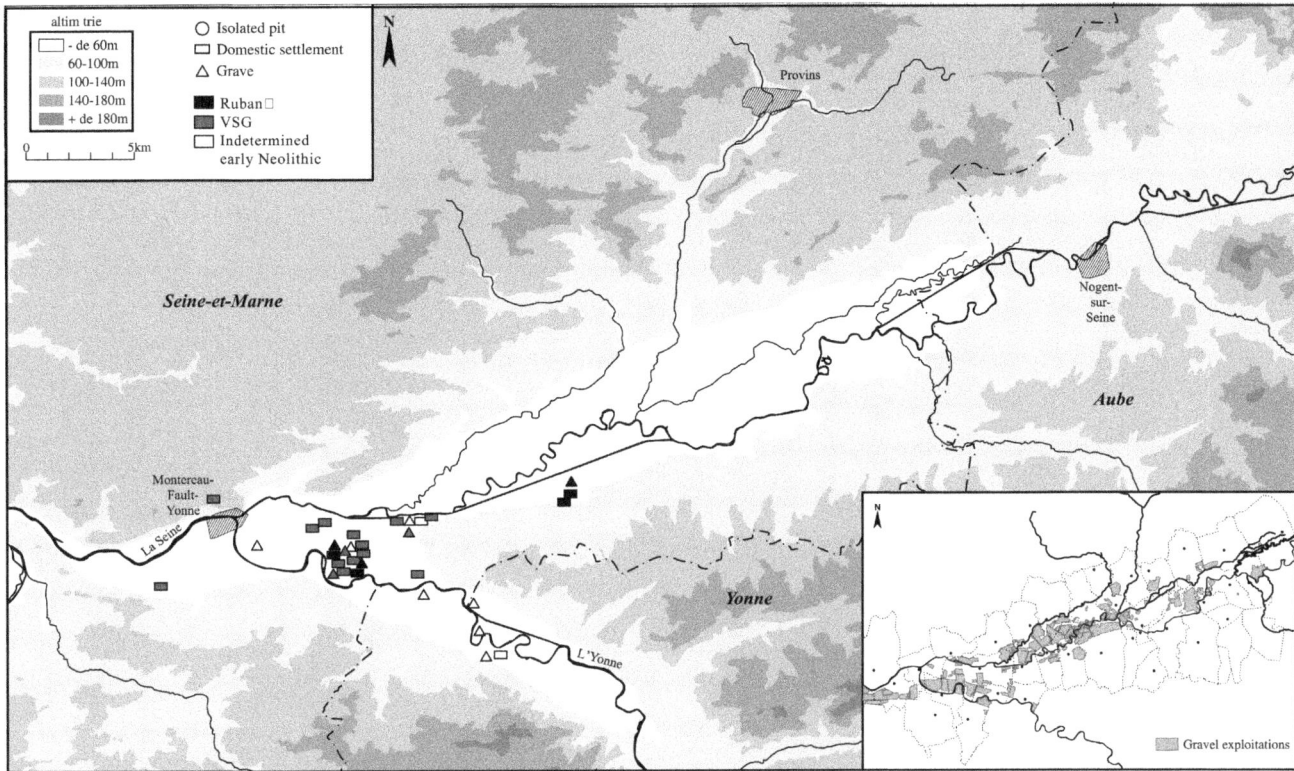

Figure 5. Early Neolithic settlements in the zone of confluence of the rivers Seine and Yonne (Data base : Centre Départemental d'Archéologie de la Bassée, P. Pihuit/I.N.R.A.P., *del.*).

outcrops, in the north of the area.

Finally, I must recall that the area of Seine valley around Barbey, between Montereau and Marolles and between Marolles and Châtenay, has been largely excavated due to the industrialized gravel extraction of the Seine valley. The Neolithic settlements are well known and we have an exhaustive view of their implantation. We can see on the map that most of the early Neolithic sites are concentrated in the area of Marolles/Barbey (fig. 5). In the rest of the valley, the settlements are more sporadic. The Marolles/Barbey sector is also characterized by settlements from the Rubané to the end of Villeneuve-Saint-Germain.

The management of raw material on the Rubané sites of this sector, is homogeneous and similar to other Rubané settlements. However, from early on in the Villeneuve-Saint-Germain period, the lithic industries differ from settlement to settlement. The typological composition of flake tools of Marolles "Le Chemin de Sens" is distinguished by an exceptional proportion of borers and numerous limestone pearl rough outs. This data, combined with the presence of sandstone polishing blocks, indicates that there was an ornament workshop (Augereau & Bonnardin 1998). The borers were probably used for the boring of discoïdal pearls. I must also recall the Bartonian flint workshop of Barbey "Le Chemin de Montereau". Later on, the Marolles "Les Près Hauts" site is characterized by an another form of specialization : this site contains the waste products of limestone (calcareous) and

shale (schist) bracelet workshops. But this specialization is not represented in the lithic industry.

The end of early Neolithic is characterized by a specialization of activities shown by the lithic industries and other data in the Marolles/Barbey sector. Certain settlements of this sector have a long chronology, with the appearance of specialized activities during the early Neolithic. This and the probable product distribution from these workshops, recall, in spite of chronological difference, the archaeological models established for the Linear Band Keramik in the Merzbach valley where central places have been defined by a long chronology and specialized functions (Lüning 1998, Zimmermann 1995). These settlements are also considered as fundation sites occupied from the early Band Keramik phase to the end of the sequence. I know that in the south-east of Paris Basin and, particularly, in the Seine valley, research is still at an early stage to be able to definitively establish a similar model. We need to continue to characterize lithic industries in relation to the representation of tool types and functional analysis and also to distinguish the settlements in relation to their meat supply, their bone industry, their pottery, etc. In this sector, we are in the early stages of this research, which is programmed to continue in the near future.

Acknoledgements

I would like to thank Rebecca Peake (I.N.R.A.P.) for her precious help for the English writing of this paper.

81

Bibliography

AUGEREAU, A., 1993, *Evolution de l'industrie du silex du Vème au IVème millénaire avant J.-C. dans le Sud-est du Bassin parisien*. Thèse de doctorat, Université de Paris I, 3 vol.

AUGEREAU, A., 1997, Analyse spatiale et organisation techno-économique au Néolithique ancien dans le sud-est du Bassin parisien: l'exemple de la taille du silex à Barbey "Le Chemin de Montereau" (Seine-et-Marne). In *Espace physiques espaces sociaux dans l'analyse interne des sites du Néolithique à l'âge du Fer*, Actes du 119e congrès national des sociétés historiques et scientifiques, Amiens, 1994, edited by G. Auxiette, L. Hachem & B. Robert. Paris: Comité des travaux historiques et scientifiques, p. 200-215.

AUGEREAU, A. & BONNARDIN, S., 1998, Marolles-sur-Seine "Le Chemin de Sens" (Seine-et-Marne) et la fabrication de la parure en calcaire au Néolithique ancien. *Bull. de la Société Préhistorique Française* 95, 1, p. 23-39.

AUGEREAU, A. & GOUGE, P., 1995, *Un habitat du Néolithique ancien à Marolles-sur-Seine "Les Prés Hauts Deuxième Vallée"*. DFS de sauvetage urgent. Paris : Afan Centre-Ile-de-France, Bazoches-les-Bray : CDA Bassée ; Saint-Denis : SRA Ile de France.

BOSTYN, F., 1994, *Caractérisation des productions et de la diffusion des industries lithiques du groupe néolithique du Villeneuve-Saint-Germain*. Thèse de doctorat, Université de Paris X, 2 vol.

BOSTYN, F., 1995, Variabilité de l'économie des matières premières lithiques dans le groupe de Villeneuve-Saint-Germain. In *Actes du 20e colloque interrégional sur le Néolithique*, Evreux, 1993. Rennes : Suppl. à la *Revue Archéologique de l'Ouest* 7, p. 31-41.

BOSTYN, F., LANCHON Y., 1992, *Jablines "Le Haut Château" (Seine-et-Marne). Une minière de silex au Néolithique*. Paris : Document d'Archéologie Française 35.

CARRE, H., 1984, Habitats danubiens Seine-Yonne. Les maisons de Passy. In *Influences méridionales dans l'est et le centre-est de la France au Néolithique: le rôle du massif central*, actes du colloque interrégional sur le Néolithique, le Puy-en-Velay, octobre 1981. Clermont-Ferrand : Cahier du Centre de Recherches et d'Etudes Préhistoriques de l'Auvergne 1, p. 15-24.

LÜNING, J., 1998, L'organisation régionale des habitats rubanés : sites centraux et sites secondaires (groupements de sites). In *Organisation néolithique de l'espace en Europe du Nord-Ouest*. Actes du 23ème colloque sur le Néolithique, Bruxelles, 24-26 octobre 1997. Bruxelles : Anthropologie et Préhistoire 109, p. 163-185.

MEUNIER, K., 2000, *Le site néolithique et protohistorique de Gurgy "Les Grands Champs" (Yonne)*. DFS de sauvetage urgent. Moulins-lès-Metz : Afan Grand-Est ; Dijon : SRA Bourgogne.

MORDANT, D., 1991, Le site des Réaudins à Balloy (Seine-et-Marne). Premiers résultats. *Actes du 15e colloque interrégional sur le Néolithique*, Châlons-sur-Marne, octobre 1988. Châlons-sur-Marne : Association Régionale pour la Protection et l'Etude du Patrimoine Préhistorique, p. 33-43.

PRESTREAU, M., 1992, Le site néolithique et protohistorique des Falaises de Prépoux à Villeneuve-la-Guyard (Yonne). *Gallia Préhistoire* 34, p. 171-207.

RENAUD, S. & GOUGE, P., 1992, *Barbey, Le Chemin de Montereau, le Buisson Rond. Carrière de la Compagnie des Sablières de la Seine. 10 millénaires d'occupations humaines : rapport de synthèse*. Dammarie-les-Lys : Programme d'intervention archéologique dans les carrières de granulats de la Bassée (Seine-et-Marne), vol. II.

SEGUIER, J.-M., 1995, *Un gisement archéologique de l'interfluve Seine/Yonne du Paléolithique supérieur à l'Antiquité tardive à Marolles-sur-Seine (Seine-et-Marne)*. DFS de sauvetage urgent. Paris : Afan Centre-Ile-de-France ; Bazoches-les-Bray : CDA Bassée; Saint-Denis : SRA Ile de France.

ZIMMERMANN, A., 1995, *Austauschsysteme von Silexartefakten in der Bandkeramik Mitteleuropas*. Bonn : Universitätsforschungen zur prähistorische Archäologie, 26.

	Rubané						VSG						Final VSG					
	Balloy (campagne 1988)		Barbey Le Buisson Rond		Passy Les Graviers		Marolles Le Chemin de Sens		Villeneuve-la-Guyard		Barbey Le Chemin de Montereau		Marolles Les Près Hauts (st.1, 2, 3)		Gurgy Les Grands Champs (st. 16, 17, 18, 19)		Passy La Sablonnière	
	N	%	N	%	N	%	N	%	N	%	N	%	N	%	N	%	N	%
Local flint	12916	99.45	1246	95.04	25282	99.44	13055	99.71	27006	99.77	9114	96.44	9162	99.42	798	81.35	11770	98.91
Fine-grained fli	54	0.42	62	4.73	141	0.55	37	0.28	60	0.22	222	2.35	37	0.40	181	18.45	117	0.98
Bartonian flint	17	0.13	3	0.23	1	0.00	1	0.01	3	0.01	114	1.21	16	0.17	2	0.20	13	0.11
TOTAL	12970	100	1308	100	25423	100	13092	100	27066	100	9336	99	9199	100	979	100	11887	100

Table 1. Flint raw material distribution amongst all the artefacts.

	Rubané						VSG						Final VSG					
	Balloy (campagne 1988)		Barbey Le Buisson Rond		Passy Les Graviers		Marolles Le Chemin de Sens		Villeneuve-la-Guyard		Barbey Le Chemin de Montereau		Marolles Les Près Hauts (st.1, 2, 3)		Gurgy Les Grands Champs (st. 16, 17, 18, 19)		Passy La Sablonnière	
	N	%	N	%	N	%	N	%	N	%	N	%	N	%	N	%	N	%
Local flint retouched flakes	237	52.78	62	32.46	1008	67.16	109	43.78	543	52.21	394	52.46	100	44.05	23	25.00	530	70.01
Local flint "plein débitage" blade products	146	32.52	89	46.60	378	25.18	124	49.80	436	41.92	198	26.36	71	31.28	36	39.13	110	14.53
Fine-grained flint retouched flakes	0	0.00	4	2.09	14	0.93	2	0.80	0	0.00	4	0.53	3	1.32	6	6.52	23	3.04
Fine-grained flint "plein débitage" blade products	50	11.14	33	17.28	100	6.66	12	4.82	58	5.58	115	15.31	37	16.30	25	27.17	81	10.70
Bartonian flint retouched flakes	1	0.22	0	0.00	0	0.00	1	0.40	0	0.00	6	0.80	0	0.00	0	0.00	0	0.00
Bartonian flint "plein débitage" blade products	15	3.34	3	1.57	1	0.07	1	0.40	3	0.29	34	4.53	16	7.05	2	2.17	13	1.72
TOTAL	449	100	191	100	1501	100	249	100	1040	100	751	100	227	100	92	100	757	100

Table 2. Flint raw material distribution amongst the tools.

www.ingramcontent.com/pod-product-compliance
Lightning Source LLC
Chambersburg PA
CBHW061303270326
41932CB00029B/3453